FINANCIAL INSTITUTIONS AND MARKETS IN THE FAR EAST

One of the more interesting aspects of the 1970s was the growth and development of financial institutions and markets within the Asia and Pacific region. Early in the decade few countries had financial markets of any significance: commercial banks dominated the domestic financial sectors and, in some cases, were virtually the only institutions. Today the capitalist countries of the Far East have the beginnings of, if not developed, money, securities and foreign-exchange markets, as well as a wide range of specialized financial institutions which compete with and complement the services of the commercial banks.

Financial Institutions and Markets in the Far East presents an in-depth, country-by-country coverage of these developments in China, Hong Kong, Japan, South Korea and Taiwan. Each chapter includes an introduction to the country and its financial sector; an examination of the development and operations of each type of financial institution, as well as the local money market, stock exchange and foreign-exchange markets; an analysis of the financial sector's overall performance; and finally some speculation on future developments that might occur. The endnotes for each chapter and the bibliography provide details for further research.

The book should prove a valuable reference for researchers in development and financial economics as well as international business, and for advanced graduate or undergraduate seminars. For the businessman, the book provides background on the financial sectors and is a handy financial guidebook to the region.

FINANCIAL INSTITUTIONS AND MARKETS IN THE FAR EAST

A Study of China, Hong Kong, Japan, South Korea and Taiwan

Edited by

Michael T. Skully
Lecturer in Finance
University of New South Wales

St. Martin's Press   New York

All rights reserved. For information, write:
St. Martin's Press, Inc., 175 Fifth Avenue, New York, NY 10010
Printed in Hong Kong
First published in the United States of America in 1982

ISBN 0–312–28961–8

Library of Congress Cataloging in Publication Data

Main entry under title:

Financial institutions and markets in the Far East.

Includes bibliographies.
Contents: Financial institutions and markets in
China; Financial institutions and markets in
Hong Kong/Michael T. Skully – Financial
institutions and markets in Japan/Hiromitsu Ishi –
Financial institutions and markets in South
Korea/Sang-Woo Nam and Yung-Chul Park – [etc.]
1. Financial institutions – East Asia – Addresses,
essays, lectures. 2. Finance – East Asia – Addresses,
essays, lectures. I. Skully, M. T. (Michael T.)
HG187.A2F56   332.1′095   82–5652
ISBN 0–312–28961–8   AACR2

Contents

List of Figures

List of Maps

List of Tables

Preface

One of the more interesting aspects of the 1970s was the growth and development of financial institutions and markets within the Asia and Pacific region. Early in the decade few countries had financial markets of any significance: commercial banks dominated the domestic financial sectors and, in some cases, were virtually the only institutions. Today the capitalist countries of the Far East have the beginnings of, if not developed, money, securities and foreign-exchange markets, as well as a wide range of specialised financial institutions which compete with and complement the services of the commercial banks. This book represents the first of a series of titles which provide an in-depth, country-by-country coverage of these developments and the respective financial institutions and markets as they exist today.

The information presented, unless otherwise noted, is derived from interviews and correspondence with government officials, academic researchers and business leaders within the region's financial sectors. The use of local contributors also enabled more comprehensive coverage of each country than a sole researcher might hope to accomplish. Wherever possible, references published in English have been included within the notes section at the end of each chapter and should provide the reader with a worthwhile starting point for further studies.

The task of constructing such a publication is considerable and could not have been accomplished without the assistance of a multitude of people. The willingness of the contributors to devote their time to preparing the articles, the co-operation of the numerous financial executives and government officials contacted, and the assistance of the administrative personnel and my colleagues at the University of New South Wales are particularly appreciated. Special thanks must also go to the noted Hong Kong financial economist Dr Y. C. Jao for his help and encouragement; to Robert F. Emery of the US Federal Reserve Board for the initial inspiration; to W. Y. Wong of the Bank of America, Julie L. T. Chien of the Central Bank of China, Seong-Tae Kim and Jun-Hwan Park of the Korea Exchange Bank, the research departments of the Bank of Japan, Bank of Tokyo and the Federation of Bankers' Association of Japan, J. R. Milhinch of Wales Australia Ltd, and C. E. Beckett and W. G. Izard of the Hongkong and Shanghai Banking Corporation for the specific assistance in the preparation and review of the manuscript; to T. M. Farmiloe of Macmillan for his understanding and support of the project; and to Mary Whitton and Pat McMahon for typing the many drafts.

M. T. S.

Notes on the Contributors

Ching-ing Hou Liang is a Professor of Economics and Chairman of the Department of Banking at the National Chengchi University, Taipei, Taiwan. She is well known for her research in trade development, monetary policies and financial institutions in the Republic of China and has published widely in these areas.

Hiromitsu Ishi is a Professor of Economics at Hitotsubashi University. He has been a Visiting Professor at the Universities of Michigan and New South Wales. He is well known for his research in fiscal monetary policies, taxation and the Japanese economy, and has published a number of books and articles.

Sang-Woo Nam is a Senior Fellow at the Korea Development Institute, Seoul. After graduating from the Sloan School of Management, MIT, he has been engaged in research in the fields of finance and aggregate econometric model building. His works include *Dynamics of Inflation in Korea*, *A Semi-Annual Simulation Model of the Korean Economy* and *Financial Structure, Corporate Investment and Financing Behavior in Korea*.

Yung-Chul Park is Professor of Economics at Korea University. After completing graduate work at the University of Minnesota he worked for the International Monetary Fund from 1968 to 1974. Since then he has taught at Georgetown University and Boston University. He has published extensively on money and finance and is the co-author, with David Cole, of *Financial Development in Korea*.

Michael T. Skully is a Lecturer in Finance at the University of New South Wales and is known for his research in the financial institutions and markets in the Far East countries. He has published widely in the areas of international finance and business, and his books include *Merchant Banking in the Far East*, *A Multinational Look at the Transnational Corporation* (editor), and *ASEAN Regional Financial Cooperation: Developments in Banking and Finance*.

1 Financial Institutions and Markets in China

MICHAEL T. SKULLY

INTRODUCTION

(a) The Setting

As the world's most populous country and the oldest surviving civilisation, the People's Republic of China occupies a strategic position within the Far East and with an area of 9,596,961 square kilometres controls a major portion of the East Asian land mass.

Since China's unification as a country in 221 B.C., it has been subjected to the rule of a variety of imperial dynasties and in 1912 finally became a republic. Political infighting, however, precluded the new government from effectively administering the country and difficulties posed by the Japanese occupation between 1937 and 1945 further de-stabilised the country's political and economic system. Civil war between the Communists and Nationalist forces followed the defeat of the Japanese and peace was restored only after the 1 October 1949 founding of the People's Republic of China on the mainland and the transfer of the Nationalist government to Taiwan.

After some forty years of almost constant fighting, political corruption, and frequently excessive inflation, the Chinese economy was devastated and the new government borrowed heavily from the Soviets in its reconstruction. Indeed even today large segments of China's bureaucratic and infrastructure organisation still reflect the influence of this pre-1960 Soviet advice.

Still, given the adverse effects of the 'great leap forward', the Cultural Revolution of 1966–9, and the internal power struggles of the 1970s, the Chinese people have seen a substantial improvement in their living standards since 1950. None the less in recent years there has been increasing dissatisfaction with the government's economic policies.

1

MAP 1.1   People's Republic of China

The present leadership attempted yet another massive economic restructuring programme in 1978 with the introduction of the 'Four Modernisations': the modernisation of agriculture, industry, defence, and science and technology. Unfortunately many of these projects proved too grandiose, and from an infrastructure and foreign-exchange reserve viewpoint, unattainable. They were therefore downgraded in mid-1979 to more realistic levels and future capital expenditures subjected to more control. The banking system in particular has been chosen for this monitoring role and China's financial institutions have become increasingly important as a result.

(b) An Overview of the Financial Sector

China's present financial system, patterned after the West and the Soviet Union, is still a rather recent development and has largely supplanted its original domestic institutions. As one study commented, 'the native financial institutions of China appear to have been reasonably adequate to the functions which they had to discharge before the modern era, but they were not fitted for handling the international financial transactions that resulted from trade with Western countries'.[1] To handle the new trade with the West and the foreign-exchange work it involved, the East India Company and the agency houses established local offices in China in the 1800s. These were supplemented in the 1840s with the arrival of a few Anglo-Indian banks but these proved unsuccessful. In 1858, however, the Chartered Bank of India, Australia and China (now the Chartered Bank of the Standard Chartered Group) opened a branch in Shanghai and has remained in operation since. Later, in 1865, the Hongkong and Shanghai Banking Corporation opened for business in Hongkong and Shanghai; and from the 1890s to the early 1900s, a large number of German, Japanese, Russian, French, Belgian, Dutch and American banks opened branches in China. Thus by 1932, the 32 foreign banks operating in China had branches in most of the country's principal commercial centres.[2]

Besides foreign trade financing and foreign-exchange work, the foreign bank notes were used widely as currency within China and the banks often handled the foreign capital raising, as well as much of the banking business of the government and its agencies. They also did some lending directly to Chinese merchants but for the most part dealt with local customers through the native bankers and, more importantly, the compradors. A bank's comprador was virtually responsible for its success or failure within China: he hired and guaranteed the Chinese employees of the bank as well as ensuring that all advances were repaid, and he received a salary and, more importantly, a commission on his activities in return.

Besides their involvement as compradors to the foreign banks and merchant houses, the Chinese businessmen soon formed their own Western-styled banking institutions.[3] Indeed, between 1929 and 1937, 128 new Chinese banks were established and by 1937 there were 164 modern Chinese banks with 1597 branches in the major cities.[4] However, the 13 largest of these institutions controlled around three-quarters of the local banking industry's total resources.[5]

By the mid-1930s, the existence of local institutions and the desire to exert more economic control caused the government to introduce measures to reduce the foreign banks' importance. In 1935, partially in response to Western government pressures, a central currency was introduced which also had the effect of reducing some foreign bank notes usage within the country.

The war with Japan and the civil war that followed, coupled with acute inflation, caused havoc in the banking system and in 1949 the government in Beijing (Peking) was faced with the remains of the Nationalist government-owned banks, the privately-owned Chinese banks, its own provincial and party banks, and the few remaining foreign banks. To control the industry, the government implemented a series of rationalisation measures centred around the activities of the People's Bank of China: the People's Bank absorbed the mainland operations of the National government and communist banks and in 1950 replaced the Central Bank of China as the Country's central bank.

Those private banks that remained in operation on the mainland in 1949 were also brought under direct government lending and borrowing controls. The nationalisation of business enterprises and the requirement for all but a small portion of state companies' funds to be deposited with the People's Bank gradually eroded the significance of the private banks and in 1952 those that remained were merged into the Joint Public – Private Bank. This bank continued to service an ever-shrinking private sector, and in February 1953 its operations were absorbed by the People's Bank of China and by 1956 had all but disappeared.

Thus the financial system that emerged was centred on the People's Bank of China with only the Bank of China and the Bank of Communications retaining their identities. These institutions, though, were highly specialised and offered only limited banking services. The Bank of China, for example, operated primarily as the foreign trade – foreign exchange department of the People's Bank, while the Bank of Communications served as the disbursement and funds manager for the Ministry of Finance's capital investment work: its operations were later assumed and are today performed by the People's Construction Bank of China. The Ministry of Finance also assumed control of the insurance industry and consolidated its operations into the People's Insurance Company of China. It also took responsibility for the then government agricultural bank.

The banking system performed an important monitoring role in the country's early years with the emphasis more on ensuring customers complied with their initial proposals and state directives rather than as lending institutions. The Cultural Revolution of 1966, though, brought substantial changes into the banking system as well as the country as a whole and bankers assumed a low profile within Chinese finance – consolidating their operations under the Ministry of Finance. The banks regained many of their former functions following the change of leadership in 1976 and, in support of the Four Modernisations, have gained new status with the government.

As shown in Figure 1.1 the People's Bank of China has now assumed a status equivalent to the Ministry of Finance, and the Bank of China,

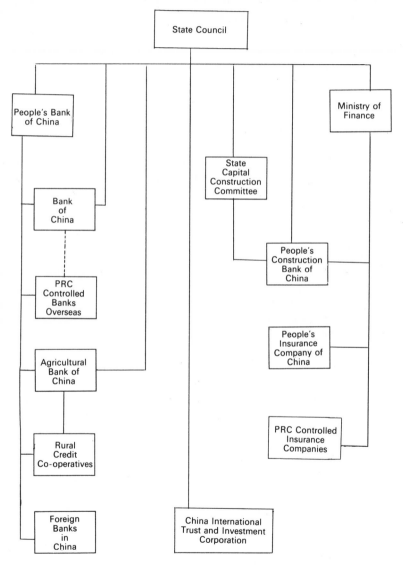

FIGURE 1.1   China's financial structure

People's Construction Bank and the Agricultural Bank of China are now all responsible directly to the Chinese government's State Council — a body somewhat equivalent to a cabinet in a Western country.

FINANCIAL INSTITUTIONS

The state planning tradition of the Soviet Union initially adopted by the People's Republic of China caused a substantial rationalisation of the country's financial institutions so that today only a few are still in operation. These include the People's Bank of China, the Bank of China, the People's Construction Bank of China, the Agricultural Bank of China, the rural credit co-operatives, the People's Insurance Company of China, and a few trust and investment and provincial investment corporations. In addition to these domestic institutions, the foreign banks operating or represented within China and those PRC-controlled financial institutions overseas are also covered briefly within the section.

(a) The People's Bank of China

The People's Bank of China was established on 20 October 1949 as part of a merger between three Communist Party-controlled banks: the Bank of Northern China, the Bank of the North Sea, and the Bank of the Peasants of the Northwest. Following the Communist Party's victory, the People's Bank became the chief banking instrument of the new government and absorbed the mainland operations and functions of the Nationalist government institutions to include those of the central bank.

Today the People's Bank serves as the key to China's financial system and, as shown in Figure 1.1, reports directly to the State Council on a similar basis to the Ministry of Finance: the heads of both institutions are also at present members of the Council. Thus, as one study explains, it 'is both an economic department of government and a state organ in its own right'.[6] The Bank performs normal central banking functions within the country, including the issue of currency and coinage, economic and financial planning, the operation of the domestic payment system, and most of the country's commercial and savings bank activities. It is also responsible for the broad supervision of the General Adminstration of Exchange Control, the Bank of China, the Agricultural Bank of China, the rural credit co-operatives, the PRC-controlled banks overseas, and, in a regulatory sense, the foreign bank branches and representative offices within China.

The People's Bank representation follows similar lines to the government with one branch in each of the country's 29 provinces, 218 central sub-branches at each prefecture, and 2220 at the county or *hsein* level. In all, there are an estimated 15,000 local offices with additional ones at the commune level, involving a staff of some 330,000. The Bank's headquarters in Beijing has a staff of 1200 and is organised into 14 departments: the names and functions of each are shown in Table 1.1. The most important of these is the planning department which is concerned with the country's monetary and economic policy.

As shown in Table 1.2 the bank obtains its deposits from enterprises, households, and government and government agencies. Deposits from

TABLE 1.1 People's Bank of China: organisational structure of headquarters

Department	Functions
1. Accounting and currency issue	Plans amount of currency issue; actual issuing of currency by PBOC branches, including county-level branches
2. Administration	Handles payroll, and operates kindergarten for workers' children
3. Advisers	n.a.
4. Bank note printing	Prints currency
5. China financial editorial	Publishes 28-page monthly *China Finance* *(Zhonggu Jinrong)*
6. Credits and loans	Extends loans to industrial and commercial departments
7. Financial research	Issues status reports on domestic and world financial situation. Sections: theory, finance, historical financial studies, and library
8. Insurance	n.a.
9. Personnel	In charge of promotions and technical education
10. Planning	Draws up national cash plan and credit plan, and plan of credit circulation; all in RMP, not foreign exchange
11. Savings deposits	Maintains national savings deposit accounts
12. Science and education	Maintains banking schools in all provinces, regions and municipalities including Beijing, Shanghai and Tianjin
13. Secretariat	Organises banking meetings
14. Supervision	n.a.

Source: People's Bank of China, 28 April 1980, as cited in *The China Business Review*. July–August 1980, p. 16.

TABLE 1.2　People's Bank of China: deposits by source

Enterprises	59.2 %
Urban households	21.3 %
Government and government agencies	19.5 %
Total	100.0 %

Source: Planning Department of the People's Bank of China, *Financial Overview of the People's Republic of China*, June 1980, p. 9, as cited in *The China Business Review*, July–August 1980, p. 15.

enterprises are the most significant. This is because of certain government directives concerning Chinese financial practice. For example, since 1950 state enterprises may hold funds on hand to cover no more than three days' worth of transactions. All additional money must be kept on deposit: deposits which earn only 1.8 per cent. Also, to limit the use of currency, all transactions over 30 Renminbi, other than salaries and agricultural purchasing, must be made by transfer:[7] as a result less than 5 per cent of all settlements in China are with cash.[8]

Personal savings are also important and in April 1980 there were more than 100 million savers in China's urban areas: a breakdown of urban and rural deposits is shown in Table 1.3. Of these funds, approximately

TABLE 1.3　Personal savings deposits: by source
(Figures in millions of Renminbi)

Year	Overall	Urban	Rural
1955	2284	1690	594
1972	5630	4456	1174
1973	6474	4924	1550
1974	7291	5540	1751
1975	8000	6000	2000
1976	15800	11963	3837
1977	17793	13219	4574
1978	20409	15490	4919
1979	28000	20157	7843
1980	30000	n.a.	n.a.

Source: Hsiao, *Money and Monetary Policy in Communist China: Xinhua News Agency*, 22 January 1974; 12 January, 1 December 1975; 27 January 1976; 8 January, 19 July 1978; 28 February, 28 July, 2 October 1979; 20 March, 1 and 3 April 1980; Peking Radio Service, 14 January 1980, as cited in *Asian Banking*, June 1980, p. 25.

82 per cent of urban and 70 per cent of rural savings are in fixed deposits. Recent increases in interest rates have caused a rapid growth in deposits in 1979 – particularly in the higher interest paying fixed deposits. As of 1 April 1980, personal savings earned 4.32 per cent for a 6-month time deposit, 5.40 per cent for 1 year, 6.12 per cent for 3 years, and 6.84 per cent for 5 years. Personal demand or current deposits, in contrast (as of 1 July 1980), earned 2.8 per cent. To attract Overseas Chinese funds as well, the People's Bank pays slightly higher rates for their deposits: 5.76 per cent for 1 year, 6.48 per cent for 3 years, and 7.20 per cent for 5 years.

The banks' deposits from government and government agencies include state grants to industry, the accounts of government departments and other state agencies as well as of the People's Liberation Army. It is expected that under the 1979 economic changes, state grants will become much less important. With these deposits, the People's Bank makes short-term loans (usually for less than a year) for working capital and capital replacement purposes. The general interest rates for loans to state and collectively-owned enterprises in mid-1980 stood at 5.04 per cent with additional penalty increases of 20 per cent on overdue loans, 30 per cent on late payments due to overstocking, and 50 per cent on late payment due to overspending on capital investments. Lower rates, however, are applied for certain types of loans. Funds for communes and state farms production expenditures or their advance purchase of certain agricultural commodities, for example, are charged 4.32 per cent, while loans for communes to acquire production equipment involved rates of only 2.16 per cent. The recent interest rate changes are particularly important for, previously, state enterprises were not charged interest for their working capital.

Besides its deposit and lending functions, the People's Bank also supervises its customer's expenditures to ensure they comply with initial plans and government directives. As one study explained, 'large enterprises often have a representative of the local People's Bank actually stationed on the site. This representative is supposed to make sure that bank credit is used for its intended purpose, to insure that accounts are kept properly, and to inspect warehouses and inventories in search of hoarding or improper use of credit for unintended purposes.'[9] These credit officers may be assigned to only one company or a number of smaller firms and their monitoring activities are a full-time occupation. Not surprisingly, auditing most of China's industry requires a substantial number of bank officers and an estimated quarter of the People's Bank provincial staff are devoted strictly to this purpose.

With the recent changes in China's economic management, the

Bank's 'watchdog' function has become more important and its lending emphasis now encourages light rather than heavy industrial development. In line with this policy its commercial credit branch in Beijing recently made its first personal (private) business loan since 1956. Such loans are now allowable to small businesses whose products or services are in short supply. The expansion of the Bank's commercial and industrial development role has caused some to suggest that a new specialist bank may be established and that eventually the People's Bank may be restructured to fulfil solely a central banking role.[10]

(b) The Bank of China

The Bank of China is the oldest of China's existing banks and can trace its origins to 1904 with the founding of the Hu-pu Bank. The Bank of China itself was formed under special legislation in 1912 as a joint government and private venture to assume the functions of the Ta Ching Bank, and by 1928 it had become the specialised bank for international remittances of the Nationalist government. In line with its international banking role the Bank of China established an extensive overseas branch network. Starting in 1936 with Singapore it soon had branch representation in Bangkok, Jakarta, New York, Saigon, Sydney and Tokyo.

With the change of government in 1949, much of the Bank's head office staff moved to Taiwan with the Nationalist government and re-established operations. The new Government, however, assumed control of the Bank's mainland operations and continued the former head office activities. The Bank of China's overseas branches, though, presented a unique problem. The Nationalist government retained diplomatic recognition for mainland China in most countries until the 1970s so the new government's political means to influence overseas branch loyalties was limited. In the end, partly due to English diplomatic recognition, the Bank of China headquartered in Beijing retained the branches in London and the then British territories of Hong Kong and Singapore; the remaining branches sided with Taipei. For some years, both banks traded as the Bank of China but finally, as other governments recognised Beijing rather than the Nationalists, the Taipei bank was restructured from an official to a private bank and renamed the International Commercial Bank of China.

Within China itself, the Beijing headquartered bank continued its international banking role for the new government and in 1953 was formally reorganised to serve in a monopoly position as China's specialised foreign-exchange bank. The legislation this entailed, however, was annulled in 1962 and, although a revised set of the Bank's Articles of Association was issued in the same year, no further legislation was introduced. At the time of writing this was still the case, but on 22 September 1980 a further revised set of articles[11] was placed into effect. Among other things they confirmed the Bank's status as a state rather than a joint public – private enterprise.[12] They also formally raised its authorised capital from 19.8 million Renminbi to 1 billion.

The new articles also clarify the bank's general purpose and areas of operations. The latter now include the:

international settlement of accounts regarding foreign trade and non-trade matters; international inter-bank deposits and loans; handling of overseas Chinese remittances and other international remittances; foreign currency deposits and loans and deposits and loans in renminbi that are related to foreign exchange business and have been approved by the People's Bank of China; buying and selling of foreign-exchange (including foreign currency); international buying and selling of gold; organizing and participating in international lending syndicates; establishing investment or joint venture banks, finance companies or other enterprises abroad and in Hong Kong, Macau and other places; in accordance with state authorization, issuing foreign currency bonds and other valuable securities; providing trust and advisory and services; [and] other banking business which the state has approved and entrusted to the bank for handling.[13]

In line with government policy, the Bank of China has recently expanded its operations into a number of new fields and can be expected to adopt further services along these lines. In Beijing, Shanghai, Tianjin, Guangdong and Fujian, for example, it may now engage in buyers' credit and bank credit guarantees; extend credit facilities to compensation trade, tourist establishments and joint venture projects with foreign business; and advise clients on the credit standings of overseas firms and markets.[14] It has also expanded its loan activities in the foreign-exchange area to provide foreign currency working capital loans to exporters and on 10 May 1979 it participated on its first Euro loan syndication.

Besides these generally banking functions, the Bank of China has also become involved in trade introductions and promotion between foreign and local business, scientific and technical exchange agreement research, and promoting China to foreign tourists.[15] In line with this latter role, the Bank has been responsible, since 1 April 1980, for the issue and sale of Renminbi denominated foreign-exchange certificates for use by foreign tourists in special Friendship Stores and other exclusively tourist facilities: foreign currencies must not be used within China. Through an agreement with the Hongkong and Shanghai Banking Corporation, the Bank of China's branches in Guanghou and Shanghai also accept Master Card and VISA bank credit cards.

To carry out these functions domestically the Bank of China has 77 branches located within China's principal ports and cities. Of its overseas branches, Hong Kong and London are the most important and the largest in terms of personnel with a staff of 400 and 150 respectively. The Singapore branch has some 90 employees and, in comparison, its Luxembourg branch, Manchester sub-branch, and Tokyo representative office are relatively small operations; a New York office is also expected shortly. These overall operations are supervised by the Bank's head office in Beijing: it has a staff of over 500 employees and is organised into the nine departments, as indicated in Table 1.4

As well as the Bank of China's recent change in articles and functions, it has taken on a new position of importance in terms of its status within the government. Previously the Bank of China had served as a *de facto* international banking department of the People's Bank. But since 1979, the Bank has operated under the direct control of the Chinese government's State Council, and People's Bank now has only a very general supervisory role (as the central bank and a government department) over its operations. Another agency also now closely involved with the Bank of China's operation, the State General Administration of Exchange Control, was also established in 1979. As its name implies it plans and administer's China's exchange control policies to include (in conjunction with the People's Bank) the setting of the foreign-exchange rates themselves. This agency, although technically separate from the Bank of China and reporting directly to the State Council, is effectively part of the Bank of China as its offices (to include its head office) are located within those of the Bank of China and it is staffed by seconded Bank of China employees.

(c) People's Construction Bank of China

The People's Construction Bank of China was established on 1 October 1954 to manage the investment project finance activities of the Ministry of Finance and it gradually assumed the operations of the reconstituted

TABLE 1.4 Bank of China: head office departments and functions

Department	Functions
1. International	Relations with overseas correspondence banks
2. General business	Coordinates foreign-exchange earnings of Chinese government and state enterprises and advises the General Administration of Exchange Control on the amount of foreign exchange to be used by local authorities
3. Foreign exchange	Acts as the clearing house of the bank's international accounts, raises funds overseas, acts in the inter-bank market, and conducts the bank's foreign-exchange operations
4. Credit	Administers the foreign-exchange component of local authorities' projects to include obtaining of the initial permission, processing the relative documentation and disbursing the end funds
5. Financial and accounting	Maintains the bank's records both locally and, through computer tie-ups, overseas. Also it is responsible for preparing the bank's own reporting to include its annual report
6. Banking	Handles the day-to-day banking transactions
7. International financial research	Compiles appropriate information on overseas economies on a regional, country and topical basis
8. Personnel	Conducts the bank's personnel administration work
9. Administration	Serves as the bank's general policy arm to include the bank's secretariat

Source: Nicholas H. Ludlow and James B. Stepanek, 'Inside the Bank of China', *The China Business Review*, July–August 1980, pp. 9–12.

Nationalist Government's bank, the Bank of Communications. As with the Agricultural Bank, the People's Construction Bank's independence has suffered various setbacks since its formation and it again became a separate entity, reporting directly to the State Council, in November 1979. Its operations, though, are also supervised by the State Capital Construction Commission and, more importantly, the Ministry of Finance.

The Bank is responsible for the administration of government appropriations to major state capital construction projects and other loans and grants for fixed asset modernisation. More recently the Bank has also been able to make loans on capital construction projects both for solely domestic and joint ventures. The Bank's role as a lending agency has taken on new importance under the government's present economic policies, as in the future capital grants are to be replaced by interest-bearing loans.

In its position as a grant administrator, the Bank's 2500 branches ensured that the funds were used appropriately and with the government's new emphasis on sound economic management this role has also been expanded. In 1977 alone, for example, it reportedly saved some 1000 million Renminbi of the state budget by eliminating redundant projects and an additional 1700 million in wasteful local projects.[16] Such successes were responsible for its new position as a lending agency, for it is hoped that wasteful or uneconomic projects will be denied funds at the very start of the allocation process.

The Bank's lending terms and conditions on its new capital construction loans are thought to be around 3 per cent interest, range from 5 to 15 years in maturity, and have 100 per cent increased interest penalty if overdue. The loans must also be made only to 'independent economic accounting systems' enterprises, not parts of government departments, and the Bank must be allowed on-site access to ensure the initial plans are fulfilled.[17] The Bank's new lending activities are expected to emphasise tourism, textiles, and other light industrial development, as well as assisting joint venture and compensation trade related construction projects.

(d) The Agricultural Bank of China

As mentioned in the development section, the Agricultural Bank has had a rather tenuous existence since its initial founding as the Agricultural Co-operative Bank in 1951, followed by a number of starts and subsequent closures.[18] Its most recent reorganisation came in February 1979 after 14 years of suspended operations. On 1 April 1979, the Agricultural Bank of China was formally re-established as a separate financial institution, operating under the direct control of China's State Council and the overall supervision of the People's Bank of China.

The Agricultural Bank operates through a national branch network of 23,000 offices, some 20,000 of which are located at the commune level. The Bank accepts deposits from and makes loans to its rural customers and supervises the operations of the rural credit co-operatives; the latter group is also subject to the overall supervision of the People's Bank.

The lack of substantial enterprise deposits or government funds makes the Agricultural Bank highly dependent on personal savings deposits. Nevertheless some 17,000 million Renminbi were loaned to Chinese agricultural over 1979 and 20,000 million were expected for 1980. These lending and deposit activities are very labour-intensive and involved a staff of some 200,000, an amount similar to that of the credit co-operatives.

(e) Rural Credit Co-operatives

Western-style credit co-operatives were first introduced in 1919 by the Futan University of Shanghai and in 1923 by the University of Nanking's Agricultural Economics Department; by 1927, 584 co-operative credit associations were in operation within the country.[19] There are now an estimated 70,000 of these associations at the rural commune level within China, with a staff of 200,000. These co-operatives function not unlike a Western credit union, in that they provide both deposit and lending facilities for their customers: their personal loan rate to commune members in mid-1980 stood at 4.34 per cent. Their operations are closely supervised by the Agricultural Bank of China and the People's Bank.

(f) People's Insurance Company of China

Long before the initiation of Western trade, the Chinese merchant guilds used a form of mutual risk sharing when transporting their goods from one part of China to another. As with the banking industry though, Western trade required different forms of financial services and the Western merchant houses were soon active in insurance as well as banking. Unlike banking, however, the merchant houses found the communication difficulties and risks with Chinese trade such that few overseas companies would handle it, and therefore, they were forced to establish their own companies for that purpose. In 1805 the foreign-owned and -controlled Canton Insurance Society became China's first insurance company, and by 1875 a number of other foreign-owned and a few small Chinese-owned local insurers had been established.[20]

As trade became more sophisticated the lack of insurance for Chinese vessels worked to the foreign merchant houses' advantage and as a result by the 1930s local Chinese-owned insurance companies had become significant. Their growth was further encouraged in 1935 by legal restrictions on the foreign companies outside of the Treaty Ports.

With the change of government in 1949, the foreign and local insurance industry virtually disappeared and the People's Insurance Company of China was established on 20 October 1949 to provide the policies necessary for China's foreign trade. People's Insurance has since specialised in ocean and inland marine, hull, aviation, cargo, land and air transport, and foreign reinsurance, and also provides fire, life, personal accident, worker's compensation and motor vehicle insurance coverage. These latter activities were once confined largely to foreign residents but, in line with the new modernisation programme, now provide the compulsory insurance on ventures with foreigners. Among some of the policies required are 'insurance of construction and installation projects, political risk and contract failure, property insurance, insurance for machine damage, business suspension, and third party liability'.[21]

In 1980 the People's Insurance Company had an estimated premium volume of some US $250 million but its business should grow rapidly. In line with this expansion programme, the Company in 1980 also established an agreement with the American Express Company subsidiary, Fireman's Fund, to act as its managing underwriter in the USA, to insure some of China's marine business and to assist in the planning of the People's Insurance domestic expansion.

The People's Insurance Company has also appointed some 300 cargo surveying and claims settlement agents in over 100 countries to act on the People's Insurance Company's behalf in the case of foreign claim situations, and it is a member of the Asian Reinsurance Corporation.

Within China, People's Insurance operates 78 branch offices in the country's principal ports and cities and has a staff of over a 1000 employees. Both the number of staff and branches, however, are likely to expand rapidly in line with the company's new responsibilities. Also headquartered in Beijing are the state-owned Tai Ping Insurance Company and the China Insurance Company, but their operations are conducted by their overseas branches. All three companies' activities are regulated by the Ministry of Finance.

(g) Trust and Investment Corporations and Other Financial Institutions

As part of the government's modernisation measures, the China International Trust and Investment Corporation (CITIC) was established as a state-owned enterprise under the direct control of the government's State Council. It commenced operation on 4 October 1979 with a paid-up capital of 200 million Renminbi and it is designed to encourage the use of foreign investment, equipment and technology within China. To this end it will assist foreign and Chinese businesses in finding and negotiating with their appropriate partners for joint ventures, compensation trade and technological licensing agreements through its Beijing office and its Hong Kong branch office. It may also issue debentures to finance these activities.

The Corporation's financial activities are still expanding but, as one observer commented, 'the China International Trust and Investment Corporation . . . seems among other things to be developing a role as a merchant bank and may even be taking on certain other banking activities, but it is not authorised to handle the international settlement of accounts'.[22]

Besides the CITIC, a number of other quasi-financial institutions have recently been established. Some of these, like the Tianjin International Trust and Investment Corporation, have taken a similar format to that of the CITIC, whereas others, like the Beijing Economic Development Corporation and the Fujian Investment Enterprise Corporation, have been established as development corporations. The financial functions of these and similar institutions is still being formalised but they will probably relate to local financing and infrastructure development for export and joint venture projects and possibly involve the raising of foreign and local capital. Some provincial investment corporations have even been reported as raising foreign capital through the issue of shares to Overseas Chinese.[23]

(h) Foreign Banks

As mentioned in the introductory section, foreign banks were responsible for developing today's banking practices in China and even now many senior Chinese bankers were initially foreign-trained. The war with Japan and the civil war that followed had forced many foreign banks to close their operations and their home country's failure to recognise the new mainland government precluded their re-establishment. The Cultural Revolution also had its effects, but nevertheless four foreign banks were able to retain their Chinese branches in Shanghai: the Chartered Bank; Hongkong and Shanghai Banking Corporation; the Hong Kong-based, Bank of East Asia; and Singapore's Overseas-Chinese Banking Corporation (OCBC) (which also has a branch office in Xiamen).

The foreign banks are rather restricted in their operations and may not even offer local chequing or savings accounts. Instead they may conduct only foreign business in respect of international trade and certain remittances. The Hongkong and Shanghai and the Chartered may also accept foreign-exchange denominated accounts from non-residents, but these funds must in turn be deposited with the Bank of China: the banks earn only a small commission for this service. As the Bank of China seeks further representation overseas – particularly in the US – additional foreign bank branches may eventually be established in Beijing and Guangzhou, as well as Shanghai.

A number of foreign banks have also established representative offices in Beijing. As of early 1981, these included the Hongkong and Shanghai Banking Corporation, the Bank of Tokyo, the Export – Import Bank of Japan, the First National Bank of Chicago, the Midland Bank, Banque National de Paris, the Bank of America, the Chase Manhattan Bank, Banca Commerciale Italiana, and Banco Nazionale del Lavoro. The Hong Kong-based Sun Hung Kai Securities also established a Beijing office in 1979. Finally the Hongkong and Shanghai Banking Corporation also maintains a trade liaison office in Guangzhou. The lack of adequate office and staff accommodation is often cited as one reason why more representative offices have not been established.

(i) Chinese Financial Institutions Overseas

As mentioned in the Bank of China section, the change of government in 1949 presented significant difficulties for those institutions with extensive overseas interests. Many of these were effectively liquidated and assets deployed elsewhere but some retained both their China head office and identity overseas. This section examines these banking, finance, and insurance interests.

(i) *Banking and finance*

Within the banking sector, these People's Republic-controlled institutions can be divided into those incorporated on the mainland and those incorporated overseas but controlled by mainland residents. With the exception of the Bank of China (discussed elsewhere) and Kwangtung Provincial Bank's Singapore branch, these institutions conduct their overseas business within Hong Kong; the names, headquarter locations, and number of Hong Kong branches are shown in Table 1.5.

At one time these banks' operations were thought to be simply those

TABLE 1.5   State-owned Chinese banks in Hong Kong

	Location of headquarters	No. of branches in Hong Kong
Mainland incorporated banks		
Bank of Communications	Beijing	22
China and South Sea Bank	Shanghai	13
China State Bank	Shanghai	12
Kincheng Banking Corp	Shanghai	14
Kwangtung Provincial Bank[a]	Guangzhou	15
National Commercial Bank	Shanghai	11
Sin Hau Trust, Savings & Commercial Bank	Shanghai	26
Yien Yieh Commercial Bank	Shanghai	13
Hong Kong incorporated banks[b]		
Nanyang Commercial Bank Ltd	Guangzhou	24
Po Sang Bank	Beijing	4
Chiyu Banking Corp. Ltd	Xiamen	7
Hua Chiao Commercial Bank Ltd	Beijing	10

[a] Under the Pinyin system this is now the Guangdong Provincial Bank.
[b] Location of majority of shareholders given.

of *de facto* branches of the Bank of China,[24] but they are in fact not subordinate. As one Chinese banker reportedly explained, 'we are all sister banks and no one is any more important than another. Every year, every bank in Hong Kong which is responsible to Peking, including the Bank of China, must send its statement of accounts to Peking'.[25] Nevertheless, it would not be surprising if the Bank of China had something of a 'big sister' influence on their operations – particularly in more recent years[26] as they have adopted more aggressive, Western-style banking techniques.

Besides the banking business, a number of these banks have expanded into other activities by way of subsidiary or affiliated companies – particularly deposit-taking companies. The Po Sang Bank, for example, has a wholly owned subsidiary, Po Fung Finance; the Hua Chiao Commercial Bank, Chiao Yue Finance; the Bank of China, China Development Finance Corporation; the Chiyu Banking Corporation, Chiyu Finance; Kingcheng Banking Corporation, Kincheng Finance (HK) Ltd; Yien Yieh Commercial Bank, Yien Yieh Finance Co. Ltd; and the Nanyang Commercial Bank, Nanyang Finance Co. and Nanyang Commercial Bank Trustees, as well as a number of trading and warehouse companies.[27] The Nanyang Commercial Bank has also introduced its own bank card, the Federal Card. The most significant diversification, though, has come only recently with the establishment of two deposit-taking company[28] joint ventures with foreign banks: the Kincheng Banking Corporation's Kincheng Tokyo Finance in conjunction with the Bank of Tokyo and the CCIC Finance Ltd, a consortium owned 30 per cent by the First National Bank of Chicago, 30 per cent by the Industrial Bank of Japan, 30 per cent by the Bank of China and 10 per cent by the PRC-controlled China Resource Company. It is thought that these latter institutions may play an important role in China's foreign loan raisings – particularly Euro bonds – when they eventuate.

(ii) *Insurance*

As mentioned in the People's Insurance Company of China section, two state–private joint companies, China Insurance Company Ltd and Tai Ping Insurance Company Ltd, are also headquartered in Beijing but conduct most of their business overseas. The China Insurance Company operates through branches in Hong Kong, Singapore and Macau; and the Tai Ping through branches in Hong Kong and Singapore. Both underwrite ocean marine, fire, life, personal accident, workers' compensation and motor vehicle insurance. The locally incorporated Ming An Insurance Company in Hong Kong is also believed to be PRC-controlled and active in these areas.

FINANCIAL MARKETS

As with banking and insurance, China's financial markets developed initially with a dual personality. The native financial market comprised by native bankers[29] and their guilds were once an important facet of local banking and finance, but were quickly surpassed by the markets which developed around the Western banks. Further competition came as the modern Chinese banks became more important and by the late 1930s the 'modern' money market together with that of the foreign banks comprised the bulk of the market.

Similarly in the securities industry, China's two major stock exchanges, in Shanghai and Hong Kong, were both established by foreign interests. Indeed it was not until 1940, when 'Chinese Stock Promotion Committee' was formed by a group of Shanghai banks and trust companies, that local interest even initiated an informal trading system: at its peak the shares of 76 companies were admitted for trading – twenty-two of which were banks.[30]

As none of these markets survived the Japanese invasion and the civil war, China's present financial markets date from the banking system's re-establishment and the government's more recent modernisation programme. For discussion purposes these are divided between the inter-bank market, the foreign-exchange market, and bond raisings.

(a) The Money Market

The lack of banks within China precluded the development of a local inter-bank market but there is nevertheless a type of market – perhaps more correctly an intra-bank market – operating within the People's Bank of China. Within this, the provincial branches of the Bank periodically match their Renminbi position with the head office at the rate of 0.27 per cent per month. More importantly, there is also some fund interaction between the Bank and the rural credit co-operatives: deposits from the credit co-operatives with the People's Bank of China earn interest at the rate of 3.24 per cent per annum; and loans by the Bank to these institutions, when made, are charged at 2.16 per cent.[31]

(b) The Foreign-Exchange Market

A very recent addition to China's financial market was the development in late 1980 of what the regional press referred to as a 'rudimentary foreign-exchange market' for Chinese enterprises.[32]

Since the early 1950s all state enterprises have been required to sell their foreign-exchange earnings to the Bank of China but, under a new system, these companies may retain some (around 10 per cent) of these funds as an added incentive for exporting. These, mainly US dollars, may then be resold to other companies on a spot basis through a foreign-exchange facility established in the Bank of China's Guangdong (Canton) branch. Before bidding, however, prospective purchasers must first hold a government-approved foreign-exchange spending quota or permit. Previously, once approval was obtained, the state automatically provided the foreign-exchange required. If there was a national foreign-exchange shortage, the firm would just have to wait – regardless of the profitability of the project. In line with its present market forces strategy, the government's new system allows companies the choice of waiting or bidding for another firm's foreign-exchange holdings. The effective exchange rates on these funds have thus far been considerably above the official exchange rate and are in line with the government's recent two-tiered foreign-exchange rate policy: as of 1 January 1981 money was exchanged on the basis of 2.8 Renminbi to the US dollar on trade transactions, compared to the official rate of 1.5. This encourages a greater export effort on the part of Chinese industry while restricting imports.

Within the buying and selling process the Bank of China acts solely in a brokerage capacity (rather than as a dealer) and simply matches the buyers' and sellers' requirements; it receives a commission of 0.25 per cent from both parties for its services. Eventually the Bank hopes to operate exchange facilities in all of China's principal trading cities.

(c) Bond Raisings

Since the founding of the People's Republic, neither government nor state enterprise public capital raisings have been particularly popular, but there have been some exceptions. Fujian Province's Fukien Overseas Chinese Investment Corporation, for example, was said to have raised close to US$13 million prior to 1960 through the sale of its bonds to Overseas Chinese. The government and various other government agencies also raised some domestic and overseas funds through debt issues in the government's early days.

A move towards self-reliance, though, limited the amount of these raisings and as part of the Cultural Revolution an effort was made to free the Chinese government from its previous debt obligations – a goal achieved by 1968. An attitude against foreign borrowing remained for some years afterwards and, even as late as 1977, official statements on the evils of foreign capital were seen in the press. More recently, with the emphasis on modernisation, the government has taken a new attitude on foreign borrowing and investment and various types of government and private credit agreements have since been arranged. Even so Chinese government officials have indicated that they are as yet unwilling to conduct any substantial Euro market borrowings: those obtained will be done strictly on a project-by-project basis.[33]

The establishment of a variety of trust and investment corporations and provincial development corporations suggest that additional funds may be obtained through local authorities' debt issues as well. To this end, for example, the Investment Enterprise Corporation of Fujian province recently issued 500-, 5000-, and 50,000-Renminbi denominated bonds yielding 6 per cent on eight-year maturities, 7 per cent on 10-year maturities, and 8 per cent on 12-year maturities – issues particularly designed to appeal to Overseas Chinese. The Fujian provincial government has also recently arranged two ordinary foreign borrowings in its own right guaranteed by the Bank of China. Bank of China officials have reportedly indicated that China would like to raise funds through more sizeable bond issues in the future, but there are many technical matters still to be resolved.[34]

Within China itself, however, bond issues have recently come back into favour and in early February 1981 (after this chapter had been prepared) the government announced a 5 billion yuan issue of Treasury Bonds. The securities will be issued with a 10-year maturity in eight different denominations ranging from 10 to 1,000,000 Renminbi. The bonds will yield 4 per cent in interest with the principal and interest repaid in five equal instalments starting in the sixth year. They will be sold to state-owned enterprises, collectives and local government agencies as well as to individuals and are designed to soak up some of the excess liquidity in the economy and provide a less inflationary means of financing the government's budget deficit.[35]

ANALYSIS

China's financial system has proved its viability under a wide range of government policies and those of the post-1979 era seem particularly to favour the banking industry. As one observer explained, 'Chinese bankers have come into their own. In fact, the years 1979 and 1980 may well be called the years of the bankers.'[36] The move to a partially market force system will mean many more changes in the economy than just charging loan interest. Mention has been made of the accounting and now allocation role placed on the banking system, but allowing consumers to influence the market will bring other changes as well. Thus far, for example, the banks have had to increase their interest rates on deposits. As more choice becomes available on the market the need to postpone consumption, and hence save, will be removed and consumer savings will occur only if the interest offered allows them sufficient compensation. Corporations' financial attitudes will be similarly effected. In addition to this change, the People's Bank, in its central banking capacity, may also need to take some forms of monetary policy actions as price competition replaces rationing within many sectors of the economy.

To this end there has been much discussion of the need for specialisation within the banking system, and the renewed independence of the Bank of China, the People's Construction Bank and the Agricultural Bank of China reflects this trend. The demand for commercial banking expertise and the potential need for central banking skills suggest that the specialisations required within the People's Bank might be better served by separate institutions, and that a specialist industrial/commercial bank, a central bank, and possibly even a savings bank should be established. These additional institutions, each serving its own special market, would also fit well within the new emphasis on profit and loss accountability within the banking system as each customer grouping – commercial, consumer, and government business – would then be forced to cover its own costs and any present subsidies would be eliminated. The major difficulty with such moves, in addition to differing political interests, is that of staffing. Few Chinese bankers have substantial lending experience and their resources might suffer if stretched too thinly. As much of the government's present economic policy rests on the ability of the nation's bankers to allocate and properly monitor investment, it can only be hoped that these shortages will be quickly overcome.

TRENDS AND PREDICTIONS

Since 1977 the Chinese government has worked to expand China's involvement in foreign trade and generally promote the development of the Chinese economy. The Four Modernisations programme, though admittedly over-zealous, reflects the enthusiastic spirit in which the government has tried to modernise Chinese agriculture, industry, defence, and science and technology. Admittedly many projects later proved impracticable but the realisation that this was the case in mid-1979 and the government's subsequent policy of readjustment, reconstruction, ccnsolidation and improvement still augurs well for China's economic management abilities.

One of the key changes has been the move toward decentralisation and the use of market forces rather than regulation to achieve certain goals. Thus, in limited areas and industries, it will be the management who decide production and pricing policies and who will be responsible for the profit or loss that results. The replacement of previously interest-free government grants with interest-bearing loans is also part of this transformation process and will place even more demands on the Chinese banking system. While the Cultural Revolution and time have robbed the banks of many of their experienced older staff and precluded younger officers from gaining the same exposure to lending and funds accountability, the banks' experience thus far suggests that they will be able to handle these new requirements.

China's overall economic future on the whole is also bright. Unlike many developing countries it has maintained tight control of its own resources and is now attempting to utilise foreign technology fully in their development. The recent cancellation of many substantial foreign-related investment projects may affect some companies' willingness to assist in the future, but fortunately Chinese market and labour forces are still sufficiently attractive to most firms. There are also many shortages in infrastructure, raw materials and labour skills which may slow the rate of growth.

Indeed it was physically impossible for the country to have achieved the short-term goals that many overly optimistic observers had suggested. Nevertheless China has extensive coal and oil reserves and is already the world's third largest producer of energy. In the long run, the development of these energy reserves and China's labour force should help to ensure China's future economic prosperity and even the fulfilment and surpassing of the government's initial modernisation goals.

NOTES

1. G. C. Allen and A. G. Donnithorne, *Western Enterprise in Far Eastern Economic Development* (London: George Allen & Unwin, 1954) p. 102.
2. Ibid. p. 106.
3. The Imperial government was first involved itself in 1897 with the Imperial Bank of China, and, more importantly, in 1904 with the establishment of the Hu-pu Bank (later the Ta Ching Bank) which was reconstituted in 1912 as The Bank of China, an institution which exists today.
4. Albert Feurerwerker, *The Chinese Economy, 1912–1949* (Ann Arbor: University of Michigan Press, 1968) p. 57.
5. In the mid-1930s, when reportedly 140 modern Chinese banks were in operation, the 13 largest banks controlled 78 per cent of the local bank assets. It is doubtful that the 14 new additions by 1937 had substantially changed this position (John G. Gurley, *China's Economy and the Maoist Strategy* (New York: Monthly Review Press, 1976) p. 267).
6. *Banking Structure and Sources of Finance in the Far East* (London: Financial Times Business Publishing, 1980) p. 340.
7. Leo Goodstadt, 'China's Resilient Bankers Emerge from the Shadows', *Asian Banking*, June 1980, p. 26.
8. *Banking Structure and Sources of Finance in the Far East*, p. 341.
9. Gordon Bennett (ed.), *China's Finance and Trade: A Policy Reader* (London: Macmillan, 1978) p. 143.

10. Pauline Loong, 'A Second Look at the Role of Socialist Banking', *Far Eastern Economic Review*, 19 December 1980, pp. 41–2.
11. Jerome A. Cohen, 'The Bank of China Clears up its Legal Status', *Euromoney*, December 1980, pp. 108–13, discusses the specifics of the new articles and their significance in terms of international bank guarantees.
12. According to its previous articles, as recent as 1962, it was still described as a joint public–private bank and prior to the Cultural Revolution its few remaining private shareholders still received dividends. Apparently, outside shareholders were recently contacted or their shares otherwise acquired as the new articles make no provision for certificates or the rights of private shareholders.
13. Article 5 as cited in *Euromoney*, December 1980 p. 109.
14. *The People's Republic of China: A Business Profile*, 3rd edn (Hong Kong: Hongkong and Shanghai Banking Corporation, 1980) p. 32.
15. Ibid., p. 56.
16. Leo Goodstadt, 'China's Resilient Bankers Emerge from the Shadows', p. 28.
17. 'China's Financial Institutions', *The China Business Review*, July–August 1980, p. 18.
18. The frequent opening and closing of the bank seemingly relates to political or bureaucratic infighting as certain groups tried to remove the People's Bank's control over that aspect of the economy.
19. Frank M. Tamagna, *Banking and Finance in China* (New York: Institute of Pacific Relations, 1942) p. 42.
20. G. C. Allen and A. G. Donnithorne, *Western Enterprises in Far Eastern Economic Development*, pp. 120–1.
21. 'China's Foreign Insurance', *China Economy and Trade*, vol. 6 (1980) p. 1.
22. Jerome A. Cohen, 'The Bank of China Clears up its Legal Status', p. 113.
23. *Asia 1980 Yearbook* (Hong Kong: Far Eastern Economic Review, 1980) p. 157.
24. Y. C. Jao, *Banking and Currency in Hong Kong: A Study of Postwar Financial Development* (London: Macmillan, 1974) p. 39.
25. As cited in Cheng Huan, 'Peking Calls the Tune for Chinese Banks', *Asian Finance*, September 1975, p. 19.
26. 'Beijing's Banks Capitalise on Xianggang', *Asian Banking*, July 1980 p. 52, discusses some of the PRC banks recent operational changes and new ventures.
27. Jo McBride, 'The Growing Rewards of Ping-Pong Economics', *Asian Banking*, July 1980, pp. 37–41, discusses some of China's other investments in Hong Kong business.
28. A discussion of deposit-taking company operations can be found in M. T. Skully, *Merchant Banking in the Far East*, 2nd edn (London: Financial Times Business Publishing, 1980) pp. 58–109.
29. A native bank was usually founded by one family group or clan as a single proprietorship or small partnership to accept deposits, make loans and handle the remittances and exchange of money within the country (Frank M. Tamagna, *Banking and Finance in China*, pp. 57–81).
30. Ibid., p. 298.

31. 'China's Financial Institutions', *The China Business Review*, July–August 1980, pp. 15 and 18.
32. Pauline Loong, 'Have Dollar, Will Sell', *Far Eastern Economic Review*, 9 January 1981, pp. 53–4, discusses this development in more detail.
33. *The People's Republic of China: A Business Profile*, p. 27.
34. Comments dated as of July 1980 as cited in *The China Business Review*, July–August 1980, p. 10. Also see Leo Goodstadt, 'Hope Springs Eternal in China's Bond Market', *Asian Banking*, May 1980, for further details of the market's expectations.
35. *The Asian Wall Street Journal*, 12 February 1981.
36. V. G. Kulkarni, 'China's Bankers Step Out of their Shell', *Bankers Handbook for Asia, 1979–80* (Hong Kong: Asian Finance Publications, 1980) p. 19.

2 Financial Institutions and Markets in Hong Kong

MICHAEL T. SKULLY

INTRODUCTION

(a) The Setting

Located near the mouth of the Pearl River on the coast of Southern China, Hong Kong remains one of the last major possessions of the once vast British Empire. Established as a naval base and trading post under the Treaty of Nanking in 1842, the Colony's original territory of some 32 square miles was expanded to cover the Kowloon Peninsula and Stonecutters' Island (another 3.75 square miles) under the First Convention of Peking in 1860, and the New Territories (some 365.75 square miles) on a 99-year lease signed under the Second Convention of Peking in 1897.[1]

Under British rule, the Colony has survived the numerous political and economic changes of mainland China and has developed into the most important centre for entrepôt, or re-export, trade within the Far East. As Hong Kong's own industrial base grew, entrepôt trade declined in relative importance (24.5 per cent of exports in 1978) but as China's trade with the West has expanded, Hong Kong has seen the importance of this activity re-emerge, both in absolute and relative terms (an estimated 27.8 per cent in 1980).

With an average growth in GDP over 1976 – 9 of some 12.5 per cent the Colony has shown a good economic growth record since the 1975 recession,[2] but this performance has been somewhat marred by the acceleration of inflation in the last few years: 5.8 per cent in 1978, 11.6 per cent in 1979, and an expected 14 per cent in 1980. Fortunately, government capital works spending and its handling of budget surplus (once a major inflationary factor) have changed significantly in the last few years, and much of today's inflation is a function of imported price increases rather than government policy. Nevertheless, further changes in government attitudes both in economic and political areas, such as refugee handling, coupled with increased China trade looks well for the Colony's immediate economic future.

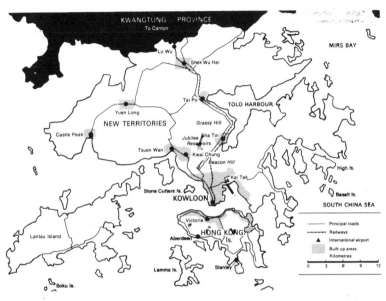

MAP 2.1   Hong Kong

Source: Department of Trade and Resources, *Businessman's Guide Hong Kong* (Canberra: Australian Government Publishing Service, 1979).

It has traditionally been political rather than economic matters which have been the major concern of the Colony's investors. First, there was the overall question of the Colony itself – would the Peking government allow it to continue or press for the British withdrawal. Secondly, what would happen after midnight 30 June 1997 when the lease on the New Territories, over 90 per cent of the Colony's land mass, expired. Finally what long-term effects would China's *rapprochement* with the West have on Hong Kong's entrepôt and own export trade.

In terms of the Colony's future the fear has not been that the Chinese might take the Colony by force, but that they would not renew the lease for the New Territories when it expired. It is important to stress,

however, that the Chinese government does not recognise any of the
treaties on which Hong Kong is based and considers all property still
part of China. Therefore the expiration date is a moot point: the
National People's Congress includes delegates representing not only
Hong Kong but Macau and Taiwan as well. The significant fact, though,
is that as a by-product of China's new foreign and economic policies,
Hong Kong finally received some official attention and in late 1978 Sir
Murray MacLehose became the first Hong Kong Governor officially to
visit Peking. Subsequent Chinese statements on both the lease and
Colony's overall future have also been encouraging. Substantial investment by China-controlled enterprises within the Colony and the number
of Hong Kong – China joint venture projects within Guangdong
Province further suggest that the Colony will continue. Indeed Hong
Kong's position as China's second largest trading partner (after Japan)
and most important source of foreign-exchange, together with its
potential for technical and production joint ventures with China, is in
itself good assurance for the future. The key, as Hong Kong's Governor
explained is that 'Hong Kong continues to exist because China wants it
to'.[3]

(b) An Overview of the Financial Sector

Because it was a trading post and entrepôt trade centre, Hong Kong's
financial institutions developed around international trade: the foreign
banks concentrated on international trade financing and foreign
exchange, and insurance companies on cargo and hull insurance. Local
commerce and the everyday needs of the Colony's largely Chinese
population were handled by merchant traders, private money lenders
and remittance houses: family-financed businesses were the rule rather
than the exception.

The Nationalist Chinese government's loss of the mainland in the late
1940s, though, greatly changed Hong Kong's economy and, through it,
the financial sector. A substantial influx of mainland Chinese, many
with extensive industrial experience and capital backing, and the partial
closing of the mainland forced Hong Kong to develop its own industrial
base. The new labour, expertise and capital helped create the export-
orientated light manufacturing industry base which today, together with
the shipping, insurance, and banking industries, comprise the major
portion of the Hong Kong economy.

As the local economy changed so did the Colony's financial sector and
as Hong Kong's economic performance and low taxation base attracted

overseas investment more financial institutions established local operations. The entrepôt trade provided a natural base for the Colony's regional financial role and it was partly for this reason that the Bank of America approached the Colony prior to selecting Singapore as the home of its new Asian dollar market: the Colony would not remove its 15 per cent interest withholding tax nor license additional foreign banks. Nevertheless, from 1969 Hong Kong continued to attract new financial institutions in spite of, rather than because of, government policy. Indeed much of its growth in the early 1970s can be attributed to surplus funds within developed countries and, following the Sterling Area's contraction in 1972, its relatively free exchange controls. The true catalyst, though, was the 1972 – 3 real estate and stock market boom which publicised Hong Kong within international financial circles and gave most international financial institutions sufficient reason to open in Hong Kong. As a result of these new entries Hong Kong grew to become an international financial centre and one of the most important in Asia. As one banker explained, 'Hong Kong now possibly ranks as the third largest financial centre in the world, and certainly in foreign bank presence it is second only to London'.[4]

FINANCIAL INSTITUTIONS

As a result of the government attitude against regulation and inter-ference in the private sector, it is almost impossible to collect statistics on the total assets of the Colony's financial institutions. Indeed, it is difficult even to determine the various types of institutions within the Colony and the relative numbers of each. But even with limited quantitative material, there is little question that the commercial banks are the most important single group and the institutions can be classified into their normal bank and non-bank groupings. The different types of insti-tutions are listed in Table 2.1.

(a) **Banking Institutions**

There is basically only one type of banking institution in Hong Kong – the commercial banks. There are no central or development banks, and savings and trust banking services are provided by the commercial banks themselves rather than by separate institutions. Although not a bank, the Colonial Government Monetary Affairs Branch and its Exchange Fund fulfil some banking functions and are discussed within this section.

TABLE 2.1   Types of financial institutions in Hong Kong

The Exchange Fund
Commercial banks
Deposit-taking companies
Other finance companies
Insurance companies
Hong Kong Export Credit Insurance Company
Pension funds
Unit trusts and mutual funds
Credit unions
Co-operative societies
Pawnbrokers
Private money lenders
The Development Loan Fund
The Home Ownership Fund
The Lottery Fund
Hong Kong Building and Loan Agency

(i) *The Monetary Affairs Branch and the Exchange Fund*

Unlike the other countries examined in this book, Hong Kong operates without a central bank. However, while many have suggested that such an institution should be established, many of its functions are already provided through the Financial Secretary's Monetary Affairs Branch and the Exchange Fund.

The Monetary Affairs Branch is made up of two major components: the Monetary Foreign Exchange and Banking Division and the Exchange Division. The former is concerned with foreign-exchange operations, monetary policy, banking, international inter-government financial institutions, Home Ownership Scheme mortgage finance, and economic research, while the latter is responsible for the management and operations of the Exchange Fund itself.

The Exchange Fund

The Exchange Fund was established in 1935 to regulate the exchange value of the Hong Kong dollar and is at present managed by the Monetary Affairs Branch of the Government Secretariat under the control of the Financial Secretary. The Fund provides the backing for the colony's legal tender and now serves a role not unlike that of an informal currency board.

Through the colony's two note issuing banks, it regulates the amount of Hong Kong dollar bank notes on issue. These banks may issue bank notes worth up to HK$95 million against approved securities, but for the most part Hong Kong bank notes are issued against non-interest-bearing certificates of indebtedness purchased from the Exchange Fund. These certificates are then issued or redeemed in line with changes in the levels of currency outstanding and provide the notes' legal backing.

In addition to its own investments the Exchange Fund also holds the foreign currency assets of the Colonial government. Recently the government transferred most of its local dollar holdings to the Fund so that, as one publication explained, the Fund 'effectively has become the banker to the government'.[5] The control of such an asset base together with the imposition of 100 per cent liquidity ratio on the short-term deposit of these, compared to 25 per cent in normal deposits with the licensed banks, also allows the Fund some influence on the money supply through its choice of deposit maturities. Moreover, as the then Financial Secretary, Sir Philip Haddon-Cave, pointed out, 'the Exchange Fund can act as a bank of last resort through its ability to supply Hong Kong dollars in the foreign exchange market'.[6]

While the Fund still has responsibility for managing the value of the Hong Kong dollar with respect to foreign currencies, since the floating of the Hong Kong dollar on 26 November 1974 there has been much less need for market intervention. For the most part, this intervention is confined to smoothing out erratic movements in the exchange rates.

(ii) *Commercial banks*

As at 1 October 1980 Hong Kong had 115 licensed banks with 1123 branches operating within the Colony. This represented one branch per every 4363 people: a ratio even exceeding those of many developed countries. The banks have traditionally dominated the local financial sector and still comprise the largest of the institutions. Though the growth of the deposit-taking companies may appear to have detracted somewhat from their overall importance, it should be remembered that licensed banks control a large number, particularly the more important, of the deposit-taking companies and, to a lesser extent, other financial institutions.

This discussion first examines the various types of banks in Hong Kong, then their regulation, funding and loan activities.

Types of banks
Hong Kong's commercial banks can basically be divided into five different, though very much inter-related, groups: the note issuing banks, the state-owned Chinese banks, other local Chinese banks, fully

licensed foreign banks, and the more recent restricted foreign banks. The relative importance of each group in terms of numbers and total branches is shown in Table 2.2. Though not licensed to conduct local banking, other foreign banks may obtain approval to open local representative offices for liaison work within the colony.

TABLE 2.2   Types of banks in Hong Kong: the total numbers and branches of each (as of 1 October 1980)

No. of banks	Type of bank	No. of branches
2	Note issuing banks	337
13	Chinese state banks	182
29	Local Chinese banks	403
30	Ordinary foreign banks	160
41	Restricted foreign banks	41
115		1123

Note issuing banks: The note issuing banks, the Hongkong and Shanghai Banking Corporation and the Chartered Bank, are the largest banks within the Colony and dominate much of the local banking practices. In co-operation with the Exchange Fund, the two banks' notes serve as the Colony's local currency. Of the HK$7920.27 million worth of bank notes on issue at the end of 1979, 78.1 per cent were issued by the Hongkong and Shanghai Banking Corporation and 21.9 per cent by the Chartered. Their relative importance in terms of branches is shown in Table 2.3.

TABLE 2.3   Note issuing banks in Hong Kong (1 October 1980)

Bank	Country of incorporation	No. of branches in Hong Kong
Hongkong and Shanghai Banking	Hong Kong[7]	248
Corporation Chartered Bank	UK	89
		337

In addition to their age [8] and size, the note issuing banks are also of importance to the Colony in that they conduct much of the banks' negotiations with the government as the rotating Chairman of the Exchange Banks' Association, operate the banks' clearing system within the Colony, and provide *de facto* lender of last resort support to the financial system.[9]

Chinese state banks: There are 13 banks in Hong Kong owned by the People's Republic of China. As shown in Table 2.4, nine of these are incorporated in mainland China and four are mainland China controlled, Hong Kong incorporated banks. These banks are active in the financing of China's foreign trade with Hong Kong and other countries, handling the remittances made by Overseas Chinese to Chinese residents, and supporting other mainland-controlled business activities in the Hong Kong, such as retailing, warehousing, cold storage, factories, property investment, insurance, oil storage and travel services.[10] More recently these banks have substantially changed their local policies and now aggressively seek additional deposits and lending business in the local market. As one study commented, 'to achieve these ends, the PRC banks have also recently installed a centralised computer system, acquiried more premises, and set up deposit-taking subsidiaries'.[11]

Local Chinese banks: The other local Chinese banks were once a more distinct group but as a function of the government moratorium on new

TABLE 2.4   State-owned Chinese banks in Hong Kong (1 October 1980)

	No. of branches in Hong Kong
Mainland incorporated banks	
Bank of China	11
Bank of Communications	22
China & South Sea Bank	13
China State Bank	12
Kincheng Banking Corp.	14
Kwangtung Provincial Bank	15
National Commercial Bank	11
Sin Hua Trust, Savings & Commercial Bank	26
Yien Yieh Commercial Bank	13
Hong Kong incorporated banks	
Nanyang Commercial Bank Ltd	24
Po Sang Bank	4
Chiyu Banking Corp. Ltd	7
Hua Chiao Commercial Bank Ltd	10
Total branches	182

bank licensing many were partly acquired by foreign and sometimes other local banks. Thus the foreign affiliated concerns perform similarly to their foreign licensed counterparts while some of the smaller local banks retain their traditionally strong involvement in gold trading, securities and real estate financing, and even some consumer lending. As *Asian Finance* once described them, 'the locally-owned small banks spread throughout the Colony largely cater for the numerous shopkeepers, and act as deposit-taking houses for the common man.[12] A listing of the locally incorporated banks together with their affiliations is shown in Table 2.5.

TABLE 2.5   Licensed local banks in Hong Kong (1 October 1980)[a]

Bank name	Institutional affiliation and percentage owned	Branches in Hong Kong
Bank of Canton	Security Pacific National Bank USA (72%)	12
Bank of East Asia Ltd	None	34
Chan Man Cheong Finance Company[b]	None	1
Chekiang First Bank Ltd	Dai-Ichi Kangyo Bank, Japan (33%)	8
Commercial Bank of Hong Kong Ltd	Tokai Bank, Japan (10%)	8
Dah Sing Bank Ltd	None	10
Far East Bank Ltd	Citibank NA, USA (76%)	23
Grindlays Dao Heng Bank Ltd	Grindlays Bank, UK (100%)	17
Hang Lung Bank Ltd	None	16
Hang Seng Bank Ltd	Hongkong and Shanghai Banking Corporation, Hong Kong (61%)	44
Hong Kong Chinese Bank Ltd	None	7
Hong Kong Industrial & Commercial Bank Ltd	Overseas Trust Bank, Hong Kong (94.34%)	17
Hong Kong Metropolitan Bank Ltd	BCCI Holdings, Luxembourg (66.4%)	13
Hong Nin Bank Ltd	None	5
Ka Wah Bank Ltd	Yu Chuan Finance Ltd, Malaysia (74%)	14
Kwong On Bank Ltd	Fuji Bank, Japan (55%)	17
Lee Shing[b]	None	1
Liu Chong Hing Bank Ltd	The Mitsubishi Bank, Japan (25%)	25

TABLE 2.5 (*Contd.*)

Bank name	Institutional affiliation and percentage owned	Branches in Hong Kong
Ming Tai Finance Company[b]	None	1
Overseas Trust Bank Ltd	None	32
Shanghai Commercial Bank Ltd	Wells Fargo Bank, USA (10%)	23
Tai Sang Bank Ltd	None	5
Tai Yau Bank Ltd	None	1
Union Bank of Hong Kong Ltd	None	11
United Chinese Bank Ltd	None	13
Wayfoong Finance Ltd	None	1
Wing Hang Bank Ltd	Irving Trust Co., USA (51%)	12
Wing Lung Bank Ltd	Chartered Bank Ltd, UK (13.3%)	18
Wing On Bank Ltd	None	14

[a] Excludes the note issuing Hongkong and Shanghai Banking Corporation and the People's Republic of China controlled Nanyang Commercial Bank Ltd, Po Sang Bank, Chiyu Banking Corp., and Hua Chiao Commercial Bank Ltd.

[b] The Chan Man Cheong Finance Company, Lee Shing, and Ming Tai Finance Company while licensed as banks under the 1948 Banking Ordinance were unincorporated enterprises and therefore unable to use the word 'bank' in their name under the 1964 ordinance. They nevertheless remain licensed banks as does the Hongkong and Shanghai Banking Corporation's Subsidiary, Wayfoong Finance Ltd.

Ordinary foreign banks: Foreign banks could open branches in Hong Kong with little difficulty prior to 1965 and these banks, once opened, were subject to no different regulation than local incorporated banks. With the exception of the Chartered Bank, one of the two note issuing banks, however, few have established extensive branch networks within the Colony. The Banque Nationale de Paris with 19 branches has the largest representation of the non-Chinese foreign banks, with Chase Manhattan and the Banque Belge pour l'Etranger SA tying for second place with 13 branches. Other foreign banks generally operate with only a couple of branches and many with just one office. A listing of these banks and the number of their respective branches is shown in Table 2.6.

Restricted foreign banks: From 1965 to 1978 the government imposed a moratorium on new banking licences within the Colony. This was lifted in respect of foreign banks on 15 March 1978 but new applicants were subject to three conditions: they must be incorporated in countries with effective banking supervision, have total assets (less contra items) of at

TABLE 2.6 Foreign banks with normal licences (as of 1 October 1980)

Banks	Country	No. of Hong Kong branches
Algemene Bank Nederland, NV	Netherlands	10
American Express International Banking Corp.	USA	5
Bangkok Bank Ltd	Thailand	4
Bank Negara Indonesia 1946	Indonesia	2
Bank of America National Trust & Savings Assoc.	USA	8
Bank of India Ltd	India	2
Bank of Tokyo Ltd	Japan	5
Banque Belge pour l'Etranger	Belgium	13
Banque de l'Indochine et de Suez	France	9
Banque National de Paris	France	19
Barclays Bank Limited	UK	5
Chase Manhattan Bank NA	USA	13
Chung Khiaw Bank Ltd	Singapore	2
Citibank NA	USA	12
Equitable Banking Corporation	Philippines	1
European Asian Bank	Germany	6
Four Seas Communications Bank Ltd	Singapore	1
Indian Overseas Bank Ltd	India	7
Korea Exchange Bank	Korea	3
Malayan Banking Berhad	Malaysia	2
Mercantile Bank Ltd	UK	2
National Bank of Pakistan	Pakistan	4
Overseas-Chinese Banking Corporation Ltd	Singapore	2
Overseas Union Bank Ltd	Singapore	3
Rainer International Bank	USA	8
Sanwa Bank Ltd	Japan	3
Sumitomo Bank Ltd	Japan	2
Underwriters Bank (Overseas) Inc.	USA[a]	1
United Commercial Bank Ltd	India	4
United Overseas Bank Ltd	Singapore	2

[a] Actually incorporated in the Cayman Islands but a subsidiary of the USA's Continental Illinois National Bank.

least US$3000 million, and allow some form of reciprocity in their country of incorporation for Hong Kong banks. While the latter condition excluded banks from countries such as Australia, the other restrictions were not significant in international banking terms and the Colony was soon flooded with applications. Indeed the position was such that the granting of new licences was temporarily suspended on August 1979 to allow the government to decide on the criteria for further approvals. Nevertheless some 41 new banks from 12 different countries were granted permission to open a local branch: a listing of these institutions and their respective home countries is shown in Table 2.7. These banks, however, differ from previous foreign entries in that they may have only one office within Hong Kong. This condition was to ensure these banks' activities would be confined largely to wholesale rather than retail banking.

Bank representative offices: While not licensed for banking within Hong Kong, foreign banks nevertheless maintained a representative office for liaison with local businesses and financial institutions. These offices are covered in part under the Banking Ordinance as they first require permission to use the word 'bank' in their name before opening in Hong Kong. They are not allowed to conduct banking businesses but in practice many representative offices actively solicit deposit for and arrange loans from their offshore branches as well as advising Hong Kong residents on economic and trade matters within their bank's operating areas. The recent failure of the Australian-based Nugan Hand group and the role played by its local representative office has resulted in a tightening-up of the regulations and their enforcement.

Regulation
The Hong Kong government has traditionally had a bias against regulations and as long as the system worked well the government left business largely to its own devices. This is true of the banking industry and, as one writer put it, prior to 1964 'even barber shops in Hong Kong were more closely regulated than banks'.[13] However, the banking crisis of 1963 forced the issue and the Banking Ordinance of 1964 resulted, as did a moratorium on new banking licensing.

Since that time the Banking Ordinance has been amended and supplemented by numerous regulations. Today, banks incorporated in Hong Kong require a paid-up capital of HK$10 million and must gradually establish a reserve of a similar amount. Licensed foreign banks must ensure that their assets, less contingencies, in Hong Kong exceed their deposit liabilities by at least HK$10 million. The same bank regulations apply to all local incorporated banks as well as to all foreign banks, but are subject to different degrees of attention. It is the government's policy to look to the monetary authorities of the country in which a foreign bank is incorporated for the detailed regulation of such institutions. The local incorporated banks are viewed differently and the Banking Commissioner is concerned with all the locally-

TABLE 2.7   Foreign banks with restricted licences (as of 2 January 1981)

Banco di Roma	Italy	1
Banco Melli Iran	Iran	1
Bank of Montreal	Canada	1
Bank of Nova Scotia	Canada	1
Bank of Scotland	UK	1
Bank of Seoul and Trust Company	Korea	1
Banque de Paris et des Pays-Bas	France	1
Banque Worms	France	1
Canadian Imperial Bank of Commerce	Canada	1
Chemical Bank	USA	1
Commerzbank AG	Germany	1
Credit Lyonnais	France	1
Credit Suisse	Switzerland	1
Crocker National Bank	USA	1
Deutsche Bank AG	Germany	1
DG Bank Deutsche Genossenschaftsbank	Germany	1
Dresdner Bank AG	Germany	1
First National Bank of Boston	USA	1
First National Bank of Chicago	USA	1
Fuji Bank	Japan	1
Hanil Bank Ltd	Korea	1
Industrial Bank of Japan Ltd	Japan	1
Lloyds Bank International Ltd	UK	1
Manufacturers Hanover Trust Co.	USA	1
Mellon Bank NA	USA	1
Midland Bank Limited	UK	1
Morgan Guaranty Trust Co.	USA	1
National Westminster Bank Ltd	UK	1
North Carolina National Bank	USA	1
Northern Trust Company	USA	1
Philippines National Bank	Philippines	1
Republic National Bank	USA	1
Royal Bank of Canada	USA	1
Royal Bank of Scotland Ltd	UK	1
Société Generale	France	1
State Bank of India	India	1
Swiss Bank Corporation	Switzerland	1
Toronto-Dominion Bank	Canada	1
Union Bank of Switzerland	Switzerland	1
United California Bank	USA	1
Westdeutsche Landesbank Girozentrale	Germany	*

* To open in early 1981.

incorporated banks' operations regardless of their location. It is also expected that gearing ratio restrictions will be introduced in the future and there are rumours that the present capital requirement for Hong Kong banks may be increased from HK$10 to 50 million.

All banks in Hong Kong are required to maintain an amount equal to at least 25 per cent of their deposits in liquid assets and 100 per cent in the case of Exchange Fund deposits for 7 days or less. These liquid assets are comprised of two tiers of which the banks must maintain at least 15 per cent of their deposits in the first category. The first category includes cash, foreign currency, gold, demand or call deposits with other banks and Hong Kong-registered deposit-taking companies, overseas bank issued certificates of deposit, UK treasury bills and other money market instruments specified by the Financial Secretary. The remainder of the 25 per cent liquid asset requirement may be fulfilled by holding money at short notice with other banks and Hong Kong-registered deposit-taking companies, overseas issued bills of exchange, Hong Kong or UK government or government guaranteed securities with less than 5 years maturity, and other governments' securities specified by the Financial Secretary.

The government has no specific legislative means to set interest rates but in practice it has worked in conjunction with the Exchange Banks' Association to achieve the desired results; the government's use of morale suasion has increased dramatically since 1978. The Association, under an interest rates cartel agreement, sets the maximum rates members can offer on savings accounts and time deposits of one year or less. Membership of the Association, however, has been voluntary and the enforcement of its policies is only through peer group pressure. In December 1980, however, legislation was introduced to incorporate the Association into a statutory body known as the Hong Kong Associations of Banks and require all licensed banks to belong and follow its rulings. It also formalises the requirement for the body to consult the Financial Secretary before finalising its decisions.[14] It is also possible that a more comprehensive system of interest rate controls may result from these changes. As the Financial Secretary, Sir Philip Haddon-Cave explained, 'in the absence here in Hong Kong, for valid operational reasons, of some form of centrally determined discount rate, and in the absence of any means whereby money market rates can be directly influenced, deposit rates set under interest rate agreement have to play an important role in the management of our monetary affairs'.[15]

Funding

Banks in Hong Kong traditionally relied on demand deposits as their major source of funds but as the Colony developed this position changed dramatically. First, demand deposits dropped from 75 per cent of deposits in 1955 to 23 per cent in 1979. Secondly, the amounts due to banks abroad grew from just another liability to, as shown in Table 2.8,

TABLE 2.8   Liabilities of Hong Kong licensed banks (figures in HK$ million as of 31 July 1980)

37.4%	Deposits	82847
41.4%	Amounts due banks abroad	91824
8.4%	Amounts due deposit-taking companies	18528
12.8%	Other liabilities	28457
100.0	Total liabilities	221656

Source: *Hong Kong Monthly Digest of Statistics*, July 1980, p. 37.

the banks' single most important source of funds; these changes reflect the increasing awareness of investment alternatives among Hong Kong depositors and the growth of Hong Kong as an international financial centre.

In terms of the banks themselves the bulk of deposits are raised by the Hongkong and Shanghai Banking Corporation, the Chartered Bank, and the locally-incorporated Chinese banks. Indeed as one study commented, 'it is widely believed that the bank [the Hongkong and Shanghai Banking Corporation] and its subsidiaries control about two-thirds of the Colony's banking assets and deposits'.[16] This position has restricted the growth of the other foreign banks which must rely on borrowing on the local inter-bank market or raise the funds overseas. These banks have understandably been the most interested in developing the use of Hong Kong dollar certificates of deposits and bankers acceptances in the local money market. US dollar certificates of deposit, such as the floating and fixed rate issues used in Singapore, have been precluded in Hong Kong due to the Colony's 15 per cent interest witholding tax. However, in 1980 one bank succeeded in resolving this problem and as a result Hong Kong-issued US dollar CDs can be expected to become a more important funding source.

Competition for time deposits of one year or less and savings deposits are restricted under the Interest Rate Agreement of the Exchange Bankers' Association. The agreement, signed on 1 July 1964, was established to protect the industry from over-competition for deposits. Under this plan member banks pay no more than a certain interest rate for savings deposits, and in the case of time deposits the agreed maximum rates are tiered in favour of the smaller and weaker local banks. Basically it divides Hong Kong's banks into five categories. The Hongkong and Shanghai Banking Corporation and most foreign banks comprise the first group of banks and it is for them that the basic 7-day, 3-month, 6-month and one-year time deposit rates are set. Each of the subsequent four banking categories may then pay increments of 1/4 per cent more. Thus group 2 can pay 1/4 per cent more than the base rate, Group 3, 1/2 per cent; Group 4, 3/4 per cent; and Group 5, 1 per cent.[17] A listing of the banks and their categories is shown in Appendix 2.1.

In late 1980 the agreement set the maximum rates for savings deposits at 11 per cent and the Group 1 time deposit rates at 11 per cent for 7-day call money, 13 per cent for 3-month –, 14 per cent for 6-month –, and 14.5 per cent for 12-month deposits. The rates, of course, represent only the maximum and the banks may pay less if they wish. Also there are no restrictions on the interest rates paid on time deposits for periods over one year. As mentioned in the regulation section, the interest rate agreement has recently taken on a new importance to the banking community and its related interest rate working committee has met on a bimonthly basis since early 1979. The controls on interest rates for short-term funds have caused banks to concentrate on competing for over 12-month deposits and use other means to obtain short-term funds. These other ways include using deposit-taking company subsidiaries (not covered by the Exchange Banks' Association) to compete for funds, devising new instruments not covered by the Association, seeking swaps in the foreign-exchange market, creating extensive local branch networks, and introducing a variety of personal customer services such as automatic cash dispensers, cheque cards, and bank credit cards.

Advances
Banks in Hong Kong have traditionally used overdrafts and discounting facilities as the primary means of advancing funds. Technically over-draft loans are of a short-term nature but in practice many are effectively a form of medium- to long-term finance. While the foreign banks traditionally concentrated on international trade financing and foreign-exchange, their expansion into other forms of lending within the domestic market has resulted in some changes in local banking practice, and the types of loans and collateral required now vary considerably from bank to bank.[18] Very large loans are handled through loan syndications and may be arranged, as with other forms of finance, in either Hong Kong dollars or foreign currencies. Most local and some foreign banks are also involved in hire purchase and consumer lending, and both the VISA and Master Card bank credit card systems are locally represented. Owing to the local tax laws, leasing has not been important except for offshore business.

As shown in Table 2.9, of the loans and advances made in Hong Kong, general commerce comprises the largest of the 14 different

TABLE 2.9   Bank loans and advances in Hong Kong (figures for the end of June 1980)

Percentage		HK$ million
14.4	Manufacturing	10587
0.1	Agriculture and fisheries	75
11.6	Transport and transport equipment	8510
0.8	Electricity, gas and telephone	620
11.9	Building and construction	8725
31.4	General commerce	23157
0.6	Hotels, boarding houses and catering	419
4.5	Financial concerns	3285
0.9	Stockbrokers	655
7.5	Individuls to purchase residential properties	5531
3.6	Individuals for other business purposes	2651
5.1	Individuals for other private purposes	3753
7.6	All other purposes	5593
100.0	Total loans and advances in Hong Kong	73561

Source: *Hong Kong Monthly Digest of Statistics*, August 1980, p. 40.

lending groups and the manufacturing sector the second largest. While similar figures are not available for loans and advances made overseas (25.8 per cent of total loans and advances and, as shown in Table 2.10, 11.6 per cent of total assets), government agencies and transport equipment would rate together with general commerce and manufacturing in importance.

Although the rates on loans and advances are subject to neither government regulation nor an interest rate agreement, the savings and time deposit rates set by the Exchange Banks' Association greatly influences the rates charged as do the decisions of the Hongkong and Shanghai Banking Corporation and the Chartered Bank. Indeed, until very recently, the former's prime or best lending rate served as the basis for much of the bank lending rates within the Colony.[19] In September 1980, the best lending rate stood at 10.5 per cent. Traditionally loan syndications for Hong Kong dollar borrowings were not an important part of local banking: most large loans were denominated in US dollars. The only major loan syndicate was that organised for the Hong Kong dollar government's Mass Transit Railway HK$600 million borrowing. However, during 1980 a number of private sector Hong Kong dollar

TABLE 2.10   Assets of Hong Kong licensed banks (figures as of 31 July 1980)

Percentage		HK$ million
0.8	Cash	1632
25.4	Short-term claims on banks abroad	56307
10.3	Time deposits on banks abroad	22475
7.1	Amounts due from Deposit-taking companies	15841
33.3	Loans and advances in Hong Kong	73722
11.6	Loans and advances abroad	25680
2.8	Investments in Hong Kong	6135
—	Investments abroad	182
5.3	Other assets in Hong Kong	11656
3.4	Other assets abroad	7756
100.0	Total assets	221656

Source: *Hong Kong Monthly Digest of Statistics*, July 1980, p. 37.

syndications were arranged and such arrangements are expected to continue. The major reason for this development was the change in the structuring of the loan charges. They are now often based on a margin over the bank's cost of funds rather than over the traditional prime lending or base lending rate of the major banks. The increased use of Hong Kong dollar certificate of deposits has encouraged foreign banks to participate in more syndications. The most important private sector syndication to date was HK$6.7 million China Cement loan syndication led by the Bank of China in early 1980. Reflecting this new trend, half of the loan was charged at a margin over the prime lending rate and half over the Hong Kong Interbank Rate. It is expected that the Hong Kong Interbank Offered Rate, or HIBOR will become an important facet in both Hong Kong and foreign currency (mainly US dollar) lending.

In terms of foreign currency loans and loan syndications, Hong Kong banks and deposit-taking companies have long played an important role within Asia. In the past Hong Kong offshore lending profits were effectively tax-free but interest paid on deposits were subject to a 15 per cent witholding tax. In contrast, interest on deposits with Singapore Asian Currency Units were not taxed, but there was a 10 per cent tax on their offshore lending profits. The logical course then was to raise deposits in Singapore's Asian Currency Market and relend them from Hong Kong. The taxation position, good office staff, accountants, lawyers and printing, excellent air transport and telex communications facilities, and the largest concentration of foreign banks outside New

York and London all added to the Colony's attraction for loan syndications, and the Colony's banks offshore borrowing and lending grew accordingly. On 1 April 1978, however, the Colony's Inland Revenue Ordinance was modified to subject profits on offshore transactions arranged in Hong Kong to the normal 17 per cent profit tax. Loans, simply booked or garaged in Hong Kong remained free of local tax but income from loans without a substantial intervention of other branches would be considered Hong Kong-derived business and taxed locally.[20]

Many bankers responded with talk of shifting their lending operations to other Asian financial centres, and perhaps closing their Hong Kong operations. Although no banks left, the taxes did affect offshore lending: total advances abroad declined from HK$19,634 million in February 1978 to hit a low of HK$15,827 million in August. Lending has since increased, possibly as a result of the new banks; but even by the end of 1978, advances abroad still totalled only HK$16,411 million. In contrast, local advances increased continually through the year. Offshore lending finally recovered in full by October 1979 and showed further increases over 1980 but there seems little doubt that some banks redirect some syndication work to other centres as a result of the taxation. Even so, foreign currency offshore loan syndications remain an important activity among Hong Kong banks and deposit companies. During 1980 the industry has set some new records in terms of the amounts syndicated: the 10-year US$680 million loan to India in late 1980 was Asia's largest commercial syndicated credit thus far.

(b) Non-banking Financial Institutions

Hong Kong's non-banking sector might well be divided into two parts: regulated and non-regulated financial institutions. The non-regulated institutions not surprisingly exhibit the greatest variety and include such traditional Chinese institutions as money changers, traders, remittance houses, rotating credit societies, and unlicensed private money lenders, as well as a variety of Western institutions, such as hire purchase and leasing companies, not raising monies from the public. The regulated institutions, on which this section concentrates its discussion, include deposit-taking companies, the insurance industry, export credit insurance and financing, pensions funds, unit trusts and mutual funds, credit unions, co-operative societies, pawnbrokers, private money lenders, the Development Loan Fund, Home Ownership Fund, the Lottery Fund, and the Hong Kong Building and Loan Agency. Besides these institutions, some mention should be made of the traditional

British and Chinese 'Hongs' or trading groups[21] which operate in both the regulated and unregulated sectors. In some respects not unlike the Japanese trading houses, these firms control a substantial portion of the Hong Kong economy and can allocate funding through affiliated financial institutions or place it directly between group members.

(i) *Deposit-taking companies*

The moratorium on new bank licensing did not preclude institutions entering the market as quasi-banks and by 1975 some 2000 finance companies had registered for operations in Hong Kong. While some of these institutions were no more than corporate shells, many were effectively Chinese money lenders and still others mortgage companies, hire purchase firms, leasing companies, merchant banks and *de facto* commercial banks. The rapid increase of fringe banking institutions caused the enactment of the Deposit-Taking Companies Ordinance on 8 January 1976. A listing of the 302 companies now registered under the Ordinance is shown in Appendix 2.2

As its name implies, the Ordinance was designed to cover those institutions raising deposits from the public[22] and limit their effect on the licensed banks. Basically, the regulations require that companies have a paid-up capital of HK\$2.5 million, accept public deposits of no less than HK\$50,000 and loan no more than an amount equal to 25 per cent of the shareholders funds to any one customer. It also established a Deposit-Taking Companies Advisory Committee to advise the government in respect of the Ordinance. The Ordinance was later amended to provide for greater reporting, the appointment of a Commissioner of Deposit-Taking Companies, and a liquid asset ratio. This was later set at 30 per cent on deposits of seven days or less, and 15 per cent on all other deposits to be held in the form of cash, bank deposits, short-term deposits with other deposit-taking companies, readily marketable foreign currency certificates of deposits issued outside Hong Kong, and specified Hong Kong money market instruments.

The inclusion of a wide range of finance companies, merchant banks and other financial institutions under the same legislation complicates the analysis of their operations. Generally though, merchant bank styled deposit-taking companies are involved in the 'money market and foreign-exchange, short- and medium-term loans in Hong Kong and foreign currencies; project finance; local and international loan syndications; local and international underwriting, private placements and trading of equity and debt securities; trade finance; quotations and listing assistance; acquisitions, mergers, and joint venture evaluation and advice; venture capital; lease finance and leverage leasing; portfolio management and investment advice; and other assorted financial and general consultancy services'.[23] In contrast, the finance company styled firms concentrate on shorter-term· lending, hire purchase finance, mortgage loans, leasing, factoring, and block discounting. While others, mainly Chinese-owned ventures, discount postdated cheques, and finance securities trading and real estate.

As shown in Table 2.11, 40.9 per cent of deposit-taking funding was from banks overseas and some 30.3 per cent from public deposits. However, much of the former probably related to the merchant banks activities and the latter to those of the more finance company styled institutions. This is particularly true in the case of licensed bank-owned

TABLE 2.11   Hong Kong deposit-taking companies' assets and liabilities (as of end of August 1980)

Percentage			HK$ million
	Liabilities		
30.3	1. Deposits from the public		31203
16.2	2. Amount due to banks in Hong Kong		16681
40.9	3. Amount due to banks abroad		42145
12.6	4. Other liabilities and reserves		12963
100.0			102992
	Assets		
—	1. Cash		5
19.9	2. Amount due from banks in Hong Kong		20528
21.8	3. Amount due from banks abroad:		
	I. Demand and short-term claims	13510	
	II. Time Deposits	8902	22412
49.8	4. Loans and advances:		
	I. Hong Kong	24784	
	II. Abroad	26485	51269
3.3	5. Investments:		
	I. Hong Kong	1478	
	II. Abroad	1922	3400
5.2	6. Other assets:		
	I. Hong Kong	2485	
	II. Abroad	2893	5378
100.00			102992

Source: Hong Kong Monthly Digest of Statistics, August 1980, p. 38.

deposit-taking companies which can be used by their parent banks to avoid EBA set interest rates. Indeed a government survey in October 1979 found that 80 of the 264 deposit-taking companies were subsidiaries of licensed banks and accounted for 70 per cent of all deposits and subsidiaries of non-licensed foreign banks comprised another 5 per cent.[24] Furthermore, whereas on average deposit-taking companies obtain some 20 per cent of their deposits on a payable on demand or up to 7-day notice basis, the firms owned by licensed banks had some 60 per cent of their funds on short notice.

In terms of advances, at the end of June 1980 deposit-taking companies' loans and advances made in Hong Kong were directed 6.3 per cent to manufacturing, 40 per cent to transport and transport equipment, 0.3 per cent to public services, 14.6 per cent to building and construction, 14 per cent to general commerce, 15.8 per cent to individuals to purchase residential property, 17 per cent to individuals for other purposes, and 18 per cent to other purposes. As is shown in Table 2.11 these advances, though, comprised less than half of the companies' advances as the rest are made outside Hong Kong. As with the funding side, most overseas advances relate to merchant bank activities while much of the loans in Hong Kong – particularly those to individuals – are the finance company advances.

There is no control over deposit-taking company interest rates as yet but there are definite indications that the government plans to extend its regulation of the industry – both in response to the Nugan Hand and a few other deposit-taking company problems and because of the growing importance of the deposit-taking companies themselves. In late 1980, for example, the industry's assets of HK$103 billion equalled almost half of the banking systems HK$229 billion. One rumour is that the government might suggest the merging of the two associations which at present represent the industry into one body which no doubt it hopes may fulfil a similar role as the new Hong Kong Association of Banks. Another possibility is for the paid-up capital to be increased from HK$2.5 to HK$5 or 10 million. Also the HK$50,000 deposit size may be lessened in the case of firms with a capital base of HK$50 million and possibly increased or the term deposit extended for the less capitalised firms.

(ii) *Insurance*

The insurance industry in Hong Kong is closely connected with the Colony's role as an entrepôt trading centre and some British affiliated companies trace their local operations back to the very establishment of the Crown Colony. As a reflection of its position as a major international insurance centre (particularly in respect to cargo and marine insurance), most of the world's major general insurance companies are registered for business within the colony.

As with banking, the industry developed with little restriction from the government, and of the 348 companies registered in Hong Kong many were established when the incorporation of a HK$2 paid-up capital company and the lodgement of an appropriate deposit was adequate for entrance into the industry: foreign companies needed only to lodge the deposit. At present the government regulation is fragmented with certain portions of the business covered by their own legislation: the Fire and Marine Insurance Companies Deposit Ordinance, the Life Insurance Ordinance, the Fire Insurance Ordinance, and the Motor Vehicles Insurance (Third Party) Ordinance. There is no specific Insurance Commissioner and the legislation is enforced by an Assistant Registrar within the Registrar of Companies office. As the government's Registrar General, himself commented in 1977, the insurance industry is 'an incredibly unregulated industry – even by Hong Kong standards'.[25]

This position, however, is changing and new legislation is expected to set a minimum capital requirement, solvency tests and twice-yearly reporting. Already an interim set of regulations has established a minimum of HK$5 million paid-up capital for new companies and a Motor Insurance Bureau was established to protect the public against uninsured risks or hit-and-run drivers. Thus far, however, general accident and medical insurance remain uncovered by the proposed legislation as does reinsurance, but such matters should receive more attention as a result of the government's new interest in the Colony's financial affairs. Indeed, as the government report on diversification pointed out, one area 'which would tend to limit its potential as an insurance and reinsurance centre is the relatively low level of regulation of the Hong Kong insurance market'.[26]

Under the present legislation it is possible for the same company to be registered to sell both life and the various types of general insurance in the Colony (see Table 2.12). The presence of so many, however, somewhat overstates the present number of actual operating companies for, as was the case with deposit companies, the imposition of even these rather loose controls was followed by a substantial influx of new companies, companies wishing to establish a position in the local market in case further entry might be precluded.

Of the companies registered for the life business, for example, only a

TABLE 2.12 Hong Kong insurance companies by country of incorporation and business transacted

Country of incorporation	Number of companies	Class of insurance business transacted			
		Life	Fire	Marine	Motor vehicle (Third Party Risks)
Australia	6	1	5	5	2
Bahama Islands	3	2	1	1	—
Bermuda	6	5	1	—	—
Brunei	1	1	—	—	—
Canada	5	4	1	1	—
Cayman Islands	1	1	—	—	—
China	3	2	2	2	2
Finland	1	—	1	1	—
France	5	—	5	5	1
West Germany	2	—	1	2	—
Hong Kong	168	52	138	130	39
India	5	1	4	3	4
Ireland	2	—	2	1	1
Italy	2	—	1	2	—
Japan	7	—	7	7	5
Luxembourg	1	1	—	—	—
Malaysia	2	—	2	2	—
Netherlands	4	—	4	4	4
New Zealand	3	—	3	3	3
Norway	1	—	—	1	—
Philippines	3	—	2	3	2
Singapore	6	2	4	3	1
Sweden	1	1	1	1	—
Switzerland	7	3	2	4	2
Thailand	1	1	1	1	
United Kingdom	61	17	42	45	24
United States of America	41	21	19	16	15
Total	348	115	249	243	101

Note: Of the 180 foreign insurance companies, 63 operate through agents in Hong Kong.
Source: Insurance Registry, Registrar General's Department, Hong Kong, 1980.

dozen or so are of significance in the market (particularly American International Assurance and Manufacturers' Life): 52 of the 115 authorised companies are incorporated outside Hong Kong.

Life policies are at a particular disadvantage in the local market as the extended family concept of the traditional Chinese culture has long served as a *de facto* insurance role for most Hong Kong residents.

Furthermore, the purchase of life insurance is considered by some to be unlucky and, more importantly, there are no tax advantages for doing so. Up to now endowment policies have been the biggest sellers but the realisation by more Western Chinese for the need of life cover and the additional retirement funds required with the breakdown of the traditional extended family are causing some growth in life, group life, and insurance-linked provident funds sales.

While not suffering the same marketing problems, general insurance companies too, have not had a substantial influence on the domestic financial market. Foreign ownership dominates the industry with 180 of the 348 companies incorporated outside Hong Kong and many locally incorporated firms foreign-controlled. Traditionally many of these assume little of the risk they underwrite and instead rely heavily on reinsurance treaties with their overseas parents. Similarly, much of their investments are made overseas. There have been some changes in the practice, though, in recent years and now some local companies, often in conjunction with overseas firms, are writing and assuming much of the risk on international as well as local business.

(iii) *Export credit insurance and financing*

The Hong Kong Export Credit Insurance Corporation was established as a statutory body under the Hong Kong Export Credit Insurance Corporation Ordinance by the Colonial government on 23 December 1966 as a means of assisting Hong Kong exporters; it has a paid-up capital of HK$20 million and a government guarantee over its liabilities up to HK$2000 million. Through its government support, the company offers coverage against losses due to non-payment by overseas buyers: — normally commercially uninsurable risks. The Corporation under its Ordinance may charge premium rates only sufficient to break even and is a member of the International Union of Credit and Investment Insurers, otherwise known as the Berne Union.

Exporters receive most of their finance from the commercial banking system, but in certain cases the banks' efforts are supplemented by a specialist lender, Hong Kong Fintracon Ltd. Hong Kong Fintracon is a private sector consortium effort established in 1973 by four of the Colony's major banks to assist in financing Eastern European countries' imports of Hong Kong goods.

(iv) *Pension funds*

In the early 1970s, few companies offered employee pension plans. Special contracts were often written for the senior expatriate managers but not other employees. However, as the skilled labour market grew tighter and living standards improved, superannuation plans, generally non-contributory ones, have grown important within the Colony, and at the end of March, 1980 there were 2051 approved retirement and pension funds in operation.[27]

In response to this demand, the Hongkong and Shanghai Banking Corporation introduced its own pooled Central Provident Fund in 1975 and today a number of banks, insurance and deposit-taking companies service this market with full portfolio management and administration facilities. There has been some suggestion that the government might establish a central retirement fund itself but this is unlikely in the near future.

(v) *Unit trusts and mutual funds*

For the most part Hong Kong investors prefer to invest directly in the local share market rather than to use unit trusts or mutual funds. As a result neither these nor local investment companies have raised much local funds within the Colony. But this has not precluded overseas funds management (both corporate and individual portfolios) from developing into an important source of local investment or local investors making their overseas investments through this medium. Indeed in 1980, the 35 funds managed from Hong Kong had assets of more than US$400 millions.[28]

Abuses by some overseas funds sold to Hong Kong residents resulted in a government study in 1971 and recommendations to control what was previously a largely unregulated industry. Thus the Hong Kong Code on Unit Trusts and Mutual Funds, issued under the Securities Ordinance, came into force on 5 July 1978. The code, which is administered by the Office of the Commissioner for Securities through a six-man Committee on Unit Trusts, requires the funds' trust deeds, accounts and promotional material be filed with the Commission for approval and for the funds to obtain authorised status before being sold locally: there were 73 funds authorised for sale in the Colony at the end of 1980.[29]

(vi) *Credit unions*

Until the 1960s there were very few credit unions in Hong Kong: most were related to Catholic religious organisations. In the late 1960s, however, a number of employer-related organisations were formed and, with the encouragement and assistance of the industry's association, the

Credit Union League of Hong Kong, some 22 credit unions were established over 1967 – 9.[30] The increased numbers brought the introduction of the Credit Union Ordinance of 1968 on 6 November, and the appointment of a Registrar of Credit Unions; in practice, the latter function is performed by the Director of Agriculture and Fisheries who supervises other co-operative societies. Of the 60 credit unions registered in Hong Kong in December 1980, 30 were related to associations (such as religious groups), 24 to employee groups, and 6 to public housing estate communities.

The Credit Union League, through its own training programmes, publicity efforts and assistance visits, has been instrumental in the credit unions success. The League, under the Credit Union Ordinance, also operates the Colony's credit union stabilisation fund, designed to help credit unions avoid temporary liquidity problems, and affords access to specialised loan protection and savings life insurance schemes. Of the 48 credit unions actively in operation in December 1980, all but six were members of the League.

As in most developed countries, the credit unions obtain their funding from their members' share purchases (*de facto* deposits) and invest much of these funds in loans to members. As of 30 September 1980 the 51 active credit unions in Hong Kong had 12,427 members, HK$12,028,802 in shares and HK$10,662,622 in loans outstanding. While the numbers of credit unions are likely to increase, their relatively small individual size limits their effects on other institutions within the financial sector.

(vii) *Co-operative societies*

The co-operative societies date from the early 1950s and can be divided into farming, fishing and urban societies: their names imply the areas of operation. In at least the first two cases, these producer-related societies generally provide more than just a deposit and lending facility to their members and actually assist in the bulk buying of materials and marketing products. In addition to funds from members, these societies also receive financing from a number of private, government and international sources.[31] Of the urban societies all but 15 are co-operative building societies formed by various civil service employee groups. Besides member deposits, these societies in the past have received land and special loan fund assistance from the government. The remaining urban societies include apartment owners' societies, consumers' societies, and salaried workers' thrift and loan societies.[32]

The societies operate under the Co-operative Societies Ordinance and are under the control and supervision of the the Registrar of Co-operative Societies. As a reflection of the initial importance of the agricultural societies, the government's Director of Agriculture and Fisheries serves as the Registrar. As of the end of 1980 there were 79 farming, 66 fishing, and 253 urban co-operative societies.

(viii) *Pawnbrokers*

Prior to the establishment of the deposit-taking companies and the expansion of commercial banks into personal lending, the pawnbrokers were an important source of consumer and small business finance, and even today serve an important function within certain sectors of the community.

Pawnbroking is regulated under the Pawnbrokers Ordinance of 1964 and the licensing controlled by the Commissioner of Police. Among other matters, the Ordinance sets the maximum interest rates to be charged on the types of articles pledged, the length of pledges, hours of business, the obligation to issue pawn tickets, and the need to determine the true particulars of the pawners. The provisions also allow the Courts to order the disposal of pawned items subsequently found to be stolen.

As of December 1980, there were 150 licensed pawnbrokers in Hong Kong.

(ix) *Private money lenders*

Licensed money lenders in Hong Kong, together with the pawnshops, represent only a small portion of the informal financial system operating within the local Chinese business community. As with the pawnshops, they represent a traditionally important source of consumer, as well as small business, credit.

The finance offered is generally of a short-term nature and, in the case of businesses, is often made against the security of a post-dated cheque. Individual borrowers are quite a different matter and as the regional press described some money lenders' operations, these 'loan sharks' would keep as collateral, passbooks of bank savings accounts (into which salaries in Hong Kong are often paid directly), passports, vehicle log books and identity cards. Use of triad muscle was normal, which has led to a real fear among loan sharks' victims of being "chopped to death".[33]

Under the old Moneylenders Ordinance of 1911, the government had little control over these lenders' basic operations and they could effectively charge what interest they liked. Fortunately, though, the Hong Kong Courts held that rates over 4 per cent per month are excessive and this placed some restraints on their charges.[34]

The old legislation was recently replaced by the Money Lenders Ordinance of 1980 and the Money Lenders Regulations of 1980. This formalises the interest rate controls and classifies rates of more than 4 per cent monthly extortionate and subject to adjustment by the courts. More importantly, rates exceeding 6 per cent monthly are prohibited and, regardless of whether one is a licensed money lender or not, offenders are subject to a fine of up to HK$100,000 and two years in prison.

As the new Ordinance will come into operation on 12 December 1980, the establishment of its associated Money Lenders Registry is not complete. However, according to the Companies Registry, there were some 1510 money lenders registered in Hong Kong as of 31 March 1980.

(x) *The Development Loan Fund*

The Development Loan Fund was established on 1 November 1958 to finance low-cost housing schemes and other social and economic development projects within the Colony. It is primarily funded from the government and in the 1980/81 Budget was allocated some HK$1.83 billion. It also obtains money from the interest on and the repayment of its loans to other government-sponsored bodies such as the Hong Kong Housing Society and the Hong Kong Housing Authority. These loans are intended to be self-liquidating and allow the government to separate its re-occurring expenditures from those of its longer-term capital investments.

Besides public housing developments, which account for some 80 per cent of its loans, the Fund finances educational, medical, reclamation, infrastructure projects, and over 1978/79 commenced an interest-free loan scheme for certain tertiary students. It also serves as the government holding company and is the registered owner of the government's interests in the Hong Kong Building and Loan Agency, the Hong Kong Air Cargo Terminals Limited, and the Cross Harbour Tunnel Company Limited.

(xi) *The Home Ownership Fund*

The Home Ownership Fund was established by the government in 1977 to finance the construction of flats for sale to families with incomes below a certain level and generally works in conjunction with the government's Housing Authority. Special mortgage arrangements, which include government guarantees against default, are then established with other financial institutions to allow nominated purchasers to obtain 90 per cent financing over 15 years at a concessional rate of interest.

(xii) *The Lottery Fund*

The Lottery Fund was established by the government in 1956 to finance the development of social welfare services by the way of grants and loans funded in part from the profits of the government and private sector run lotteries.

(xiii) *Hong Kong Building and Loan Agency Ltd*

The Hong Kong Building and Loan Agency was formed in 1964 under the sponsorship of the Colonial government, England's Commonwealth Development Corporation, and the Colony's four major banks, to assist in financing home purchases of middle income earners: families with incomes between HK\$700 and 6000 per month. All six sponsors are shareholders in the Agency and control some 75 per cent of the shares in this stock exchange listed, public company.

As a result of the government's Finance of Home Ownership Committee recommendations, the agency notes are government guaranteed and include as specified liquid assets under the Banking Ordinance. In 1979 the agency lent approved applicants up to 80 per cent or HK\$250,000 on mortgages of up to a 15-year maturity at an adjustable interest rate (then 14 per cent) reflecting the institution's cost of funds.

FINANCIAL MARKETS

Given Hong Kong's position as an international financial centre, one would expect its local markets to be highly developed. This is true in respect of those markets directly connected with their overseas counterparts such as in foreign-exchange and Asian dollar bond trading. The largely domestic markets, though, have not yet reached the same level of development: the local money market, for example, is only now beginning to use financial instruments. This section briefly examines the present state of these local markets, looking first at the local money market, then the foreign-exchange market, stocks and bonds markets, and the commodities markets.

(a) The Money Market

The money market in Hong Kong can generally be divided into four major subcomponents: the inter-bank market, the inter-deposit-taking company market, the general money market and the foreign currency deposit portion of the foreign-exchange market.[35]

(i) *The inter-bank market*

Dealings between the major banks in Hong Kong have always been part of local financial practice but an active inter-bank market in itself did not really develop until 1959.[36] The market traditionally involves overnight call and other short-notice deposits up to one week but sometimes longer maturities are available; financial instruments are seldom used. Participation is limited to Hong Kong licensed banks and authorised brokers and is subject to the general control of the Exchange Banks' Association. In practice, the Hongkong and Shanghai Banking Corporation by its size alone can influence the inter-bank rates and thus much of the general interest rates and monetary conditions within the Colony. It and other banks with large domestic branch networks, such as the Chartered and Chinese banks, are generally net lenders to the foreign banks, many of whom depend on these funds for their operations. The great range of possible rates (between 4 per cent and 19 per cent on 24-hour-call money over much of 1980) and the tendency in the past of the inter-bank rates to sometime rise above the prime lending rate caused many foreign banks to avoid relending from this source. The development of lending at a margin over a bank's cost of funds, though so far limited, may encourage some banks to make more use of inter-bank funding.

(ii) *The inter-deposit-taking-company market*

As bank advances (even at call) to deposit-taking companies are not eligible for bank liquidity purposes, the deposit-taking companies are precluded from direct participation in the inter-bank market. Thus an inter-deposit-taking-company market developed in the early 1970s to cover their short-term liquidity requirements. Like the inter-bank market, it operates almost entirely on a deposit rather than an instrument basis. While maturities range from up to a month to some times 6 to 12 months, most are overnight or 24-hour-call placements.

(iii) *The general money market*

The general money market is the least developed as there is no secondary market or even well-established, negotiable Hong Kong dollar-denominated financial instruments within the Colony. The recent rise in interest rates, the increased numbers of financial institutions, and particularly the increased interest rate competition by deposit-taking companies have brought the introduction of a number of financial instruments: Hong Kong dollar certificates (CDs) and negotiable certificates of deposits (NCDs) bills of exchange, and bankers' acceptances.

One potential for secondary trading is the Hong Kong dollar negotiable certificates of deposit. There have been several unsuccessful attempts in the past: Slater Walker Hutchinson in 1973 and American Express Finance in 1974/75. A more promising effort, however, came in July 1977 when Wardley, supported by the Hongkong and Shanghai Bank, issued fixed-rate instruments with maturities up to five years. Chase Manhattan Asia's NCDs soon followed with Jardine Fleming as the principal market maker but used a floating (rather than a fixed) rate set at the average of the Hongkong and Shanghai and the Chartered Banks' best lending rates with a minimum of $5\frac{1}{2}$ per cent per annum. Other Hong Kong dollar CD issues followed with their own formulas and offered either fixed rates or various floating rates linked with the prime lending or inter-bank rates. Eventually a market-wide formula will be established and true secondary trading of these instruments may result. An adequate secondary market is particularly important as the government has indicated its reluctance to specify Hong Kong dollar certificates of deposits as a bank liquid asset until this is achieved. In the meantime, they have added another source of potential deposits for the Hong Kong banks.

An attempt to introduce commercial paper to the local market was made unsuccessfully in 1976 with Bancom International's Dow Chemical Pacific HK$10 million bills of exchange issue. A more promising attempt was accomplished in February 1979 when seven institutions lead by Trident International Finance, arranged a HK$270 million bills of exchange discount facility for the Mass Transport Railway Corporation.

Finally in respect of bankers acceptances, Citibank in mid-1979 introduced a HK$10,000 and a HK$500,000 90-day bill for individual and corporate or institutional investors respectively. As with the other instruments mentioned, arrangements were made with another company to maintain a secondary market in these securities, but as yet true secondary trading has yet to develop.

The absence of a viable secondary market in any of these securities is due largely to governmental factors: the lack of central bank direction and a 'lender of last resort'; and the lack of government securities. In other countries, the government or central bank developed the secondary market. In contrast, the *de facto* lender of last resort, the Hongkong and Shanghai Banking Corporation, needs neither a discount nor a commercial paper market and, since such a market would assist its competitors, has understandably not worked toward its development. Similarly while the introduction of government securities, like bonds or treasury notes, would provide a most useful starting place from which secondary trading within the money market might develop, there seems little likelihood of such issues being made. Thus for the immediate future, the market will continue to be primarily deposit-based.[37]

(b) The Foreign-exchange Market

As the absence of foreign-exchange controls allows money raised overseas to be converted into Hong Kong dollars or lent directly on the local market, the local deposit, foreign currency deposit and foreign-exchange markets operate as one. Deposit-taking companies and foreign banks in particular obtain Hong Kong dollars through 'swap' transactions in the spot and forward markets, allowing them to sell foreign currencies for Hong Kong dollars with an agreement to repurchase them at a fixed date at a price reflecting market interest rates and exchange risks. Furthermore, as interest on foreign currency assets are generally free from profits and withholding taxes, often have better yields, and sometimes better foreign-exchange risk potential, than the local alternatives, many companies invest much of their funds in foreign currencies. Finally, as one government official noted, 'the residual source of liquidity for the banking system as a whole is the foreign-exchange market, and the ability of each individual bank to acquire Hong Kong dollars, at a price, against the sale of US dollars',[38] an ability assured through the activities of the government's Exchange Fund.

As a reflection of Hong Kong's US and international trade and investment, US dollar-Hong Kong dollar transactions are most active in the foreign-exchange market and account for some 25 per cent of transactions. The remainder involve other Hong Kong dollar and strictly third country transactions. In the latter case, US dollar – Japanese yen transactions are the most important.

At one time the Exchange Banks' Association was very much in control of foreign-exchange transactions, at least within the banking sector, with its members and the brokers following a predetermined spread of rates. The entry of non-exchange bank members, such as merchant banks, in the early 1970s soon destroyed much of the cartel's effectiveness and since 1973 the Association's so-called 'agreed merchant rates' serves only as a reference guide in the market.[39] The entry of these other financial institutions into the market also resulted in the establishment of the Hong Kong Forex Club.

As the market developed, so did its attractions to other financial institutions increase. As access to a foreign-exchange licence is not difficult, a wide range of institutions are now involved in the market but the commercial banks, deposit-taking companies, and international money or exchange brokers are the most active. Since its exclusion from the Sterling Area in 1972, Hong Kong has also seen the international scope of its transactions expand significantly, both in the spot and forward markets. Indeed, since 1978 the Federal Reserve has frequently used the Hong Kong foreign-exchange market in support of the US dollar.

(c) The Stocks and Bonds Markets

The securities industry in Hong Kong is unique within Southeast Asia as it is one of the oldest, with share trading dating back to 1866,[40] and has the largest number of individual stock exchanges. Of the four exchanges, the Hong Kong Stock Exchange is the oldest, dating to 1891, while the other three are products of the Hong Kong share market boom of the late 1960s to early 1970s: the Far East Exchange Ltd (commenced 17 December 1969); the Kam Ngan Stock Exchange Limited (15 March 1971); and the Kowloon Stock Exchange Limited (5 January 1972). These latter markets were formed by Chinese brokers dissatisfied with the Hong Kong Stock Exchange and further exchanges would have been founded but for the introduction of the government's Stock Exchange Prohibition Ordinance in February 1973

There is little economic justification for the separate exchanges and, as shown in Table 2.13, over the years the Kowloon Stock Exchange has become very much less important. A variety of merger talks have

TABLE 2.13   Hong Kong securities exchanges by percentage of market turnover
(1972–80)

	Far East Exchange Limited (%)	Hong Kong Stock Exchange Ltd (%)	Kam Ngan Stock Exchange Ltd (%)	Kowloon Stock Exchange Ltd (%)	Total Trading (HK$ million)
1972	42.27	24.74	18.05	14.94	42885.11
1973	32.60	25.23	25.39	16.78	48880.44
1974	44.16	21.42	26.66	7.76	11436.7
1975	45.61	24.26	27.10	3.03	10359.91
1976	45.74	24.24	28.55	1.47	13155.93
1977	47.31	26.46	25.71	0.52	6126.74
1978	50.07	19.39	30.10	0.44	27419.01
1979	45.83	21.87	32.06	0.25	25632.74
1980	45.56	20.25	33.94	0.25	95684.71

occurred in the past without success and as a result the government announced its intention to legislate a merger. Thus in May 1980 a working party chaired by the Commissioner for Securities drew up plans for the formation of the Stock Exchange of Hong Kong with its initial shareholders coming from the members of the present four exchanges. New members, however, are required to have a net worth of at least HK$1 million. The government hopes to complete the rationalisation and have the new Exchange in operation by early 1984 at the latest.

The securities industry is regulated under the Securities Ordinance 1974 by the Office of the Commissioner for Securities. The Commissioner is also responsible for insider trading, through the Insider Dealing Tribunal, and takeovers, through the Committee on Takeovers and Mergers. Investors also have some protection through the Stock Exchange Compensation Fund. At the end of 1980 there were 110 corporate and 1060 individual dealers, 86 corporate and 140 individual investment advisers, 880 dealers' representatives, and 66 investment advisers' representatives registered under the Securities (Dealers, Investment Advisers and Representatives) Regulations of 1974.

Since the share boom peaked on 9 March 1973, there have been few new listings, and share issues have been a relatively minor source of corporate funding. 1980, however, has seen considerable change and by early November 1980 more than HK$4.46 billion had been raised – mainly through the sale of loan stock with warrants.[41]

In contrast to their recent popularity, debt issues have not been popular among either Hong Kong corporations or investors. From a corporate viewpoint, Hong Kong's low profit tax eliminates much of the benefits normally associated with the tax deductability of interest payments. Also, as it leaves more money after tax available to the corporation, self-financing through retained earnings is more feasible than in other countries and removes some of the pressure to obtain external financing. Furthermore, it is rumoured that, at least at one time, the Colony's major banks were not pleased with their customers having such issues. To investors, too, straight corporate debt issues had little appeal. Local Hong Kong corporate issues were subject to the 15 per cent withholding tax; furthermore, local interest rates were lower than those overseas and foreign securities offered less political risk. Therefore local Hong Kong dollar bonds issues must either be convertible securities or include warrants to purchase ordinary shares, and this is still the case. Some exceptions to this 'no ordinary debt' rule were the government-guaranteed HK$400 million Mass Transit Railway Corporation 10 year loan stock issue in 1976 and three offshore Hong Kong dollar issues (Bermuda subsidiaries of Hong Kong Land and Jardine Matheson and the Canadian province of Manitoba) raised in 1977.

While local investors prefer equities when investing locally, they have not been so adverse to buying foreign currency denominated securities. As a result, Hong Kong traders have built up a substantial level of Asian and Eurocurrency bond transactions within the international bond markets.[42] Indeed, given local investor interest and, more importantly, the amount of overseas investment funds under management within the Colony, Hong Kong is considered by some 'to be the biggest international bond centre outside Europe'[43] and a leading centre for the underwriting of Asian dollar bonds.

(d) Commodities Markets

The Hong Kong Commodity Exchange was established in 1977 and commenced trading in cotton futures on 9 May 1977. It has since added sugar, soybeans and, on 19 August 1980, gold futures contracts to its trading markets. Until late 1979 with the introduction of soybeans futures, the Exchange's activity was quite slow. However, soybeans added substantial volume and gold futures are expected to be even more successful: an indication of the contracts' relative importance is shown in Table 2.14.

The Commodity Exchange operates under the Commodities Trading Ordinance of 1976 and its members under the Commodities Trading (Dealers, Commodities Trading Advisers and Representatives) Regu-

TABLE 2.14　Hong Kong commodity trading (by types of contracts)

Type of contract	Amount traded (US$)	Percentage of total
Cotton	106979	3.7
Sugar	82203	2.9
Soybeans	438330	15.3
Gold	2234878	78.1
Total	2862990	100.0

Note: The above figures are for October 1980 only.
Source: *Hong Kong Monthly Digest of Statistics*, October 1980, p. 47.

lations of 1976. Membership is restricted to Hong Kong residents and its 122 full members must have a net worth of at least HK$2 million. As of the end of 1980 there were 89 corporate and 157 individual commodities dealers; 949 commodity dealers' representatives, 8 corporate and 13 individual commodity trading advisers and 12 commodity trading advisers' representatives. The public are protected in their dealings with members and, to a lesser extent, with non-members of the Exchange by the Commodity Exchange Compensation Fund.

As with other futures contracts, the new gold market was established in line with the international practice of quoting prices in US dollars for a standard 100-ounce contract of 99.5 per cent fine gold delivered in London at a future date, but the trading language on the floor differs as it is officially Cantonese. The Exchange received many membership applications as a result of the gold futures and the market is expected to draw considerable business from Japanese traders as well as Hong Kong futures business previously conducted on the Gold Exchange of Singapore.

Besides the Commodities Exchange, there has traditionally been an informal local futures market between the major international commodity houses in Hong Kong – particularly in gold futures. These transactions are conducted in line with the contracts handled on the New York Commodities exchange. The major difference between these and the new local contracts is that delivery is to New York rather than London. Such transactions will no doubt continue, but will be less important in the future.

The Chinese Gold and Silver Exchange Society (the Kam Ngan) developed from an association of Chinese goldsmiths operating in Hong Kong's Western District. It has been active in Hong Kong since the early 1900s but was formally registered in 1920. Unlike markets overseas, the society has retained much of its early traditions and trade neither in the standard contract size nor gold purity of other markets. It instead uses the old Chinese measurement, the tael (approximately 1.2 fine ounces) and a slightly less pure 99 per cent fine gold. Furthermore, the transactions are denominated in Hong Kong rather than US dollars.

While the market's transactions are concerned with spot (physical gold) transactions, in practice traders can create a *de facto*, undated futures contract by paying a premium, rather than immediate settling, and keeping their position open. This may be accomplished in either gold or silver, but in practice gold dominates the market and despite its name, the exchange only resumed silver transactions in June 1978 after a 43-year embargo. While increased speculation in both gold and silver have caused substantial trading for the Society and its 195 members, over 1980 the government has had to tighten its control over all gold dealers in the Colony, and in August 1980 passed the Commodities Trading (Amendment) Ordinance 1980.

The Chinese Gold and Silver Exchange Society's operations, like those of the futures market, are also supplemented by informal gold trading between the Hong Kong offices of the international gold bullion dealers. These transactions are conducted in line with those at the London Gold Market and, as the Hong Kong market closes just before London opens, it often sets the basis for the initial London prices. The Colony's removal of import and export restrictions on gold in 1974 and the attractiveness of gold as an investment medium has seen the international side of the Hong Kong gold spot market grow substantially in recent years.

The spot and futures exchange markets, together with their less formal local counterparts, have assisted Hong Kong development into the world's fourth largest gold market after London, Zurich and New York.[44] Its significance was also assisted by the establishment of an active gold market in the United States in the mid-1970s, as the Colony forms a valuable link between the American closing and the European opening prices.

ANALYSIS

In terms of its development, Hong Kong's financial sector has had a rather mixed experience due at least in part to the government, or rather the lack of government, involvement in this area. As the then Colonial Chief Secretary, Sir Denys Robert, explained the Hong Kong government's policy, 'on the whole, we have tried to leave it to private business and financial people to work things out with our help. We don't try to take things over, because bureaucrats are rotten businessmen.'[45] This approach within the financial sector – intervention only when absolutely necessary – is a major factor in Hong Kong's position today as an international financial centre. Indeed as one report concluded, 'this approach seems to have served Hong Kong well and we see no reason for any major departures from it'.[46]

Selective intervention is still not without its faults and Hong Kong's mixed development can be traced directly to this policy. Lack of adequate regulations, for example, has probably hindered the local insurance and securities industries. Lack of government policy and action similarly affected the money and bond markets and limited the creation of many specialist financial institutions. Moreover, lack of government planning in the provision of adequate infrastructure – particularly with respect to communications – may hamper the Colony's medium-term future as an international financial centre. Finally, the government's lack of adequate statistics has meant that, when intervention was made, the policy makers had neither adequate information on which to base their decision nor sufficiently accurate feedback to evaluate the effects of their actions.

As mentioned in the discussion of the insurance industry, the government wishes to consolidate the present four ordinances into one comprehensive piece of legislation for the industry, but as yet has failed to do so. The problem is apparently the lack of sufficient parliamentary-style legislative draftsmen to produce the ordinance. In the meantime the existing legislation covers only fire, marine, life and motor vehicle insurance. Firms selling other forms of general insurance or strictly reinsurance are not covered by any of the present regulations. Furthermore, even firms covered by the existing ordinances are free to do much as they please: government intervention is possible only after something has gone wrong. Such conditions do little to foster a good reputation for the industry and what with Singapore's efforts in the reinsurance area, business will undoubtedly be lost unless action is taken.

The securities industry, too, suffers from the lack of regulatory attention. The fact that the Colony has four exchanges is only because the government did not act quickly enough to prevent their formation. The lack of protection under the Companies Act for minority shareholders, inadequate corporate reporting requirements, and out-of-date controls over mergers and takeovers do little to encourage local long-term investors. Instead, the present situation argues for short-term trading and an environment where a long-term investment is one left over the weekend. The Office of the Securities Commissioner has acted with respect to the unit trust industry and toward unifing the exchanges, but there is still much that the government could do to assit the securities markets in performing a more valuable economic function.

In the development of their local money markets other countries have benefited from the assistance of their central bank and specialist financial institutions such as discount houses or official money market dealers. Unfortunately there are no such institutions to help the local market in the Colony and the *de facto* lender of last resort for the financial sector, the Hongkong and Shanghai Banking Corporation, has no reason of its own to create one. Nevertheless, the creation of such a market is important. As the President of the Hong Kong Forex Club, Dennis Lam, warned, 'the development of an efficient money market system aided by a central bank . . . is essential if Hong Kong is to remain a major financial centre'.[47] Similarly, the former Banking Commissioner on his retirement pointed to the Colony's need for a central bank and 'the development of a secondary market to cope with refinancing of longer-term assets during times of tight money conditions'.[48] Unfortunately, recent government speeches indicate that neither a central bank nor other government support for the money market is likely.[49]

The lack of marketable government securities has also worked against the market's development and has meant that there is no natural base on which to build a secondary market for other financial instruments. Furthermore, the government has made it known that it has no intention to issue any.[50] Similarly the classification of Hong Kong issued bank certificates of deposits as a specified liquid asset (at present not the case) would do much to encourage secondary trading in these instruments. The government policy instead is to require the market to develop before so classifying them. Likewise, the use of local US dollar certificates of deposits came about only because one bank discovered a way to avoid the normal 15 per cent interest withholding tax: the government did nothing to encourage their use or trading. The withholding tax issue has also worked against Hong Kong companies using local debt securities and denies local businesses access to an otherwise important source of long-term capital. The provision of incentives for Hong Kong registered pension funds, unit trusts, and insurance companies to invest in local debt securities would greatly assist in the growth of this market.

On an infrastructure basis, too, the government's postponement of the replacement of Hong Kong's international airport, Kai Tak, may also adversely effect the financial sector. As the present airport will reach full capacity in 1983, transport to and from Hong Kong by then may prove difficult. To continue as a financial centre, the government must monitor changes in transport and communications technology and ensure the Colony's own facilities are kept fully up-to-date.

Finally, the government must improve its statistical and other information gathering and feedback techniques. Mistakes have seemingly been made in the past because of poor data and, as the Financial Secretary himself admits, 'a better understanding of the influence of monetary aggregates must await the forthcoming improvements in the quality of the monetary statistics we collect'.[51] Similarly he sees the greater use of professional associations in addition to the various ordinances' formal advisory committees as another means to improve the quality of information collected and disseminated.

More meaningful statistics are particularly important as, since the Colony's initial experiences with rapid inflation in 1977, the government has become increasingly interventionist (by Hong Kong standards) and since 1978 has attempted – through moral suasion, the 100 per cent liquidity ratio on short-term Exchange Fund deposits, the liquid asset ratio for deposit-taking companies, and increased regulation of the financial sector – to influence the growth of Colony's money supply: an effort which has had questionable success. As the regional press commented, 'the big question mark which overhangs the inflation situation in Hong Kong is the now quite staggering rate of increase in the money supply, despite successive sharp increases in interest rates'.[52] The problem is not just that the statistical information available has proved insufficient, but that the government's present financial regulatory powers, not developed for monetary control purposes, were inadequate. As one study concluded, 'there is an urgent need to review the existing institutional and legal framework so that excessive growth of money and credit can be brought under control'.[53]

TRENDS AND PREDICTIONS

As mentioned at the start of this chapter, Hong Kong's future, and hence the future of its financial sector, is dependent on two important factors:[54] first, its relations with China and status after the expiration of the lease on the New Territories; and secondly, the long-term effects of improved Chinese – Western relations on the Colony's traditional entrepôt trade and financial go-between roles.

From a political standpoint, the Colony's position seems to have improved in China's post-Mao era. The Chinese leaders have held meetings with the Colonial government and the overall relations between the two have been much more favourable. Some progress, too, has been made with respect to the New Territories. As the Chinese Foreign Minister, Huang Hua, explained, 'the lease is due to expire in 1997. So there is still time. The basic attitude of the Chinese Government in this matter is that when the time comes for resolution we will take into consideration the interests of investors so that their interests will not be hurt.'[55] Similarly, Vice-Premier Deng Xiaoping in 1979 requested the Colony's Governor, Sir Murray MacLehose, to 'ask investors in Hong Kong to put their hearts at ease'.[56] Such comments cannot help but imply that the issue will eventually be resolved favourably.

The new reapproachment between China and the West, while possibly improving the Colony's political future, has also produced fears that these improved Chinese links with the West might damage Hong Kong's traditional importance in Chinese trade. Furthermore, government-to-government and other major financial negotiations might be done directly between Peking and Tokyo, London or New York rather than through Hong Kong's financial sector. Finally, the foreign investment that results from these improved relations with the West may well be directed into industries not unlike those operating in the Colony and eventually replace Hong Kong's export products in the international market.

There appears to be some danger that all three events may possibly occur and to that extent adversely affect some of Hong Kong's present business. But to suggest that this will mean an end to Hong Kong or even severe damage to its economy neglects the ability and, more importantly, the adaptability of Hong Kong businessmen. Even as the Western trade officials were negotiating their agreements, Hong Kong entrepreneurs were establishing joint venture production and assembly works, particularly within the neighbouring province of Guangdong. Border plants and compensation trading agreements between Chinese enterprises and Hong Kong businessmen have been particularly encouraged by the Chinese government and three special export processing economic zones in the south of Guangdong (Shenzhen and Shekou near Hong Kong and Zuhia near Macau) have been established specifically for such purposes.

With China providing less expensive labour and factory space and the Hong Kong businesses the industrial expertise and marketing skills, these joint ventures should allow much of the Colony's otherwise labour-intensive industries to maintain their international competitiveness. Such co-operation between China and Hong Kong businesses helps to ensure the Colony's own future as well.[57] As one writer concluded, 'China wants to capitalise on, not offset, Hong Kong's achievements in finance and industry.[58] Similarly Hong Kong's port facilities, English legal system, and other infrastructure and financial centre advantages suggest Hong Kong will continue to play an important role in China's 'Four Modernisations' policy.

As a financial centre, too, Hong Kong's future seems assured for at least the short term. However, the expense of local operations in Hong Kong and recent measures by the Singapore government to improve Singapore's position as a regional financial centre cannot help but effect the level of Hong Kong business. Similarly, the 17 per cent profits tax on offshore bookings has detracted from certain business being placed within the Colony.[59] These adverse facts, however, have been more than offset by the drawing power of Chinese trade and the Colony's relatively close proximity to international borrowers such as the Philippines, South Korea, Taiwan and, eventually, China. Indeed in the short term, only a substantial liberalisation of Tokyo's foreign exchange controls could affect the Colony's position in the region. The longer term, however, is a quite different matter. As a government study warns, 'there is no room for complacency. There are other financial sectors eager to replace Hong Kong as the leader and likely to move swiftly to fill any gaps left in the market by Hong Kong. Thus . . . [the government must] . . . be prepared to change its policies and its regulatory system as circumstances alter.'[60] Only time will tell whether the Colony's government officials will be able to adapt successfully from their past policies on non-intervention in the market place to one of assisting the financial sector to meet future needs.

APPENDICES

Appendix 2.1 Exchange Banks' Association Members by Interest Rate Agreement Category (as Set 24 March 1977)

Category 1

Algemene Bank Nederland, NV
American Express International Banking Corporation
Bangkok Bank Ltd
Bank Negara Indonesia 1946
Bank of America NT & SA

Bank of Canton Ltd, The
Bank of India
Bank of Tokyo Ltd, The
Banque Belge pour L'Etranger SA
Banque de l'Indochine
Banque Nationale de Paris
Barclays Bank International Ltd
Chartered Bank, The
Chartered Finance (Hong Kong) Ltd
Chase Manhattan Bank NA, The
Citibank, NA
Dao Heng Bank Ltd
Equitable Banking Corporation
European Asian Bank
Far East Bank Ltd
Hang Seng Bank Ltd
Hongkong and Shanghai Banking Corporation, The
Indian Overseas Bank
Korea Exchange Bank
Kwong On Bank Ltd
Mercantile Bank Ltd
National Bank of Pakistan
Rainier International Bank
Sanwa Bank Ltd, The
Sumitomo Bank Ltd, The
Underwriters Bank Incorporated
United Commercial Bank
Wayfoong Finance Ltd
Wing Hang Bank Ltd

Category 2

Bank of China
Bank of Communications
Bank of East Asia Ltd, The
Chekiang First Bank Ltd
China & South Sea Bank Ltd, The
China State Bank Ltd
Hang Lung Bank Ltd
Hong Kong Industrial and Commercial Bank Ltd
Hua Chiao Commercial Bank Ltd

Kincheng Banking Corporation
Kwangtung Provincial Bank, The
Liu Chong Hing Bank Ltd
Nanyang Commercial Bank Ltd
National Commercial Bank Ltd, The
Overseas Trust Bank Ltd
Shanghai Commercial Bank Ltd
Sin Hua Trust Savings and Commercial Bank Ltd
Union Bank of Hong Kong
Wing Lung Bank Ltd
Wing On Bank Ltd, The
Yien Yieh Commercial Bank Ltd

Category 3

Chiyu Banking Corporation Ltd
Chung Khiaw Bank Ltd
Commercial Bank of Hong Kong Ltd, The
Dah Sing Bank Ltd
Four Seas Communications Bank Ltd
Hong Kong Chinese Bank Ltd, The
Ka Wah Bank Ltd
Malayan Banking Berhad
Malayan Finance Corporation Ltd, The
Oversea-Chinese Banking Corporation Ltd
Overseas Union Bank Ltd
United Chinese Bank Ltd
United Overseas Bank Ltd

Category 4

Po Sang Bank Ltd.

Category 5

Hong Kong Metropolitan Bank Ltd
Hong Nin Savings Bank Ltd
Tai Sang Bank Ltd
Tai Yau Bank Ltd

Not subject to the agreement while operating under restricted licence

Chan Man Cheong Finance Company

Lee Shing
Ming Tai Finance Company

Appendix 2.2 Registered Deposit-taking Companies in Hong Kong (as of 1 January 1981)

ABN Finance Ltd
Acme Finance Ltd
Advance Finance Ltd
Allied Capital Resources Ltd
American and Panama Finance Company Ltd
American Express Finance Ltd
American United Finance Ltd
ANZ Finance (Far East) Ltd
Argo Enterprises Company Ltd
Asean Merchant Credit and Investment House Ltd
Asia Alliance Finance and Investment Ltd
Asia Pacific Capital Corporation Ltd
Asiavest Ltd
Astro Asia Finance Ltd
ATB Finance Ltd
Atlantic Capital Ltd
Australia–Japan International Finance Ltd
Ayala Finance (HK) Ltd
Ayudhya Finance Ltd
BA Asia Ltd
BA Finance (Hong Kong) Ltd
Bancom International Ltd
Barclays Asia Ltd
Barclays Asian Finance Ltd
Baring Brothers Asia Ltd
BCCI Finance International Ltd
Beacons Finance Ltd
Belgian Finance Company Ltd
BfG Finance Asia Ltd
BNP-Daiwa (Hong Kong) Ltd
BNP Finance (Hong Kong) Ltd
BNS International (Hong Kong) Ltd
Bonsun Finance Ltd
British Columbia Financial Corporation (HK) Ltd
Broad Rich Company Ltd

BT Asia Ltd
BT Finance Ltd
Bumiputra Malaysia Finance Ltd
Canadian Eastern Finance Ltd
Canton Pacific Finance Ltd
Caranip Finance Company Ltd
CBC International Finance (Asia) Ltd
CCIC Finance Ltd
Central Asia Capital Corporation Ltd
Central Finance Ltd
Central Leasing (Hong Kong) Ltd
CF Finance Company Ltd
Charoen Pokphand Finance Company Ltd
Chartered Credit (Hong Kong) Ltd
Chartered Finance (Hong Kong) Ltd
Chase Manhattan Asia Ltd
Chau's Brothers Finance Company Ltd
Cheerful Finance Company Ltd
Che Hsing Finance Company Ltd
Chemical Asia Ltd
Chiao Tung Finance Company Ltd
Chiao Yue Finance Company Ltd
Chiap Hua Credit Ltd
Chiap Luen Finance Ltd
China Development Finance Company (Hong Kong) Ltd
Chiyu Finance Company Ltd
Chow Sang Sang Finance Ltd
Chow Tai Fook Finance Ltd
Chung Nam Finance Company Ltd
Commerce International Finance Company (Asia) Ltd
Commercial Development Finance Ltd
Cosmos Finance Ltd
Creditland Finance Ltd
Credit Lyonnais Hong Kong (Finance) Ltd
Credit Suisse Finance Ltd
Crocker International (HK) Ltd
Crown Prince Finance Ltd
CTB Australia Ltd
Dah Sing Finance Ltd
Dai-Ichi Kangyo (Hong Kong) Ltd
Daiwa Overseas Finance Ltd

Daiwa Securities (HK) Ltd
DB Finance (Hong Kong) Ltd
DBS Asia Ltd
Deak & Co. Finance Ltd
DG Capital Company Ltd
Diamond Lease (Hong Kong) Ltd
Dollar Credit and Financing Ltd
Dominican Finance Ltd
Dow Finance Corporation Ltd
Dubai Oriental Finance Ltd
East Asia Finance Company Ltd
Estate Finance Ltd
E. Tung Finance Ltd
Europa Finance (International) Ltd
European Asian Finance (HK) Ltd
Express Finance and Investments Ltd
Filinvest Finance (HK) Ltd
Financial and Investment Services for Asia Ltd
First Bangkok City Finance Ltd
First Canadian Financial Corporation Ltd
First Chicago Hong Kong Ltd
First Dallas Asia Ltd
First Hong Kong Credit Ltd
First Metro International Investment Company Ltd
First National Boston (Hong Kong) Ltd
Five Rams Finance Company Ltd
FNCB Financial Ltd
Foreign Exchange & Investment Ltd
Forest Ocean Finance Ltd
Forex Finance Ltd
Fuji International Finance (HK) Ltd
GU Finance Ltd
General Credit Finance and Development Ltd
Golden Finance Ltd
Golden Hill Finance Company Ltd
Grindlays Finance Ltd
GSP Finance Company Ltd
Gulf Finance Company Ltd
Habib Finance International Ltd
Hamburg LB International Ltd
Hang Lung (Finance) Company Ltd

Hang Seng Finance Ltd
Hang Wo Finance & Investments Ltd
Harbour Finance Company Ltd
Harvest Finance Company Ltd
Hawaii Financial Corporation (Hong Kong) Ltd
HBZ Finance Ltd
Henderson International Finance Ltd
HICB Finance Ltd
Hill, Samuel & Company Ltd
Hoarestott Finance Ltd
Hock Finance Holdings Ltd
Hocomban Finance Ltd
Hondela Finance Ltd
Hong Fok Finance Company Ltd
Hong Nin Finance Ltd
Hung Kai Finance Company Ltd
IBJ Finance Company (Hong Kong) Ltd
IBU International Finance Ltd
ICB Finance Ltd
Impact Finance Ltd
Inchroy Credit Corporation Ltd
Indosuez Asia Ltd
Indosuez Finance Hong Kong Ltd
Inter-Alpha Asia (Hong Kong) Ltd
Japan Leasing (Hong Kong) Ltd
Jardine Fleming & Company Ltd
JCG Finance Company Ltd
J. P. Morgan (Hong Kong) Ltd
Ka Wah International Merchant Finance Ltd
KB Luxembourg (Asia) Ltd
Kian Nan Financial Ltd
Kincheng Finance (HK) Ltd
Kincheng-Tokyo Finance Company Ltd
King Chong (Finance) Ltd
King Fook Finance Company Ltd
King's Finance Company Ltd
Kingson Finance Ltd
Kleinwort, Benson Ltd
Kleinwort, Benson (Hong Kong) Ltd
Korea Associated Finance Ltd
Korea Commercial Finance Ltd

Korea First Finance Ltd
K-Rex Finance Ltd
Kuala Lumpur Finance Company Ltd
Kuwait Pacific Finance Company Ltd
Kwong Lee Finance Ltd
Kwong On Finance Ltd
Kyowa Finance (Hong Kong) Ltd
LBI Finance (Hong Kong) Ltd
Legarleon Finance Company Ltd
Liu Chong Hing Finance Ltd
LTCB Asia Ltd
Luxembourg Finance Company Ltd
MAIBL Bermuda (Far East) Ltd
Malahon Credit & Finance Ltd
Malaysia America Finance Corporation (HK) Ltd
Man Sun Finance (International) Corporation Ltd
Manila CBC Finance (Hong Kong) Ltd
Manila & Hong Kong Capital Corporation Ltd
Manufacturers Hanover Asia, Ltd
Manufacturers Mutual Finance Ltd
Marac Hong Kong Ltd
Merban Asia Ltd
Merchant Guaranty Ltd
Metropolitan Finance Corporation Ltd
Middle East Finance International Ltd
Midland Finance (HK) Ltd
Mitsubishi International Finance Ltd
Mitsui Finance Asia Ltd
Mitsui Trust Finance (Hong Kong) Ltd
Multi-Credit Finance Company Ltd
Multinational Securities and Investment Company Ltd
Nanyang Finance Company, Ltd
Natcan Finance (Asia) Ltd
National Westminster (Hong Kong) Ltd
NCNB (Asia) Ltd
Neways Finance Ltd
Nippon Credit International (Hong Kong) Ltd
N. M. Rothschild & Sons (Hong Kong) Ltd
Nomura International (Hong Kong) Ltd
Nordic Asia Ltd
OCBC Finance (Hong Kong) Ltd

Oman International Finance Ltd
Ong Finance (HK) Ltd
Ontario Finance and Investment Company Ltd
Orient Leasing (Asia) Ltd
Orion Pacific Ltd
OTB Finance Ltd
OUB Finance (HK) Ltd
Overseas Express Finance Corporation Ltd
Overseas Union Finance Ltd
Panin International Finance Corporation Ltd
Pan Seas Finance & Investment Ltd
Paribas Asia Ltd
Philippine Finance and Investment Company Ltd
Philmont Finance and Investment Company Ltd
Philtrust Finance Ltd
Pierson, Heldring & Pierson NV
PNB International Finance Ltd
Po Fung Finance Company Ltd
Producers Finance and Investment Ltd
Public Finance (HK) Ltd
Rainier International Finance Company Ltd
Renown Credit Ltd
RNB Finance (Hong Kong) Ltd
Robina Credit Ltd
Royal Scot Finance Company Ltd
Roy East Investments Ltd
Sai Shing Investment & Finance Ltd
Saitama International (Hong Kong) Ltd
Sanwa International Finance Ltd
SBC Finance (Asia) Ltd
SB India Hong Kong Finance Ltd
Scandinavian Far East Ltd
Schroders & Chartered Ltd
Seattle First Asia Ltd
Search Asia Ltd
Security Pacific Credit (Hong Kong) Ltd
Shacom Finance Ltd
Sharikat Safety Finance Company (Hong Kong) Ltd
Siam Commercial Finance Ltd
Sin Hua Finance Company Ltd
Sing-Ho Finance Company Ltd

Sino-Thai Finance Ltd
Siu On Finance Company Ltd
Solid Pacific Finance Ltd
Southeast Asia Properties & Finance (Credit) Ltd
State Investment House (Hong Kong) Ltd
Stephens Finance Ltd
Stephil Ltd
Sumitomo Finance (Asia) Ltd
Summa International Finance Company (HK) Ltd
Sun Hung Kai Finance Company Ltd
Sun Light Finance Company Ltd
Sun Poh Shing Finance Company Ltd
Tai Sang Finance Ltd
Taiyo Kobe Finance Hong Kong Ltd
Takugin International (Asia) Ltd
Tat Lee Finance Singapore Ltd
Tesoro Finance & Investment Company Ltd
Tetra Finance (HK) Ltd
Thai Farmers Finance and Investment Ltd
Thai Mercantile Development Finance Ltd
Thai-Overseas Investment & Finance Company Ltd
Thai United Finance Company Ltd
The China State Finance Company Ltd
The Great Eagle Finance Company Ltd
The Hong Kong Chinese International Finance Ltd
The Malayan Finance Company Ltd
The Sumitomo Trust Finance (HK) Ltd
The Wales Australia Ltd
The Wing On Finance Company Ltd
The Yien Yieh Finance Company Ltd
Thye Hong Commercial & Finance Company Ltd
Times Finance Ltd
TKM (Far East) Ltd
Tokai Asia Ltd
Tokyo Finance (Asia) Ltd
Tokyo Leasing (Hong Kong) Ltd
Toronto Dominion (Hong Kong) Ltd
Toyo Trust Asia Ltd
Trade Development Finance (Asia) Ltd
Uban-Arab Japanese Finance Ltd
Union Finance Ltd

United Chinese Finance Company Ltd
United Merchants Finance Ltd
Vernes Asia Ltd
Vietnam Finance Company Ltd
Wa Pei Finance Company Ltd
Wardley Ltd
Washington International Ltd
Wayfoong Credit Ltd
Wells Fargo Asia Ltd
Western International Capital Ltd
WestLB Asia Ltd
Whitehall Finance Ltd
Widely Credits Ltd
Wing Hang Finance Company Ltd
Wing Hong Finance and Management Ltd
Wing Lung Finance Ltd
Wisdom Finance Company Ltd
WOC Finance Company Ltd
Worms Asia Ltd
Yasuda Trust and Finance (Hong Kong) Ltd
Yick Yuen Finance and Development Ltd

NOTES

1. Peter Wesley-Smith, *Unequal Treaty 1898–1897* (Hong Kong: Oxford University Press, 1980) provides the background of the Colony's three acquisitions and concentrates on the various legal aspects of the lease.
2. Alvin Rabushka, *Hong Kong: A Study in Economic Freedom* (Chicago: University of Chicago Press, 1979) discusses some of the reasons behind Hong Kong's success.
3. *Financial Times*, 9 July 1979.
4. W. L. C. Brown (Chief Manager of the Chartered Bank in Hong Kong), 'The Turkeys which Voted for an Early Christmas', *Far Eastern Economic Review*, 4 April 1980, p. 68.
5. *Hong Kong 1980: A review of 1979* (Hong Kong: Government Printer, 1980) p. 43.
6. *Insight*, July 1978, p. 36.
7. Though locally incorporated, the Hongkong and Shanghai Banking Corporation is generally considered in Hong Kong as British and classified with the foreign banks in the Exchange Banks' Association interest rate agreement.
8. The Chartered Bank is now the oldest in the Colony (it established local operations in 1859) and the Hongkong and Shanghai Banking Corporation commenced locally in 1865.

9. In its role as a *de facto* lender of last resort, the Hongkong and Shanghai Banking Corporation has provided funds not only to other financial institutions but to non-financial companies as well. The most significant of the latter was its HK$156 million rescue in 1975 of the Hutchinson Group.
10. Cheng Huan, 'Peking Calls the Tune for Chinese Banks', *Asian Finance*, September 1975, p. 19, provides greater details of these activities.
11. Y. C. Jao, 'Hong Kong as a Regional Financial Centre: Evolution and Prospects' (an unpublished paper, 1980) p. 43. One of these banks, the Nanyang Commercial Bank has also recently introduced its own bank card, the Federal Card.
12. *Asian Finance*, 15 March 1977, p. 86.
13. Robert F. Emery, *The Financial Institutions of Southeast Asia: A Country by Country Study* (New York: Praeger, 1970) p. 117.
14. For anti-trust reasons most American banks are happy to place cartel agreements under legislation. Also see John Mansfield, 'Breaking the Rules of the Bank Cartel', *Asian Money Manager*, December 1980, pp. 41–2, for some examples of the ease with which the cartel rules could be avoided under the old system.
15. As cited in Anthony Rowley, 'New Influence on Interest', *Far Eastern Economic Review*, 12 December 1980, p. 68.
16. The Banker Research Unit (ed.), *Banking Structures and Sources of Finance in the Far East* (London: Financial Times Business Publishing, 1980) p. 187.
17. Rate increment of the Interest Rate Agreement has varied over time and initially provided a tiering of $\frac{3}{4}$ per cent, $1\frac{1}{4}$ per cent, and $1\frac{3}{4}$ per cent respectively over the Group 1 rates. Y. C. Jao, *Banking and Currency in Hong Kong: A Study of Postwar Financial Development* (London: Macmillan, 1974) p. 54.
18. Now instead of just an overdraft facility tied to the prime rate, Hong Kong-based borrowers can choose: loans tied to the Hong Kong Interbank Offered Rate (HIBOR) or fixed rate, Hong Kong dollar term loans; short-, medium-, long-term overdraft styled loans denominated in most convertible currencies; custom-designed project finance; trade finance; various types of more specialised discounting facilities; indirect financing such as guarantees, performance bonds, confirming letter of credit and syndicated guarantee facilities – see M. T. Skully, *Merchant Banking in the Far East*, 2nd ed. (London: Financial Times Business Publishing, 1980) p. 75.
19. On 26 April 1979 the Hongkong and Shanghai Banking Corporation, Chartered Bank, and Hang Seng Bank introduced a concessional prime rate (then $1\frac{1}{2}$ per cent below the normal rate) on loans for importing foodstuffs and certain raw materials.
20. The Third Inland Revenue Ordinance Review Committee (partly responsible for the move) was appointed in 1976 to improve the equity of the Colony's tax system. The Committee wished to maintain the principle that income arising 'through or from the carrying on by the bank or other financial institutions of its business in the Colony' be taxed there. Unfortunately, they found that much offshore lending instigated by or arising from work done within the Colony was still tax-free. The amendments following the Financial Secretary's announcement were designed to tax this income but allow revenue from bookings not instigated from within the colony to continue tax-free.

21. The Jardine, Hutchinson Whampoa, Wheelock Marden and Swire groups represent the most important of Hong Kong's so-called traditional British 'Hongs', and Y. K. Pao and his World International complex, Cheung Kong, C. Y. Tung complex, Kadoorie, and the Stelux and Carrian groups are among the better-known Chinese groups—*Asian Finance*, 15 March 1980, provides a good discussion of both types of organisations.

22. Companies which did not raise funds from the public (in other words were self-financed or financial institution financed) did not require registration under the Ordinance and thus still operate outside its control. Although most are small, often family, businesses, some subsidiaries of financial institutions and hire purchase and leasing company subsidiaries of manufacturing companies are large organisations in their own right but not under the Ordinance.

23. M. T. Skully, *Merchant Banking in the Far East*, p. 65.

24. As cited in Leo Goodstadt, 'Hong Kong Government's Plans to Put Deposit-Taking Companies in Their Place', *Asian Banking*, July 1980, pp. 30–1.

25. Mr P. Jacobs as cited in *Asian Finance*, October 1977, p. 15.

26. *Report of the Advisory Committee on Diversification 1979* (Hong Kong: Government Printer, 1979) p. 208.

27. Approval in this case is from the Commission of Inland Revenue and relates to the tax exemption the earnings within such funds enjoy.

28. Leo Goodstadt, 'Asia's Mutual Funds Bloom in Hong Kong', *Asian Banking*, September 1980, p. 28.

29. Ibid., p. 28.

30. Robert F. Emery, *The Financial Institutions of Southeast Asia*, p. 123.

31. *Report of the Advisory Committee on Diversification 1979*, p. 128. Some of these funds include the Kadoorie Agricultural Aid Loan Fund, J. E. Joseph Trust Fund, World Refugee Year Fund, the Fishery Development Loan Fund and the Fishing Marketing Organisation. All of these are in part administered through the Government's Agriculture and Fisheries Department.

32. Ibid., p. 128.

33. Mary Lee, 'A Crackdown on Loan Sharks', *Far Eastern Economic Review*, 12 December 1980, p. 68.

34. Robert F. Emery, *The Financial Institutions of Southeast Asia*, p. 121.

35. A number of the Chinese-oriented firms operate a very small and informal secondary market in post-dated cheques. There is some potential for trading the cheques of prime companies in the general market, but cheques can be cancelled and, if negotiable, are bearer instruments.

36. Y. C. Jao, *Banking and Currency in Hong Kong*, p. 74.

37. A more detailed discussion of the attempts and problems of developing the local money market may be found in M. T. Skully, *Merchant Banking in the Far East*, pp. 66–75.

38. P. W. Allsopp (Deputy Secretary for Monetary Affairs), 'Reflections on the Need for a Central Bank in Hong Kong', a speech to the Hong Kong Society of Security Analysts on 27 November 1980, p. 5.

39. Y. C. Jao, 'Financial Structure and Monetary Policy in Hong Kong', an unpublished paper, dated 1980.

40. Y. C. Jao, *Banking and Currency in Hong Kong* , p. 78.
41. Warrants enable the holder to purchase so many shares of the issuer's ordinary shares at a predetermined price over a set period–usually of some years' duration.
42. Unlike the stock exchanges, the international bond market has no physical site within which to trade: all transactions are accomplished by telephone or telex. Firms most active in this business are generally members of the Association of International Bond Dealers.
43. Claude Kauffman, International bond division of the Standard Chartered Merchant Bank Ltd, as cited in *Modern Asia*, April 1980, p. 24.
44. *Asian Finance*, 15 June 1977, p. 24.
45. As cited in Alan Chalkley, 'Hong Kong's Unfinished Business', *The Banker*, December 1976, p. 58.
46. *Report of the Advisory Committee on Diversification 1979*, p. 209.
47. *South China Morning Post*, 27 June 1978.
48. A speech by Mr Anthony Ockenden in 1978, cited in *The Straits Times*, 19 April 1979.
49. P. W. Allsopp, 'Reflections on the Need for a Central Bank in Hong Kong'.
50. 'The Hong Kong government has no intention of creating any marketable government debt' (ibid., p. 10).
51. Sir Phillip Haddon-Cave, as cited in Anthony Rowley, 'A Reprieve from Recession', *Far Eastern Economic Review*, 19 September 1980, p. 126.
52. Ibid., p. 126.
53. Y. C. Jao, 'Financial Structure and Monetary Policy in Hong Kong', p. 65.
54. Other matters, such as the Colony's problems with Chinese and Vietnamese refugees, rapid inflation, a trade deficit, a weakening currency, and overheating in the real estate industry and other areas of the economy, will also be important factors in the short run.
55. *Far Eastern Economic Review*, 28 December 1979, p. 6.
56. A speech by Sir Murray MacLehose dated 6 April 1979, as cited in *Modern Asia*, June 1979, p. 104.
57. China's own investments in Hong Kong were conservatively estimated at US$2 billion in 1977 (*The Times*, 31 January 1977, p. 1).
58. Mary Lee, 'A New Relaxed Feeling of Having one's Heart at Ease', *Far Eastern Economic Review*, 21 March 1980, p. 39.
59. George Forrai, 'How Good a Tax Haven is Hong Kong?', *Asian Finance*, 15 March 1980.
60. *Report of the Advisory Committee on Diversification 1979*, p. 215.

3 Financial Institutions and Markets in Japan

HIROMITSU ISHI

INTRODUCTION

(a) The Setting

The Japanese archipelago is formed by an arc-shaped group of volcanic islands stretching from the northeast to the southwest for a distance of nearly 2200 kilometres. It lies 200 kilometres east of the Korean peninsula and between the 31st and the 46th latitudes, north. This range in latitude produces various climatic contrasts while the position near the continent makes for more severe summers and winters than would otherwise be the case.

Honshu, Kyushu, Shikoku and Hokkaido are, as is to be seen in Map 3.1, the four main islands of Japan, accounting for 98 per cent of the total 377,420 square kilometres in land area. Japan is a geographically small nation relative to its population of approximately 110 million. The mountainous terrain of the islands, moreover, reduces the effective size of the nation. Three-quarters of all the land in Japan is hill or mountain land with slopes exceeding 15 per cent. Consequently, only 16 per cent of the total land area has been cultivated.

That there is an average of 290 persons per square kilometre is not a realistic measure of the population density of Japan. Population density is a function of both terrain character and the degree of urbanisation. The great majority of the Japanese have followed this pattern and have congregated in the urban centres located on the coastal plains. Roughly 80 million of the Japanese live in populous cities, most of which are densely populated areas of over 3800 people per square kilometre. The largest urban centres in Japan are the three metropolitan regions of Tokyo–Yokohama, Osaka–Kyoto–Kobe and Nagoya, all of which

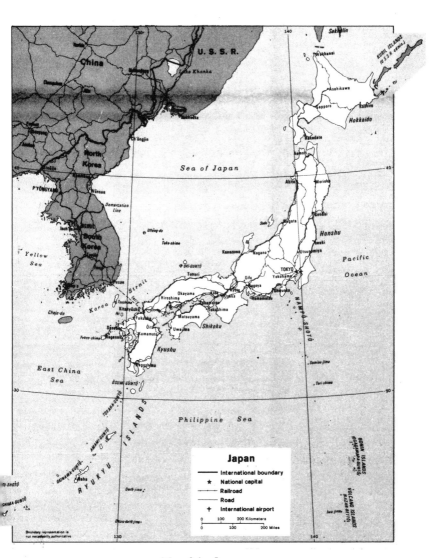

MAP 3.1   Japan

Source: United States Department of State, Bureau of Public Affairs, July 1980.

are located along the Pacific coastal belt on the principal island of Honshu.

Natural resources in Japan are limited. Almost all its raw cotton, wool, bauxite, nickel, natural rubber, crude oil and iron ore, together with countless numbers of other raw materials to varying degrees, are imported. By value, imports of raw materials, foodstuffs and chemicals account for nearly 80 per cent of total imports. While imports are large, Japan has generally maintained a substantial positive trade balance. In 1978, a surplus of 18.2 billion dollars from foreign trade was reported. Japan's trade balance for 1979, however, showed a deficit of 7.6 billion dollars, primarily due to increases in oil prices. Many predict that this deficit will increase in 1980.

Exports from Japan consist mainly of manufactured goods. The largest single export commodity in 1979, by value, was transport and equipment, which accounted for 27.4 billion dollars. Non-electrical machinery, electrical machinery, and iron and steel produced export sales of 14.1, 13.9 and 11.9 billion dollars respectively. Although Japan has achieved successes in international trade, it has been the domestic demand that has supported its economic growth. Even during the high growth period from 1951 to 1973, exports accounted for only an 8.5 per cent share of the total gross national product.[1]

During the initial postwar recovery, the reconstruction of the core of basic industries such as coal, electric power, fertilisers, chemicals, steel and shipbuilding was of primary concern. These basic industries were nurtured under the closely controlled structure established by the Allied occupation. The Korean War, which broke out in 1950 was perhaps the biggest single impetus to Japan's postwar development. Industrial production rose by 50 per cent within one year and the increased trade resulting from the war effort brought Japan a surplus in their balance of payments for the first time in the postwar era. Priority had initially been given to the core industries, but as they became secure in their development, priorities were shifted to newer industries such as electronics, optics and automobiles in order to promote import substitution. It was during the period from the early 1950s to the early 1970s that the policy of growth reigned supreme. Since the late 1960s, Japan has ranked third in total GNP, behind the USA and the USSR. Japan's postwar economic growth was unprecedented and averaged 10.8 per cent in the years between 1951 and 1973. Indeed, rapid and substantial growth was the dominant feature of the period.[2]

The oil crisis of 1973 fell hard on Japan and the real GNP actually experienced a negative growth in 1974. It was from that time that growth slowed and an emphasis began to be placed upon stable, rather than rapid growth. Even so, after the recovery from what has been termed the 'oil shock', the growth of the economy has been averaging between 5 and 6 per cent on an annual basis.

A definite pattern of reconstruction and subsequent growth developed in postwar Japan. The government implemented tariffs and quotas to protect emerging industries while providing export incentives for those industries that were sufficiently developed domestically to compete in the international market. The government in this sense created a favourable environment for economic development but the initiative to development has come entirely from the private sector. Given the high priority that has been placed on economic goals in Japan and the national consensus for the desire to be among the group of industrialised nations, business has been able to count upon a supportive government. Neither business nor government, however, act as monolithic entities within themselves and simplistic interpretations such as the 'Japan Inc.' thesis tend only to cloud the issues concerning the relations between enterprise and government in Japan.[3]

Substantial differences exist between the political parties and among the various ministries of the government bureaucracy. Although they may share common concerns on a macro-policy level, each have their own perspectives as to how those policies should be effected. This holds true even within one particular ministry as various departments which represent particular interests vie with each other for influence.

That business in Japan is dominated by giant corporations is a common but mistaken impression. The great majority of the labour force in Japan, nearly 70 per cent, are employed in small-scale operations of fewer than 100 personnel. Corporations employing over one thousand persons employ less than 17 per cent of the total labour force. Productivity in large firms, however, is almost twice that of small enterprises and the fixed assets per worker is nearly triple. It has been the large corporations, more than the small firms, that have been able to take advantage of new capital-intensive technologies and have made the high rate of investment in plant and equipment. It is they who have been given the added advantage of receiving preferential access to credit at lower rates in order to do so.

Throughout the postwar period, Japan has benefited from political stability. The Liberal Democratic Party, a conservative party, has constantly maintained a majority in the Diet, thereby reducing political turmoil which often tends to damage the normal workings of an economy. Thus, political stability has contributed much to the sustained growth of the Japanese economy.

(b) Overview of the Financial Sector

The corporate business sector in Japan is a large borrower in the financial market and the personal sector is the largest lender in the market through savings formation. This is evident from Table 3.1 in which flow of funds is observed in each sector. This pattern in and of itself is not necessarily unique to Japan, but its structure and predominance provides a marked contrast between Japan and other countries. In recent years the saving rate of individuals in Japan has been more than 20 per cent of their disposable income, greatly surpassing that of all other industrialised nations. The flow of these funds to the corporate business sector through the lendings of the financial institutions is referred to as the 'indirect financing' mechanism. In contrast, 'direct financing' or equity financing by the corporate business sector has not developed in Japan and so the funds channelled through the securities market have been relatively small. This accounts for the extremely high debt–equity ratio which is characteristic of Japanese corporate finance.[4]

Given this choice of financing-debt over equity, enterprises in Japan are dependent on banks for investment funds and so during periods of rapid industrial growth, this has led to a condition of excess borrowing or what is termed 'overborrowing'. The recent slowdown in the rate of economic growth has eased the problem but the imbalanced capital structure of corporations – small internal capital and large external capital – is still pervasive.

Related to the 'overborrowing' of Japanese corporate enterprise, banks, specifically the city banks (the largest type of commercial banks as described later), have often experienced an 'overloan' position because they have not been able to meet the demand for funds from their own deposits. The term is applied to the condition wherein city banks must rely upon borrowings from either the Bank of Japan or the call money market or both in order to meet the financial requirements of their customers. City banks are constantly short of funds and cover their shortage principally through the short-term money market. The short-term money market provides the means by which the city banks can adjust their liquidity positions with other financial institutions, which are nearly all permanently in surplus of funds. The market is, without exception, a one-way channel of funds flowing toward city banks from all other financial institutions and as such it reflects the imbalance of bank liquidity in Japan.[5]

The personal sector assumes the central role in savings formation and is the final lender in the flow of funds accounts of the overall economy.

Personal saving in Japan is still maintained at a high rate. The high economic growth rate, the bonus payment system, inadequate social security and the inadequate distribution of real assets are plausible causes for such a high saving rate.[6] Savings in Japan predominantly take the form of time deposits with financial institutions. While over 80 per cent of savings are invested in time deposits, securities investments account for only a 10 per cent share of all personal savings. It is in this sense that Japanese savers finance the loans which are made by the banks to the corporate enterprises.

A look into the flow of funds from savings to investment in the fiscal years from 1971 to 1973 shows that 46 per cent of gross savings are supplied by the personal sector. Moreover, they account for 62 per cent of the funds supplied to the financial market. Corporations led in the demand for funds as well as in gross investment by absorbing 60 per cent and using 48 per cent respectively of the total amount of these funds. The most notable of all, however, is that 92 per cent of all the fund flows in the financial market passed through the hands of intermediary financial institutions. This system of indirect finance, whereby a financial institution acts as an intermediary in connecting lenders and borrowers, is a major characteristic of the Japanese financial system.

The government in Japan exerts a great influence on monetary and economic conditions through public finance. During the occupation period of postwar Japan, the government had strictly followed the policy of a balanced budget, established under the Dodge Plan in 1949. In 1965, however, the government began to assume a new posture as a borrower by issuing bonds as a means of fund raising. Its influence in the securities market has grown and currently it accounts for nearly 30 per cent of the outstanding bonds.[7] The government acts as a lender as well by absorbing the funds collected through the nationwide network of post offices in the form of postal life insurance premiums, postal annuity funds and deposits of personal savers in the postal savings account system and then channelling them to borrowing businesses and individuals via the various government financial agencies and institutions.

Another major characteristic of the financial system in Japan is the control of the interest rate structure. The interest rates were first regulated in Japan by the enactment of the Temporary Interest Rates Adjustment Law in 1947. Owing to the continuing demand for funds being in excess of the availability of supply, however, this law has remained in effect. The result of the restriction of the market adjustment function of interest rates by their strict regulation, however, has been to

TABLE 3.1 Flow of funds accounts: financial transaction accounts for 1978 (¥ billion)

	Financial institutions Assets	Financial institutions Lia-bilities	Bank of Japan Assets	Bank of Japan Lia-bilities	Private fin. inst. Assets	Private fin. inst. Lia-bilities	Banks Assets	Banks Lia-bilities	Other fin. inst. Assets	Li bili
A Deposits to Bank of Japan	266.1	266.1		266.1	265.2		255.9		9.3	
B Currency		2087.3		ª2332.4	221.8		107.3		114.5	
C Demand deposits		602.3				6649.4		4308.5	128.4	24
D Time deposits		22416.5				15143.2		8587.3	469.2	70
E Free yen deposits & foreign currency deposits		1376.0				376.0		1345.9		
F Government current deposits		132.9		132.9						
G Trust		212.7				2812.7	21.7		−16.4	28
H Insurance		4547.8				2913.3				29
I Securities	22045.5	4038.1	ᵇ3195.2		14828.0	3340.2	5978.4	1899.3	8849.6	14
J Short-term govt. securities	4795.9		2107.7		−2.4				−2.4	
K Government bonds	8635.9		1142.6		7237.3		4708.9		2528.4	
L Local government bonds	2089.2				2033.3		488.5		1544.8	
M Public corporation bonds	2267.2	698.3	−55.1		1622.7		272.1		1350.6	
N Bank debentures	1484.3	2367.3			1290.1	2367.3	−49.1	1756.4	1339.2	6
O Industrial bonds	785.1				666.5		−38.0		704.5	
P Stocks	1929.3	142.6			1921.9	142.6	576.5	107.6	1345.4	
Q Securities investment trust	58.6	795.0			58.6	795.0	19.5		39.1	7
R Bonds in foreign currency		34.9				35.3		35.3		
S Bank of Japan loans	436.5	436.5	436.5			436.5		384.6		
T Call money	−74.5	−74.5			−74.5	−74.5	−87.4	−325.5	12.9	2
U Bills bought & sold	571.8	571.8	−150.0		721.8	571.8	67.1	664.8	654.7	−
V Loans	26502.8					16883.7	10839.7	89.3	7452.6	13
W Loans by private fin. inst	16883.7					16883.7	10839.7	89.3	7452.6	1
X Loans by public fin. inst.	9619.1									
Y Trade credit										
Z Deposits to trust fund bureau		4250.8								
a Gold & foreign exchange reserves	...		...							
b Foreign trade credits	644.1	564.4			644.1	564.4	644.1	564.4		
c Foreign direct investment										
d Other foreign claims & debts	3221.0	1142.8			2799.3	1145.0	2115.9	1149.2	683.4	
e Other		960.9	−750.3			1411.4		1274.9		
f Financial surplus or deficit (−)		1480.9								
g Total	53613.3	53613.3	2731.4	2731.4	36289.4	36289.4	19942.7	19942.7	18358.2	18

ª Including ¥2271.3 billion of Bank of Japan notes.
ᵇ Including ¥1234.9 billion of net purchases of securities by the Bank of Japan from private financial institutions.
ᶜ Including ¥4922.4 billion of Foreign Exchange Fund Bill.

Notes:

1. Classification of transactions

   (1) Demand deposits: current deposits, ordinary deposits, special deposits, deposits for tax payments, etc.

   (2) Time deposits: time deposits, instalment savings, postal savings, etc.

   (3) Financial surplus or deficit: this is the balancing item of each sector. The 'financial deficit' (net increase in financial liabilities) corresponds to 'the excess of investment over saving' in non-financial transactions, and the 'financial surplus' (net increase in financial assets) also corresponds to 'the excess of saving over investment'. In the 'rest of the world' sector, this country's balance of payments

stunt the development of both the long- and short-term financial markets in Japan.

The discount rate, or the basic money rate applied by the Bank of Japan on its lending, is the point of reference for the entire interest rate structure in Japan. The lending rates of private financial institutions, especially the 'standard rate of interest' or prime rate, are linked to the discount rate, and so they fluctuate with it. Ceilings for short-term interest rates by law are set by the Minister of Finance, but they, together with the standard rate of interest, move by the same margin as the change in the discount rate. This practice has established a convention whereby the standard rate for all banks is set 0.25 per cent higher than

fin. inst.	Central government		Public Corporation & local authorities		Corporate business		Personal		Rest of the world		Total	
Lia-bilities	Assets	Lia-bilities	Assets	Lia-bilities	Assets	Lia-bilities	Assets	Lia-bilities	Assets	Lia-bilities	Assets	Lia-bilities
											266.1	266.1
				-0.5	208.8		1879.0				2087.3	2087.3
1.2				18.9	3505.2		3078.2				6602.3	6602.3
7273.3				646.0	3822.9		17947.6				24416.5	22416.5
											...	1376.0
	132.9										132.9	132.9
		47.2	42.7		782.3		1983.2				2812.7	2812.7
1634.5							4547.8				4547.8	4547.8
697.9	372.8	17394.3	61.5	4065.1	1076.7	2038.2	4355.3		780.1		28691.9	27535.7
	372.0	'5602.4	31.0								5602.4	5602.4
		11795.9	23.7				2070.2				11803.5	11795.9
698.3			-13.0	2319.1	614.1		91.2		782.6		2319.1	2319.1
				1747.5			86.3				2445.8	2445.8
							1212.5				2367.3	2367.3
					747.4	42.7					747.4	747.4
	0.8			19.8	442.2	1148.8	221.8		-173.9		2440.0	1291.4
					20.4		716.0				795.0	795.0
-0.4		-4.0		-1.5		142.0			171.4		171.4	171.4
											436.5	436.5
											-74.5	-74.5
											571.8	571.8
		2038.8		4489.6		10064.3		9910.1			26502.8	26502.8
				645.6		8724.1		7514.0			16883.7	16883.7
		2038.8		3844.0		1340.2		2396.1			9619.1	9619.1
					8082.7	6894.0		1188.7			8082.7	8082.7
4250.8	4250.8										4250.8	4250.8
	...									2182.4	...	2182.4
					42.0	826.8		826.8	121.7		1512.9	1512.9
					492.7	4.4		4.4	492.7		497.1	497.1
-2.2				-4.4	-78.9	-0.4		1598.1	3897.1		4740.2	5035.1
280.1	3744.1			-198.4	-174.4		-110.1				3459.6	762.5
		-10932.5	773.1	-7578.8		-2067.3		22582.2		-3484.5		
14135.6	8500.6	8500.6	773.1	773.1	17760.0	17760.0	33681.0	33681.0	3209.4	3209.4	117537.4	117537.4

is recorded from the standpoint of the foreign countries. Then the 'financial deficit' of the sector represents the favourable balance of payments (current balance) of this country.

(4) Foreign transaction items: the amount of increase or decrease of gold and foreign exchange reserves, and foreign claims and debts (both in terms of dollars) are converted into yen by the basic rate (the inter-bank rate, for the term during August and December 1971 and since February 1973).

2. In response to the reform of the flow of funds accounts (modified on 'Division of Sectors' and 'Classifications of Transactions') some figures have no linkage with those prior to October–December 1977 (figures after the retroactive reform should be referred to the July 1978 issue).

Source: The Bank of Japan.

the discount rate. Although maximum limits for deposit rates are set by the Temporary Interest Rate Adjustment Law, in actual practice the Bank of Japan announces guidelines for maximum deposit rates within the limits of the law and requests the compliance of financial institutions. Discount rate changes constituted a major instrument of monetary policy in Japan and have often been shifted upward or downward to influence business activity. As such the discount policy has been a more useful tool for effecting desirable adjustments in the economy than any other policy instruments, like open market operations and control of the reserve-ratio.

In addition to participation in the financial markets and control over the interest rate structure, the monetary authorities maintain other supervisory and guidance mechanisms over the financial sector, particularly with regard to the banks. The Bank Law in Japan authorises the Ministry of Finance to demand reports from banks in order to inspect their business whenever he deems it necessary. Moreover, the approval of the Ministry of Finance is required for the opening of any new branch office. The maximum legal limit for the establishment of new branches is set at two within a period of two years, but the Ministry may approve or disapprove of plans that fall within that limit. The Ministry of Finance has in fact had a very restrictive policy concerning the expansion of banking operations and this has been an important instrument in the supervision of bank activity.

The government has also regulated the operations of financial institutions through its structural policy of specialisation. Financial institutions are classified by the type of activities in which they are allowed to be engaged; short-term finance, long-term finance, trust business, foreign-exchange banking, mutual banking, co-operative banking and the securities business. Financial institutions have been able to broaden both their markets and their functions to a certain degree, but the government has asserted its authority to maintain the separation of activities that it felt to be desirable.

Government regulation has been positive and deliberate. It has influenced the flow of funds through financial intermediaries in order to allocate resources to the corporate sector and within that sector, to those industries designated as target industries in Japan's reconstruction programme. The financial system has been structured, then, to function in concert with industrial policy and to that extent it has contributed significantly to Japan's economic growth.

FINANCIAL INSTITUTIONS

(a) Banking Institutions

(i) *The Bank of Japan*

The Bank of Japan is the central bank. It plays a pivotal role in the financial system of Japan through its functions as the bank of issue, the banker's bank and the government's bank. Given the purpose of stabilising both the value of money and the development of the national economy, the Bank of Japan regulates the monetary system and enforces monetary policies.

Though the Bank of Japan is the sole issuing authority in Japan, the current 'Elastic Maximum Issue Limit System' stipulates that the maximum amount of legal tender which the Bank can issue is to be fixed by the Minister of Finance upon consultation with a Cabinet Council. The Bank of Japan may, however, issue additional notes provided that they do not remain in circulation above a period of 15 days.

Operating as the government's bank, it receives deposits from the central government in the form of taxes and other government revenues. The Bank can make advances to the government as well, but this practice is rare except on a very short-term basis near the end of the fiscal year. The Bank of Japan manages the Treasury Funds, encompassing not only the payments and receipts but the accounting responsibilities, including the handling of all securities either owned by or deposited with the government.

Other than its workings with the government, the Bank of Japan deals exclusively with financial institutions. Almost all principal financial institutions have contractual agreements with the Bank of Japan, but some transact only deposit business whereas others maintain both deposit and lending accounts. Current accounts or deposits of these financial institutions are placed with the Bank of Japan for the purpose of settling transactions as well as fulfilling the reserve requirement responsibilities. These deposits are utilised for transferrals of funds between district branches and settling accounts between the financial institutions through the clearing system.

There are three principal instruments of monetary policy that the Bank of Japan utilises in order to control the credit and money supply.[8] They are the Bank lending policy, the open market operations and the reserve requirement system. Although it is not a policy in the strict sense of the term, the Bank has applied what has been termed 'window guidance', or advice on the appropriate behaviour of financial institutions in the form of 'moral suasion'.

The lending policy of the Bank of Japan is effected through the alteration of credit outstanding as well as changes in the official discount rate or the 'bank rate' which are applied to those loans. In Japan, the discount rate has long been the single most potent device in the implementation of monetary policy. The effectiveness of this policy instrument derives from the financial structure of Japan wherein both banks and corporations are highly leveraged to an exceptional degree.

Because private banks depend heavily on the Bank of Japan for funds, changes in the discount rate have considerable impact on the cost of capital. The Bank of Japan has also established a system whereby ceilings are set on its lending to city banks in order to curb their dependence upon Bank loans. Lendings above the ceiling are not generally approved but should they be, a penalty rate is assessed to them.

The second policy instrument is open market operations. The Japanese capital market is undeveloped in comparison with other industrialised nations. Until 1962, securities were bought and sold by the Bank through direct negotiation with individual financial institutions. At that time the Bank of Japan began to channel cash supply through operations in the securities market as a new method of monetary adjustment. This, however, was done at fixed rates of interest and with repurchase agreements. In 1966, unconditional market operations were instituted whereby prices are determined by the market and no repurchase agreements are attached. The low interest rate policy which the government has maintained, however, has limited the impact of these operations. The Bank of Japan in recent years has been resorting to the market operation more frequently and, with the trend toward the liberalisation of interest rates, it will undoubtedly be playing an even more important role in daily monetary adjustments.

The Reserve Requirement System is the third and the most newly-developed policy instrument used by the Bank of Japan. The Law Concerning Reserve Deposit Requirement System took effect in 1957 and the reserve requirements were first established in 1959. Financial institutions are required to redeposit cash reserves with the Bank at determined rates. These reserve rates vary according to the kind of financial institution concerned and are based on both the volume and type of deposits which they hold. Although the reserve ratios in Japan have been increased gradually, they still remain considerably lower than those of other countries because most financial institutions, especially the city banks, have generally been without sufficient cash reserves as a result of their excessive lending practices.

In addition to these three orthodox policy instruments, the Bank of Japan engages in a supervisory practice known as 'window guidance'. Through this practice the Bank supplements its policy instruments by giving advice to financial institutions concerning their lending policies and fund positions. The main focus is that of monetary restraint and as such its objective is to limit the volume of commercial bank credit rather than to control the qualitative aspects of lending. Although window guidance is strictly supplementary to the orthodox policy instruments, the Bank's close contact with its client financial institutions lends great strength to this informal policy instrument.

(ii) *Private banking institutions*

Among the various financial institutions in Japan, the banks play the most prominent role. Figure 3.1 and Table 3.2 summarise the structural framework of financial institutions in Japan. The banks account for approximately 40–50 per cent of all deposits, savings, loans and discounts in Japan. The term 'all banks' is sometimes used to describe these institutions as a group but they may be best divided into three main classifications; commercial, long-term credit and trust banks. Such a classification is conventional in nature and does not necessarily coincide with legal classifications or terminology. The term 'commercial banks' for instance will not appear in the legal code but they can be identified and classified by the types of financing in which they are primarily engaged. Moreover, a word of caution might well be in order, for such classifications tend to lead to the conceptualisation of clearly defined spheres of activity. Government financial policy has been aimed toward the separation of financial markets among the various types of institutions, but the institutions themselves have been struggling against this policy and have achieved some success. Thus, most private banking institutions in Japan tend to engage in both credit-creating and credit-intermediating functions. While this compromises the use of groupings, the classifications are valid to the extent that they distinguish the various banks by the fields in which they mainly operate. This section first examines the types of commercial banks in Japan, then their operations, and finally discusses the more specialised long-term credit and trust banks.[9]

Types of commercial banks
The commercial banks in Japan may be divided into four groups: the city banks, regional or local banks, foreign banks, and the specialised foreign-exchange bank.

City banks: The city banks represent the core of the Japanese banking system. They operate on a nationwide scale but are based in metropolitan areas. At present there are 13 such banks; their names and relative importance are shown in Table 3.3. The Bank of Tokyo, although a specialist foreign-exchange bank, is considered as a city bank for statistical purposes. These banks are the most important of all private

TABLE 3.2 Fund resources of financial institutions (in billions of yen)

	End of 1965		End of 1970		End of 1975		End of 1978	
	Savings and deposits (financial resources[a])							
All banks	19364	48.2%	40420	43.5%	91574	40.0%	130115	37.4%
City banks	(10009)	(24.9)	(20449)	(22.0)	(44248)	(19.3)	(62104)	(17.9)
Regional banks	(6222)	(15.5)	(13104)	(14.1)	(30943)	(13.5)	(45579)	(13.1)
Long-term credit banks	(2444)	(6.1)	(5311)	(5.7)	(12930)	(5.7)	(18281)	(5.2)
Trust banks	(689)	(1.7)	(1556)	(1.7)	(3453)	(1.5)	(4151)	(1.2)
Trust accounts of all banks[b]	2098	5.2	5224	5.6	13105	5.7	21114	6.1
Financial institutions for small business	7298	18.2	16663	17.9	42514	18.6	61978	17.8
Mutual loan and savings banks	(2892)	(7.2)	(5685)	(6.1)	(14194)	(6.2)	(20663)	(5.9)
Credit associations	(3030)	(7.5)	(7504)	(8.1)	(18801)	(8.2)	(27163)	(7.8)
Credit co-operatives	(765)	(1.9)	(1936)	(2.1)	(4829)	(2.1)	(6907)	(2.0)
Financial institutions for agriculture, forestry and fisheries	2866	7.1	7342	7.9	18397	8.0	26330	7.6
Insurance companies[c]	2411	6.0	6637	7.1	15005	6.6	23040	6.6
Government financing[d]	6170	15.3	16735	18.0	48256	21.1	85244	24.5
Total	40207	100.0	93021	100.0	228851	100.0	347821	100.0
	Loans and securities investment (fund employment)							
All banks	22650	52.2%	46028	46.6%	102910	42.7%	147233	40.7%
City banks	(12967)	(29.9)	(25434)	(25.8)	(54345)	(22.6)	(75183)	(20.8)
Regional banks	(6505)	(15.0)	(13639)	(13.8)	(31825)	(13.2)	(47528)	(13.1)
Long-term credit banks	(2486)	(5.7)	(5384)	(5.4)	(12782)	(5.3)	(17671)	(4.9)
Trust banks	(692)	(1.6)	(1571)	(1.6)	(3958)	(1.6)	(6851)	(1.9)
Trust accounts of all banks	2241	5.2	5437	5.5	13712	5.7	19196	5.3

Financial institutions for small business	6777	15.6	16250	16.5	42132	17.5	61666	17.0
Mutual loans and saving banks	(2833)	(6.5)	(5662)	(5.7)	(13962)	(5.8)	(20620)	(5.7)
Credit associations	(2674)	(6.2)	(7278)	(7.4)	(18889)	(7.9)	(27197)	(7.5)
Credit co-operatives	(664)	(1.5)	(1766)	(1.8)	(4566)	(1.9)	(6536)	(1.8)
Financial institutions for agriculture, forestry and fisheries	2258	5.3	6716	6.8	17117	7.1	24844	6.9
Insurance companies	2163	5.0	6494	6.5	15637	6.5	23349	6.4
Government financing	7254	16.7	17845	18.1	49263	20.5	85787	23.7
Total	43343	100.0	98770	100.0	240771	100.0	362075	100.0

a Fund resources and the total of current deposits, short-term deposits, time deposits, bank debentures, trusts, and insurance.
b Trusts do not include investment trusts.
c Both life and non-life insurance companies are included in the fund employment, but only life insurance companies in the fund resources.
d The fund resources of government financing consists of postal savings, postal book-transfer savings, postal life insurance and annuity, public corporation bonds and deposits to Trust Fund Bureau.

Sources: Bank of Japan, 'Flow of Funds Accounts'.

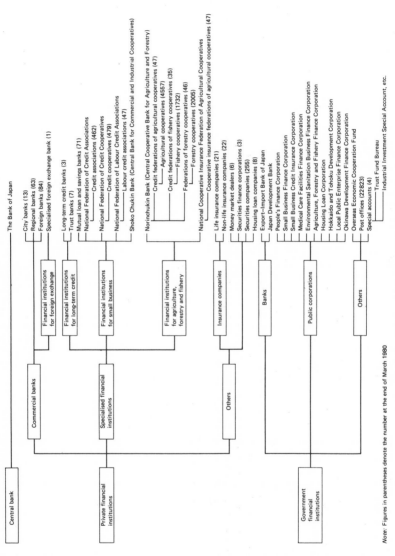

FIGURE 3.1   Financial institutions in Japan

Note: Figures in parentheses denote the number at the end of March 1980

TABLE 3.3   City banks (as of the end of March 1979)

| | | Number of branches | |
Bank	Deposits (¥ 100 million)	Domestic	Overseas
Dai-Ichi Kangyo Bank, Ltd	106132	317	7
Fuji Bank, Ltd	97073	217	7
Sumitomo Bank, Ltd	92338	199	9
Sanwa Bank, Ltd	90494	222	8
Mitsubishi Bank, Ltd	89011	197	7
Tokai Bank, Ltd	67197	214	5
Taiyo Kobe Bank, Ltd	65146	322	6
Mitsui Bank, Ltd	62295	160	9
Daiwa Bank, Ltd	57758	153	4
Bank of Tokyo, Ltd	54643	35	28
Kyowa Bank, Ltd	44676	224	3
Saitama Bank, Ltd	35663	154	3
Hokkaido Takushoku Bank, Ltd	27992	162	4
Total	(13) 890425	2576	100

Source: Federation of Bankers' Association of Japan (1979).

financial institutions with 40 per cent of all the financial resources on hand for all banks and 20 per cent of those for all financial institutions. Their principal customers have predominantly been the large corporate enterprises.[10] As such, their lendings to them have had a decisive influence on the growth of the Japanese economy. The relationship between the city banks and their corporate clients has not developed without cost, however, for the almost insatiable desire for funds by expanding industries has led to a situation in which city banks have been in a chronic state of 'over-loan'. They have also become important shareholders in the larger companies.[11]

Regional banks: Regional banks in Japan operate mainly in the prefectures and have been long thought of as 'country banks'. They currently number 63. Although some compete with city banks in size, most are medium-to small-size banks: their relative sizes are shown in Table 3.4. Each of these banks is based in a particular prefecture but in recent years they have been expanding their business over prefectual boundaries into the neighbouring prefectures. Moreover, they have expanded their activities to include the metropolitan areas of Tokyo and

TABLE 3.4 Regional banks

Bank	Deposits (¥100 million)	Number of branches	
		Domestic	Overseas
Bank of Yokohama, Ltd	29204	136	2
Chiba Bank, Ltd	19888	114	—
Shizuoka Bank, Ltd	19357	166	—
Hokuriku Bank, Ltd	18708	146	—
Joyo Bank, Ltd	18366	108	—
Bank of Fukuoka, Ltd	16262	150	—
Bank of Hiroshima, Ltd	16087	146	—
Ashikaga Bank, Ltd	16068	101	—
Gunma Bank, Ltd	13964	93	—
Hachijuni Bank, Ltd	13391	98	—
Yamaguchi Bank, Ltd	12114	135	—
Chugoku Bank, Ltd	11199	128	—
77 Bank, Ltd	11036	102	—
Bank of Kyoto, Ltd	10695	85	—
Daishi Bank, Ltd	10639	110	—
Hokkaido Bank, Ltd	10446	107	—
Iyo Bank, Ltd	10392	101	—
114th Bank, Ltd	10234	81	—
Suruga Bank, Ltd	10230	107	—
Nanto Bank, Ltd	10210	86	—
Shiga Bank, Ltd	9329	83	—
Juroku Bank, Ltd	8972	89	—
Kiyo Bank, Ltd	8871	79	—
105th Bank, Ltd	8566	95	—
Hokkoku Bank, Ltd	7589	99	—
Shikoku Bank, Ltd	7267	89	—
Higo Bank, Ltd	7124	89	—
Ogaki Kyoritsu Bank, Ltd	6975	71	—
Toho Bank, Ltd	6973	71	—
Fukui Bank, Ltd	6704	96	—
Eighteenth Bank, Ltd	6516	73	—
Kagoshima Bank, Ltd	6486	84	—
Tokyo Tomin Bank, Ltd	6403	64	—
Awa Bank, Ltd	6138	71	—
Oita Bank, Ltd	6102	88	—
San-in Godo Bank, Ltd	6047	111	—
Shinwa Bank, Ltd	6003	79	—
Bank of Iwate, Ltd	5946	81	—
Hokuetsu Bank, Ltd	5867	70	—
Akita Bank, Ltd	5581	67	—
Aomori Bank, Ltd	5576	78	—
Bank of Osaka, Ltd	5548	59	—

TABLE 3.4 (*Contd.*)

Bank	Deposits (¥100 million)	Number of branches Domestic	Number of branches Overseas
Yamanashi Chuo Bank, Ltd	5178	60	—
Michinoku Bank, Ltd	4997	74	—
Musashino Bank, Ltd	4997	55	—
Yamagata Bank, Ltd	4897	67	—
Bank of Saga, Ltd	4607	66	—
Miyazaki Bank, Ltd	4601	75	—
Bank of Ryukyus, Ltd	4327	51	—
Chiba Kogyo Bank, Ltd	4137	50	—
Senshu Bank, Ltd	3826	46	—
Bank of Ikeda, Ltd	3803	47	—
Bank of Okinawa, Ltd	3158	63	—
Mie Bank, Ltd	2755	45	—
Shimizu Bank, Ltd	2680	46	—
Kanto Bank, Ltd	2491	85	—
Ugo Bank, Ltd	2449	46	—
Tottori Bank, Ltd	2325	45	—
Shonai Bank, Ltd	2287	42	—
Tajima Bank, Ltd	1880	35	—
Tohoku Bank, Ltd	1559	37	—
Chikuho Bank, Ltd	1171	31	—
Toyama Bank, Ltd	977	27	—
Total (63)	508208	5136	2

Osaka in response to the increased economic activity between rural communities and the urban industrial centres.

The clients of regional banks have traditionally been small local businesses, although these banks have catered to large corporate enterprises during times of monetary restraint when these corporations could not find adequate financing at the city banks. An increase, however, in the regular lendings of regional banks to corporate clients has accompanied their move into metropolitan areas. These loans now account for about 40 per cent of the lending activity of regional banks.

Owing to the high level of lending to local enterprises and the low turnover of their largely personal savings deposits, the liquidity position of the regional banks has been greatly superior to that of city banks. Very few of the regional banks borrow from the Bank of Japan on a continual basis and the majority have had a persistent surplus of funds. Thus, regional banks have been able to supply a vital portion of the funds on the call loan market.

Foreign banks: Foreign banks are expanding their influence in the Japanese financial sector. By March 1979, 63 foreign banks operating a total of 84 branch offices had been established in Japan. Foreign exchange still dominates their business but they are beginning to enter the lending and deposit markets. They represent approximately 2 per cent and 1 per cent respectively of the national total of bank lendings and deposits. Foreign banks are required to obtain a license under the Bank Law as 'ordinary banks' and their business, therefore, parallels that of the Japanese commercial banks. The various foreign banks with branch operations or representative offices within Japan are listed in Table 3.5.

TABLE 3.5 Branches and offices of foreign banks in Japan
(as of the end of March 1979)

Nationality	Bank	Branches	Rep. offices	Opening
Australia	The Commercial Bank of Australia Ltd	—	1	Apr. 69
	Bank of New South Wales	—	1	Jul. 69
	The National Bank of Australasia Ltd	—	1	Jul. 69
	Australia & New Zealand Banking Group Ltd	—	1	Dec. 69
	The Rural & Industries Bank of Western Australia	—	1	Oct. 73
	The Rural Bank of New South Wales	—	1	Oct. 74
	The Commercical Banking Company of Sydney	—	1	Feb. 77
Belgium	Kredietbank NV[a]	—	1	Feb. 73
	Société Générale de Banque SA	1	—	May 73
	Banque Bruxelles Lambert SA	—	1	Aug. 74
Brazil	Banco do Brasil SA	1	—	Dec. 71
	Banco do Estado de São Paulo SA	1	—	Oct. 72
Canada	The Bank of Montreal	—	1	Apr. 62
	The Bank of Nova Scotia	—	1	Jul. 62

TABLE 3.5 (*Contd.*)

Nationality	Bank	Branches	Rep. offices	Opening
	The Royal Bank of Canada	—	1	May 70
	Canadian Imperial Bank of Commerce	—	1	Nov. 70
	The Toronto Dominion Bank	—	1	Mar. 71
Cuba	Banco Nacional de Cuba	—	1	Apr. 73
Denmark	Den Danske Bank	— -	1	Dec. 72
	Privatbanken A/S[a]	—	1	Dec. 72
Finland	Union Bank of Finland	—	1	Dec. 72
France	Banque de l'Indochine et de Suez SA	2	1	Dec. 49
	Banque de l'Union Européene SA	—	1	Jan. 68
	Credit Lyonnais SA	1	1	Mar. 70
	Banque de Paris et des Pays-Bas SA	1	—	Sep. 71
	Crédit Commercial de France SA[a]	—	1	Feb. 73
	Banque Nationale de Paris SA	1	—	Apr. 73
	Société Générale	1	—	Jun. 73
	Crédit Industriel et Commercial SA	—	1	Nov. 73
	Banque Rothschild SA	—	1	Jan. 74
	UBAF (Union de Banques Arabes et Française SA)	1	—	Apr. 75
	Paribas (Compagnie Financière de Paris et des Pays-Bas)	—	1	Apr. 76
	Credit Chimique	—	1	Dec. 77
Germany	Commerzbank AG	1	1	Oct. 61
	Bayerische Vereinsbank	1	1	Dec. 69
	Deutsche Bank	1	1	May 71
	Westdeutsche Landesbank Girozentrale	1	—	May 71
	Berliner Handels-und Frankfurter Bank[a]	—	1	Feb. 73
	Dresdner Bank AG	1	—	Oct. 73
	Simonbank AG	—	1	Jan. 75
India	Bank of India	2	—	May 50
	State Bank of India	—	1	Jan. 78
Indonesia	Bank Indonesia (Central Bank)	—	1	Mar. 64
	Bank Negara Indonesia 1946	1	—	Aug. 69

TABLE 3.5 (*Contd.*)

Nationality	Bank	Branches	Rep. offices	Opening
Iran	Bank Melli Iran	—	1	Jun. 73
Italy	Banco di Roma SpA	1	—	Mar. 72
	Banco Ambrosiano SpA[a]	—	1	Feb. 73
	Credito Italiano SpA	—	1	Jan. 74
	Banca Nazionale dell'Agricoltura	—	1	Dec. 76
Korea	Korea Exchange Bank	2	1	Jan. 67
	Bank of Korea (Central Bank)	—	1	Apr. 67
	Hanil Bank Ltd	1	—	Oct. 68
	The Korea Development Bank	—	1	Nov. 69
	Korea First Bank	1	—	Jul. 72
	The Bank of Pusan Ltd	—	1	Apr. 73
	The Cho-Heung Bank Ltd	—	1	Nov. 74
	The Bank of Seoul Ltd	—	1	Dec. 74
	The Commercial Bank of Korea Ltd	—	1	Dec. 74
Luxem-bourg	AICI Holding SA	—	1	Feb. 75
	Bank of Credit and Commerce International SA	—	1	Jan. 78
Malaysia	Bank Bumiputra Malaysia Berhad	1	—	Dec. 78
Mexico	Banco de Comercio SA	—	1	Apr. 72
	Banco Nacional de México SA	—	1	Nov. 73
	National Financiera SA	—	1	Jun. 76
Netherlands	Algemene Bank Nederland NV	3	—	Dec. 49
	Nederlandsche Middenstandsbank NV[a]	—	1	Feb. 73
	Amsterdam–Rotterdam Bank NV	1	—	Oct. 76
New Zealand	Bank of New Zealand	—	1	Nov. 69
Norway	Bergen Bank	—	1	Oct. 73
Pakistan	National Bank of Pakistan	1	—	Aug. 74
Peru	Banco de Crédito del Peru	—	1	Jan. 73
Philippines	Philippine National Bank	—	1	Dec. 69
Rep. of China	International Commercial Bank of China	2	—	Dec. 49

TABLE 3.5 (*Contd.*)

Nationality	Bank	Branches	Rep. offices	Opening
Singapore	Overseas Union Bank Ltd	1	—	May 63
	United Overseas Bank Ltd	1	—	Dec. 72
	Oversea-Chinese Banking Corp. Ltd	1	—	Mar. 73
	The Development Bank of Singapore Ltd	1	—	Oct. 77
Spain	Banco Español de Credito	—	1	Jun. 73
	Banco Hispano Americano	—	1	Jun. 78
Sweden	Skandinaviska Enskilda Banken	—	1	Jul. 70
	Svenska Handelsbanken	—	1	Sep. 72
Switzerland	Union Bank of Switzerland	1	1	Oct. 66
	Swiss Bank Corp.	1	—	Aug. 71
	Banque Scandinave en Suisse	—	1	Dec. 71
	Swiss Credit Bank (Crédit Suisse)	1	1	Aug. 72
	Swiss Volksbank	—	1	Jul. 78
	Interallionz Bank Zürich AG	—	1	Apr. 79
Thailand	Bangkok Bank Ltd	2	—	Nov. 55
UK	The Chartered Bank	3	—	Dec. 49
	The Hongkong & Shanghai Banking Corp.	2	—	Dec. 49
	Mercantile Bank Ltd	1	—	Feb. 63
	Scandinavian Bank Ltd	—	1	Jun. 69
	The National Bank of New Zealand Ltd	—	1	Aug. 69
	Grindlays Bank Ltd	1	—	Feb. 70
	Kleinwort, Benson Ltd	—	1	Dec. 70
	Barclays Bank International Ltd	1	—	Nov. 72
	National Westminster Bank Ltd	1	—	Dec. 72
	Baring Brothers & Co. Ltd	—	1	Jan. 73
	Williams & Glyn's Bank Ltd[a]	—	1	Feb. 73
	Lloyds Bank International Ltd	1	—	Dec. 73
	Schroders Ltd (J. Henry Schroder Wagg & Co. Ltd)	—	1	Apr. 74
	Midland Bank Ltd[b]	1	—	May 74
	Marine Midland Ltd	—	1	Jul. 74
	Thomas Cook Banker Ltd	—	1	Oct. 75
	European Arab Bank Ltd	—	1	Nov. 77
	Wardley Ltd	—	1	Mar. 78
	S. G. Warburg & Co. Ltd	—	1	Oct. 78

Table 3.5 (*Contd.*)

Nationality	Bank	Branches	Rep. offices	Opening
USA	Bank of America NT & SA	4	—	Dec. 49
	The Chase Manhattan Bank NA	2	—	Dec. 49
	Citibank NA	4	—	Dec. 49
	American Express International Banking Corp.	3	—	Oct. 53
	Continental Illinois National Bank & Trust Co. of Chicago	2	—	Feb. 64
	Morgan Guaranty Trust Co. of New York	1	—	Dec. 68
	Seattle-First National Bank	2	—	Apr. 69
	Rainier National Bank	1	—	Sep. 69
	Marine Midland Bank	1	—	Dec. 69
	First National Bank of Boston	1	—	Feb. 70
	Crocker National Bank	1	—	Jan. 71
	First National Bank in Dallas	—	1	Jan. 71
	Allied Bank International	—	1	Mar. 71
	Manufacturers Hanover Trust Co.	1	—	Jun. 71
	Republic National Bank of Dallas	—	1	Sep. 71
	Wells Fargo Bank NA	1	—	Nov. 71
	Security Pacific National Bank	1	—	Jan. 72
	Chemical Bank	1	—	Mar. 72
	Texas Commerce Bank NA	—	1	May 72
	United California Bank	1	—	Jun. 72
	The First National Bank of Chicago	1	—	Oct. 72
	Bankers Trust Co.	1	—	Dec. 72
	Union Bank	—	1	Jan. 73
	Irving Trust Co.	1	—	Apr. 73
	National Bank of Detroit	1	—	Oct. 73
	First Union National Bank of North Carolina	—	1	Jan. 74
	Mellon Bank NA	1	—	Feb. 74
	First City National Bank of Houston	—	1	May 74
	The Fidelity Bank	—	1	Jul. 74
	Bank of California NA	1	—	Oct. 74

TABLE 3.5 *(Contd.)*

Nationality	Bank	Branches	Rep. offices	Opening
	Pacific National Bank of Washington	—	1	Jun. 75
	First Pennsylvania Bank NA	—	1	Sep. 76
	Harris Trust and Savings Bank	—	1	Nov. 76
	Republic National Bank of New York	—	1	Aug. 77
	American Security Bank NA	—	1	Nov. 78
	California First Bank	—	1	Apr. 79

a Inter-Alpha Group of Banks.
b Midland Bank Group.

Source: Federation of Bankers' Associations of Japan (1979).

The specialised foreign-exchange bank: The specialised foreign-exchange bank was established under the Foreign Exchange Law in 1954 and at present, the Bank of Tokyo is the only financial institution to have been authorised. As its title implies, this bank is primarily engaged in foreign-exchange transactions and foreign trade financing. While it cannot make yen loans unrelated to foreign trade and exchange, it may issue debentures up to a sum equivalent to five times the amount of its combined capital and reserves. Although the Bank of Tokyo is given priority in receiving foreign currency deposits from the government, other commercial banks are authorised to conduct foreign-exchange business as well.

Commercial bank operations

In principle, commercial banks are short-term credit financial institutions the funds of which are derived from short-term deposits of two years or less. In practice, however, they have long been engaged in both short-term and long-term financing. About 25 per cent of all loans have maturity periods of over one year and many short-term loans are substituted for long-term loans in the form of continued loans through renewals. Moreover, their holdings of outstanding bank debentures and corporate bonds represent about 20 per cent and 30 per cent of the market, respectively. Thus, commercial banks exert their influence in both short- and long-term financial markets either directly or indirectly. This situation is due, in large part, to an undeveloped capital market and the subsequent channelling of the majority of personal investments into bank time deposits, 80 per cent of which are for a year or more.

Commercial banks engage in the receipt of deposits, the lending of money, the discounting of bills and notes, exchange transactions and their related services. They are not authorised to conduct any business that does not fall into one of these fields.

Deposits are the most important source of funds for commercial banks, accounting for nearly 75 per cent of their combined liabilities and debt. They are classified as either demand deposits, time deposits, or foreign currency deposits. Among these three categories, time deposits represent the great majority – 60 per cent of the total deposit amount.

Time deposits are the most popular in Japan. Over 70 per cent of the total personal deposits and more than 40 per cent of corporate deposits are of this variety. The most common type of time deposits varies only in the length of the contract terms and their corresponding interest rates. In May 1979, negotiable certificates of deposit (or CDs) were issued for the first time. With the growing financial surpluses of corporations which have accompanied the downturn in the economic growth rate, this was a necessary measure in order for the banks to be able to diversify their fund raising methods. Although limits are set upon each bank's issue amount and the term of maturity, this is a step towards liberalising the interest rate structure in Japan.

While deposits account for the major portion of the debt held by commercial banks, their major credit is derived from their lending operations. Indeed, loan activity accounts for more than 60 per cent of the total assets of commercial banks. Loans by commercial banks are three principal types: bills discounted, loans on bills and loans on deeds. They represent 20 per cent, 44 per cent, and 34 per cent respectively of the total lendings. Overdrafts do exist but they comprise only a negligible share at 2 per cent.

Businesses make up the largest group of customers for commercial banks. They borrow over 65 per cent of the total lendings made by the commercial banks. City banks direct over 60 per cent of their loans toward large corporations with capital of over one hundred million yen while regional banks do business mainly with enterprises whose capital is under that level. In the early postwar years primary industries, like agriculture, forestry and fishery, were the main recipients of bank loans but with the slowdown in plant and equipment investment, manufacturing industries now account for only 35 per cent of the total lendings whereas the service sector is absorbing 30 per cent.

Consumer credit has long been minimal, if not negligible, in the process of postwar growth. Lendings to individuals have just recently reached a 12 per cent mark. Housing loans account for the lion's share of personal borrowing because of the overwhelming demand for individual housing units which has paralleled the rise in incomes.

Investment in securities constitutes the second largest use of funds by the commercial banks, but yet it accounts for only 15 per cent of their total assets. While commercial banks can engage in the subscription of securities, they are restricted from underwriting, dealing, brokerage and distribution of securities.[12] The low level of investment in securities is an indication of the near dearth of the market. For various reasons to be explained later, the primary market for stocks is small while the secondary market for bonds and debentures remains undeveloped. Therefore commercial banks have little motivation to look to securities as instruments of investment. Consequently, the holdings of commercial banks are limited to bonds and shares of their client enterprises, government and government-guaranteed bonds or bank debentures.

Long-term credit banks
In the immediate postwar era, the Reconversion Finance Bank was established to provide the long-term funds required to begin economic reconstruction. This bank, however, was dissolved in 1952. The capital market, at that time virtually non-existent, could not even begin to supply the funds necessary to meet the continued demand for long-term funds. It was then than the long-term credit bank system was established. Today there are three such banks: their names and the

TABLE 3.6 Long-term credit banks

Bank	Deposits (¥100 million)	Number of branches	
		Domestic	Overseas
Industrial Bank of Japan, Ltd	89358	19	4
Long-term Credit Bank of Japan, Ltd	72459	16	3
Nippon Credit Bank, Ltd	47158	15	2
Total	208976	50	9

Source: Federation of Bankers' Association of Japan (1979).

relative importance of each are shown in Table 3.6. The purpose of these banks was two-fold; to relieve commercial banks of the pressure of long-term financing and to substitute as a capital market.

Long-term banks raise funds by issuing bank debentures and they are authorised to do so up to 20 times of the total amount of their capital and reserves. This is expected to be increased soon to a rate of 30 times. Debenture issuances currently account for about 70 per cent of the total debts of these banks. They are of two kinds: interest-bearing debentures sold to mainly commercial banks on a 5 year term and discount bank debentures sold to private individuals through securities companies on a 1-year term. Deposits, which can only be accepted from client enterprises and public institutions, are small and represent an amount roughly equivalent to only 16 per cent of the funds raised through the issue of debentures.

Lendings by the long-term banks occupy a 13 per cent share of all loans made by all banks. Short-term working funds within their total deposit receipts are extended, but over 90 per cent of all their loans are for periods exceeding one year. Over 80 per cent of all loans are directed toward equipment funding, a high percentage of which has gone to the steel and chemical industries.

Trust banks

Trust banks are involved in both the trust and the banking business. Though beginning as trust companies, their status was changed in 1948 in order to help them through the severe inflation of the early postwar period. Trust banks, however, now receive administrative guidance to concentrate on their trust business. Having acquiesced to the government policy of separating the banking business and the trust business, the ratio of these respective accounts currently stands at roughly 1:4 for most trust banks. The activities of the banking accounts are identical to those carried out by commercial banks.

The majority of trusts are currently money trusts, particularly loan trusts, money in trust and securities in trust. Over 90 per cent of the total liabilities of trust accounts are of the money trust type. 70 per cent of the loan trust contracts are held by individual trust depositors: an indication of the trust banks' important role as recipients of long-term savings. The major portion of operational funds, moreover, are derived from loan trusts and they have enabled trust banks to be a major participant in the field of long-term funding. Lending is made primarily for plant and equipment investment. They now supply nearly 25 per cent of all the equipment and plant loans made by all private banks in Japan. In this they rival the long-term credit banks. The names and relative importance of each of the seven trust banks are shown in Table 3.7.

TABLE 3.7   Trust banks

Bank	Deposits (¥100 million)	Number of branches	
		Domestic	Overseas
Mitsubishi Trust & Banking Corp.	61297	44	2
Sumitomo Trust & Banking Co. Ltd	58227	44	2
Mitsui Trust & Banking Co. Ltd	54877	44	2
Yasuda Trust & Banking Co. Ltd	42657	44	2
Toyo Trust & Banking Co. Ltd	35123	44	2
Chuo Trust & Banking Co. Ltd	18962	44	1
Nippon Trust & Banking Co. Ltd	10835	36	—
Total (7)	281982	300	11

Source: Federation of Bankers' Associations of Japan (1979).

(b) Other Financial Institutions

Various financial institutions, both public and private, have developed in Japan to accommodate the requirements of small businesses with regard to financing. The private institutions for small businesses are regional institutions which include mutual banks, credit associations and credit co-operatives. Mutual banks function in much the same way as commercial banks,[13] in that they rely upon the same type of deposits for funds and employ their funds through lending, investments in securities and call loans. They are rapidly acquiring similar qualities to those of the city banks with the basic difference being, of course, the size of the customers that they serve. Credit associations and credit co-operatives limit their transactions, for the most part, to their members. The National Federation of Credit Associations and the National Federation of Credit Co-operatives act as central organisations for their respective networks. The deposit business is the same as that of commercial and mutual banks. These organisations will accept deposits from non-members but they will make only a limited number of small-lot loans to non-members.

In addition to these private organisations, the Central Bank for Commercial and Industrial Co-operatives, in which the government has more than a half of the capital shares, supplies funds to co-operatives of even smaller enterpreneurs.

Financial institutions which cater to the primary sector (i.e. agriculture, forestry and fishery) are organised at a base level as co-operative associations. The activities of the fishery and forestry co-operatives are extremely limited in scope, however, so that the Central Co-operative Bank for Agriculture and Forestry in most cases provides funds directly to them. Agricultural financial institutions, on the other hand, are organised into a three-tiered system having wide-ranging capacities. Above the local co-operatives stand the credit federations of agricultural co-operatives which operate on a prefectural level. At the apex is the Central Co-operative Bank for Agriculture and Forestry that functions on a national scale.

The functions of the agricultural co-operatives are restricted to dealings with members in the areas of credit, insurance purchasing and selling. Deposits are the same type as those utilised by commercial banks. Lendings, are made for the most part on a long-term basis because of the self-sufficiency of farmers for their short-term requirements. The credit federations accept deposits from and extend loans to member co-operatives. They function, moreover, to adjust surplus or deficits of funds of the member co-operative in order to reinforce their financial activities. Recently, however, deposits have outweighed loans nearly two to one. Surplus funds have in turn been deposited with the Central Co-operative Bank for Agriculture and Forestry or loaned to other financial institutions either directly or through the call money market.

Insurance companies in Japan are strictly divided into life and non-life; no one company may engage in both. Life insurance companies invest in the long-term market and their supply of equipment loans have been of great importance. Of their operating funds 68 per cent have been channelled into lending while 22 per cent has been invested in securities. Of these securities, 90 per cent are stocks and so they have been very influential in the stock market. Non-life insurance companies are, by nature of their business, more concerned with liquidity. Hence, they are active in short-term lending and in the investment of stocks with high marketability.

Housing credit in Japan has been financed primarily by commercial banks and supplemented by the government's Housing Loan Corporation. Increased demand for private housing units coupled with the tedious and specialised nature of home financing have led, however, to the organisation since 1971 of financial companies which deal exclusively in home loans. The majority of such companies, having been established as joint ventures of several banks, rely principally upon long-term loans from the investing financial institutions for funds. Consequently, the interest rates they charge to home purchasers are relatively high and so they account for only 6.5 per cent of the outstanding balance of home financing.

The government in Japan is also engaged in extensive financial activities through its own institutions. Funds for the government banks and finance corporations come through the Industrial Investment Special Account and the Trust Fund Bureau. The Industrial Investment Special Account relies upon funds transferred from the General Account, but the Trust Bureau relies mainly upon the funds collected through the nationwide network of post offices. Postal savings have been steadily increasing in popularity over the past decade and the total personal deposits outstanding are currently approaching an amount that is equivalent to 80 per cent of the total personal deposits with all commercial banks.

The government financial institutions comprise two banks and ten financial corporations, all of which are engaged in various areas of the financial market in order to supplement the activities of private financial institutions. The Japan Development Bank was established in 1951 to encourage economic reconstruction and industrial development. The principal operation of this organisation is the lending of equipment and plant funds to those industries which are deemed important to Japanese economic and industrial development. It has supported, since its inception, the financing of such 'target' or 'key' industries as coal, electric power, chemicals, steel and shipbuilding. Loans are extended, in general, in conjunction with loans from private institutions. The Export–Import Bank began operation in 1950 for the purpose of supporting and encouraging the finance of exports, imports and foreign investments. It has primarily financed the export and import of plant and equipment on a deferred payment basis.

These two government banks generally limit their clients to large corporations and their activities to large-scale projects. Government finance corporations, on the other hand, cater to specific sectors of the economy on a small scale. Funding for these finance corporations, like the banks, comes directly from the government through the Trust Fund

Bureau and the Industrial Investment Special Account. There are ten government finance corporations which include those for special sectors of the economy such as small business, housing loans, agriculture, medical care and local public enterprise, as well as those for regional development. These finance corporation activities are supervised by those government ministries overall responsible for each respective area.

Of particular interest are those government financial institutions specialising in the support of the small business sector. For example, the Small Business Finance Corporation has supplied small businesses with equipment and other long-term financing since 1953. The People's Finance Corporation, established in 1949, also provides business loans to very small firms and individuals who find it difficult to borrow from other financial institutions. Similarly, the more than two-thirds government-owned Central Bank for Commercial and Industrial Co-operatives' main purpose is to support small business co-operatives.

FINANCIAL MARKETS

(a) The Money Market

The market for the transaction of short-term funds, generally termed a money market, initially developed in Japan during the early 1900s. The money markets in both England, particularly the bill discount market in London, and the United States provided a basic framework on which the Japanese money market was modelled. Its development in Japan, however, has been exceedingly slow until recently, and has principally evolved around the call money market. In 1971 the bill discounting market was separated from the call money market for transactions of two- to three-months' credit. As a result, the call money market discontinued transactions of over-the-month loans in 1972, thereby restricting the operations to within-the-month transactions.

At present, the call money and bill discount markets operate in Tokyo, Osaka and Nagoya, Tokyo being by far the largest, accounting for an overwhelming 80 per cent share of market transactions. The amount outstanding in each of the call money and bill discount markets at the end of 1979 was 2332 billion yen and 4403 billion yen, respectively. Although the bill discount market is larger, bills totalling 2324 billion yen were purchased by the Bank of Japan through open market operations. If the amounts purchased by the Bank of Japan are excluded, the size of the call money market is slightly larger than that of the bill discount market.

Participants in these markets are strictly limited to financial institutions. Security companies can act only as lenders.[14] In this sense, they are closed markets, unlike those in either England or the United States where both business corporations and individuals may participate.

Another characteristic of these markets in Japan is that a pattern has developed whereby the city banks are consistently the borrowers in the call money market and the sellers in the bill discount market, while all other financial institutions, including almost all the regional banks, are the lenders and the buyers. The two markets, in short, function as channels through which funds are routed to city banks from all other financial institutions. This is another manifestation of the chronic overloan and short reserve positions which have characterised the operations of city banks.

Interest rates are regulated in Japan and are generally set at lower levels than they would be under free market conditions. The call money and bill discount rates, however, are not subject to similar regulations and so they exhibit a rate structure of a substantially higher level. While interest rates are not regulated directly in those markets, the Bank of Japan exerts its influence on the market through the daily interventions aimed at adjusting both the flow and the rates of funds.

In addition to these two markets, mention should be made of two other short-term money markets which are open to both financial institutions and business enterprises. One market deals in negotiable certificates of deposits and the other deals in the trading of bonds with repurchase agreements, referred to in Japan as *Gensaki* transactions. Negotiable certificates of deposits were, as mentioned previously, introduced in May 1979 and they are expected to develop quickly as an investment market. The conditional bond market involves the buying and selling of private and public bonds with a forward repurchase agreement. Developed during the 1970s, this market has an important place in the adjustment of funds among its participants. The outstanding balance of this market now rivals that of both the call money and the bill discount markets.

As noted earlier, financial institutions are both borrowers and lenders of funds in the call and bill discount markets. Call loans dealers often act as specialised intermediaries to handle the transactions. The dealers receive temporary surplus funds and act to raise funds to meet temporary fund shortages of client financial institutions. As borrowers, the city banks are dominant and they constitute 80 per cent of call money borrowing and 90 per cent of the bill discount sales. Lenders on the call market include all other financial institutions, but trust banks, regional banks, mutual banks and the National Federation of Credit Associations predominate. The Bank of Japan is singularly the largest buyer of bills on the bill discount market, although the National Federation of Credit Associations and trust banks hold a relatively large share of the market as well.

Call funds are usually transacted through call loan dealers, but in some cases they are transacted directly between financial institutions. Call market loans are classified according to their loan periods: (1) a half-day loan, to be settled within the day of lending; (2) an overnight loan, to be repaid the following day; (3) an unconditional loan, to be settled on the condition of a one-day advance notice; (4) a fixed-term loan, made on the condition that it will be unredeemed for a set period of time, from two to seven days, including the transaction date. The majority of all loans tend to be those of the unconditional type.

Bills which are bought and sold on the bill discounting market are of two types: (1) prime commercial bills, prime industrial bills, foreign trade bills and prime single-name bills; (2) bills of exchange drawn by financial institutions to short-term dealers and accepted by the drawer institutions themselves on the security of prime bills. Almost all trading is of the bill of exchange variety owing to the fact that they allow for smoother transactions than do prime bills. The term of discounts may be four months at the longest, but most are those that extend through the first day of the second month following the discount data – referred to as over-two-month ends bills.

Rates for both call money and bill discounts are determined on the basis of bids by the lender of funds, the effective rates being a bit higher as a result of the 0.125 per cent commission taken by the dealers. Money market rates fluctuate rather sensitively, reflecting the supply and demand conditions of the market. Although under normal interest rate structures, short-term loans, owing to their emphasis on liquidity instead of return, should be set at rates lower than bank lending rates or official discount rates, this is not the case in Japan. Given the condition of city banks which perpetually rely on external funding and are consistently in a tight cash position, the demand for money market funds have always been in excess of supply. Furthermore, since they already carry sizable borrowings from the Bank of Japan, money market rates generally maintain a higher level than the discount rate which represents the lower limit.

The Bank of Japan has utilised the money market as a means of advancing its monetary policy because of the direct impact it has upon the market. By purchasing or selling bills through direct intervention in the bill discount market or by altering the volume of its direct lending to financial institutions, the Bank can greatly affect the flow of funds in the money market. When the Bank sees the need for monetary restraint, it may limit its purchases of bills and reduce its lending, causing a tight money supply.

(b) The Securities Market

Financing by the private sector in Japan has long been in favour of debt rather than equity. The large increases in investments which accompanied the rapid postwar growth of the economy have outpaced the amounts which could have been raised through internal financing. The associated growth in earnings as well as the convention of issuing equities at par value have increased the cost of equity capital. These considerations have influenced the corporate managers' bias toward indirect debt through bank financing and the interdependence between banking community and their principal corporate customers has, as a result, been strengthened. Concurrently, through the relationship between the Bank of Japan and the private banking institutions, the monetary authorities have had greater control over the allocation of resources.

The stock market has performed the functions of raising capital for business enterprises, allocating resources by establishing the cost of capital, broadening investment options and distributing ownership and income. The secondary market for equities is broad and active, and in this sense the Japanese stock market is similar to those of other developed countries. The primary or issuing market, on the other hand, is limited in scale and is not as active as the economy might indicate.

Japanese corporations have raised a great portion of their funds from external sources; over 70 per cent between the late 1950s and the early 1970s. The stock market, however, has accounted for only a small percentage of these funds. Indeed, equity issues represented an amount which was equivalent in range to only 5–20 per cent of total external financing. Although the stock market has not been a great fund raiser for the corporations, it has had an important role in allocating capital.

The stock market establishes the cost of capital and it is used as a guide by corporate managers in their budgeting decisions. Japanese management is keenly aware of the cost of capital and of the role of the equities market in this regard.

The distribution of subscription rights has been an important function of new equity issues. This is particularly so when stocks are issued at par value as was predominantly the case until the mid-1970s. Equity issues at market value increased through the early 1970s but stockholders have not reacted with pleasure in response to this trend. The value of subscription rights has been greatly reduced and the loss of preemptive rights has aroused displeasure. Moreover, after the early 1970s, shareholders have experienced a loss on new shares for the first time. The response, as a result, has not been favourable. The fact that corporations have not increased the share of equity issues at market value implies that stockholder relations are a consideration as important as fund raising in equity financing.

Individual holdings, have been steadily declining since the late 1950s when they accounted for one half of all listed shares. By the early 1970s, their share had been reduced to nearly 30 per cent. Reflecting this trend, the share held by investment trusts, which represent the investments by the personal sector, had fallen from 10 per cent to 1 per cent. These holdings have been transferred primarily to financial institutions and corporations who have increased their share from 22 per cent to 34 per cent and 16 per cent to 27 per cent respectively in the same period. In 1973, stock holdings at market value accounted for approximately 17 per cent of individual financial assets in Japan.

Although the market activity is dominated by corporations and financial institutions, the stock market provides an important opportunity to the individual saver's option for investment. Fluctuations of stock prices can be wide on a short-term basis but over the long term returns have been relatively high and the risks low. Consequently, the secondary or exchange market for stocks in Japan has been extremely active.

In addition to stock markets, the bond market is also important. Securities companies and security finance corporations are the main participants in the underwriting of bonds. Financial institutions including banks are precluded from underwriting bonds with the exception of long-term national, government, local government and public corporation bonds. Given the fact that these bonds account for just over 50 per cent of all bonds issued, however, financial institutions do exert some influence on the bond market.

The bond market includes government bonds, public corporation bonds, bank debentures and industrial bonds.[15] Long-term government bonds now account for roughly three-quarters of all government securities issued. Short-term government securities which comprise treasury bills, foreign-exchange fund bills and food bills are offered for public subscription, but owing to their low interest rates few are sold and most are absorbed by the Bank of Japan.

The Bank of Japan, as the government's agent, also handles long-term bonds, but in these cases the subscriptions and underwriting are contracted to a syndicate of financial institutions. Local government bonds and public corporation bonds, which are guaranteed by the central government, follow a similar system except that they are underwritten by a joint syndicate of financial institutions and securities companies. The subscription and underwriting of industrial bonds are handled exclusively by a syndicate of securities companies, since these types of bonds lie outside the legal operating realm of financial institutions. Bank debentures, or bonds issued by financial corporations, unlike all others, are handled by the issuing institutions.

The trading of bonds on exchanges in Tokyo and Osaka was reopened in 1966, after the government began to issue bonds regularly in the same year. Since that time the scale of the bond market has expanded and its pattern of trade has been altered so that currently the bulk of public and corporate bonds are traded in the markets. While market improvements have been partially responsible for the expansion, bond sales by city banks for the purpose of raising funds have been a significant factor in its development.[16]

The securities companies in Japan are the only institutions that are authorised to engage in the dealing, brokerage and underwriting of all securities. These companies experienced a phenomenal growth from the mid-1950s to the early 1960s when securities, mostly stocks, were being issued to finance rapid corporate growth. The subsequent slump that hit the stock market from 1963 to 1965 led to a stricter regulatory structure of the securities companies in terms of capital requirements.[17] Greater prudence in the expansion of their business activities was strongly urged. The market has, of course, regained its strength and the number of licensed foreign securities companies is growing.

Japan's securities industry is governed by legislation which has been revised repeatedly since the Second World War.[18] Most importantly, the licensing of securities companies was introduced, in lieu of simple registration, in 1965 when the Securities and Exchange Law was amended. At that time the number of licensed securities companies accounted for 277, but it tended to reduce and turned into 259 in 1975 because of mergers and bankruptcies.

Now securities companies are classified into 139 members of the securities exchanges,[19] 99 non-members and others. Among them, the four securities companies, Nomura, Nikko, Daiwa and Yamaichi, are the so-called 'Big Four' in the securities industry. Together these companies handle more than half of the securities transactions in Japan. Their relative importance and that of the other eight major companies is shown in Table 3.8.

TABLE 3.8   Major securities companies by total assets (figures in
¥ million for 31 March 1979)

Nomura Securities	713052
Nikko Securities	495157
Diawa Securities	416923
Yamaichi Securities	410990
New Japan Securities	194513
Sanyo Securities	175334
Wako Securities	147357
Okasan Securities	133967
Nippon Kangyo Kakumaru Securities	128252
Osakaya	87240
Yamatane Securities	78938
Dai-Ichi Securities	60173

Source: M. T. Skully, *Merchant Banking in the Far East*, 2nd edn (London: Financial Times Business Publishing, 1980) p. 158.

ANALYSIS, TRENDS AND PREDICTIONS

A discussion of another four major points is required to clarify the features of Japan's financial institutions and market in terms of both their past and future development: (1) government regulation of the financial sector, (2) debt financing of large corporate enterprise, (3) evaluation of the present financial structure, and (4) the progress of internationalisation.

The government regulation of the financial sector through institutional controls and the strict supervision of interest rates may well lead to an assessment of the Japanese financial system as one that is still undeveloped. One must be careful, however, not to carry this kind of argument too far, for the evolution of the present financial structure has not been a result of any inability to develop a system in which freely fluctuating interest rates determine the allocation of resources. Rather, there has been a conscious and clearly-defined policy on the part of monetary authorities in the construction of the present financial system. To a large extent the development of a financial framework within which monetary authorities could exert their monetary policies was a result of the urgent need for reconstruction and economic redevelopment in the postwar period. Given the goal of rapid economic redevelopment, the financial system has been both greatly efficient and effective.

Investment has been guided by both market forces and the implementation of government policies through the various Ministries and the Bank of Japan. A significant amount of investment has been controlled directly through government financial institutions such as government banks, public finance corporations and the Trust Fund Bureau in particular. Funds channelled through these organisations are those which are allocated on the basis of government policies and priorities.

The government preference for institutional controls over regulation by market forces is evident in its structural policy. Smooth operation of the financial system has been of prime concern to government authorities whereas competition has not. The Ministry of Finance is the sole authorising power for the establishment of bank branches and bank mergers, an authority which the Ministry has used very deliberately to either stimulate mergers or restrict expansion. Moreover, a Committee of Financial System Research, comprising a group of appointees from varied fields, is attached to the Ministry of Finance for the purpose of continually reviewing the financial system and making recommendations for improvement. This orientation towards financial policy has expressed itself in the development of specific policy objectives in Japan rather than a general framework. The supply of credit through specialised institutions and the employment of economies of scale through concentration have been the main thrust of structural policies, not the maintenance of competition and the functions of the free market. The degree of concentration among Japan's financial institutions, however, is nowhere near the very high concentration typical of most industrialised nations. The 13 city banks, 63 regional banks, 3 long-term banks and 7 trust banks are evidence of the balance which the financial structure has assumed between concentration and competition.

The maintenance of specialisation among financial institutions is yet another aspect of structural policy. Specialisation has taken on four basic forms in Japan; (1) the separation of lending, underwriting and trust operations, (2) the separation of short- and long-term finance, (3) the separation of operations based on customer size, and (4) the separation of operations focused on some particular area of the economy. The logic of specialisation rests in the reduction of risk, the reduction of conflicts of interests and the increased control afforded to regulatory agencies. In practice, however, the boundaries of activity have not been as clearly defined as one might expect. Financial institutions have been aggressively attempting to expand their markets and their sphere of activities, not without success. Short-term banks have in effect practised long-term lending through prearranged extensions; trust banks now engage in borrowing and lending activities; regional banks pursue large corporate accounts while city banks are soliciting business from smaller enterprises. The only area in which specialisation has been adhered to almost without exception is in the segregation of the banking business from the securities business.

While specialisation of financial activities may have the merits of ordering the activities of market intermediaries, the compartmentalisation of the markets and their participants has led to an imbalanced allocation of capital funds. The secular deficit in liquid funds by the city banks and the constant surpluses of almost all other financial institutions attests to this problem. As has been noted, however, the specialisation of market activities is not absolutely rigid and the government policy has permitted expansions and regroupings to some extent.

Secondly, it must be stressed that, among the varied forms of financing, corporations in Japan have opted to rely upon debt rather than equity. Equity financing through issues of stocks, for example, averaged about 18 per cent of total capitalisation for large corporations in 1972. Bond financing, owing to the low interest rates, has been similarly low. So, Japanese corporations have depended on borrowings from banks for their capital requirements. They have, in short, 'overborrowed'.

Three principal reasons lie behind the choice of corporations to be so highly leveraged. Equity financing in Japan has been, as explained earlier, very expensive because of the established practice of issuing stock at par value rather than at market value. Another reason has been the tax structure, which allows for the deduction of interest from the tax base. The third factor is rooted in the high growth rates of the economy during the postwar period. Rapid growth has made it difficult for corporations to raise internal capital proportionate to their expanding markets. None of these factors is sufficient in itself but they have all influenced corporate decision-making in favour of highly leveraged systems of capital formations.

One criticism is that heavy dependence on bank borrowing leads to excessively close relations between banks and their corporate customers. Another is the concern about the risks believed to be associated with the low equity ratio of corporate finance. Official statements in recent years have been admonishing corporations to improve their capital structure in order to reduce their risk posture.

A few principal factors have helped to reduce the exposure of corporations to the risks associated with heavy debt financing. Rapid growth of the economy eased the pressure of the debt held by corporations by providing an environment in which they could expand their sales and therefore eased the burden of the outstanding debts. Over-expansion and poor management decision-making have been on occasions redeemed by the growth of demand which soon caught up. Similarly, inflation lessened the weight of old debts. The influence of these two mechanisms on the reduction of debt assumes that a firm's expansion is proportionate to the general growth rate. The high growth rate in Japan, however, was experienced by all industries, and as such it assisted in reducing the risk of debt.

The special relations of corporations to their main banks as well as those among the network of corporate relations has been another factor in the control of risk. It is assumed in Japan that a firm's main bank takes on an added responsibility concerning its outstanding liabilities. Should it experience difficulties, other creditors have priority over the main bank's claims. This relation is a matter of convention rather than of law.

Banks perform this function for a variety of firms that cluster around it and form a kind of loose association. Members of these 'groups' come to aid each other when necessary. The main bank may assist by extending a loan or by arranging a loan from another bank while co-members who are either suppliers or customers may alter the payment terms of contracts to ease the liquidity problem of the firm in need. This kind of organisation, referred to as the '*keiretsu*' or linkage system, is a remnant of the large prewar combines and its membership is limited in most cases to large enterprises.[20]

The government is another factor which enables corporations to carry what would appear to be a great financial risk. The view that corporate failures are desirable for the elimination of inefficiency is not widely subscribed to in Japan. Economic growth has been nurtured by government policy so that relations between government and business have been characterised by co-operation and consent rather than regulation and compliance.

Third, the structure of the financial system has contributed enormously to economic growth in general and to investments in plant and equipment in particular, by influencing the direction of capital flow. During the decades of the 1950s and 1960s, industrial expansion was limited only by other factors than capital. Financing was extended as far as was possible, further in fact than the city banks could supply on the basis of their own deposits. The additional funds were supplied by resorting to the call money market and the discount window of the Bank of Japan, thereby creating the condition of 'overloan'. Given the fact that the Bank of Japan could have closed the valve on the flow of these funds, it had given tacit approval to the situation.

Overloan has not been a necessary condition in the flow of funds. It is instead an outgrowth of the institutional framework of the financial system. A freely functioning bond market would ease the demand by corporations for funds from the city banks while the lack of certificates of deposit until just last year has compelled the city banks to look to the call money market for surplus funds. Moreover, the deposit deficiency of the city banks could have been eased by being permitted either to establish branch offices more freely or to merge with regional banks. These alternatives, however, are precisely the kinds of measures that the Ministry of Finance wants to avoid because of its structural policy. It is important, then, to note that although indirect finance – encompassing both the conditions of 'overloan' and 'overborrowing' – is often cited as a major characteristic of the Japanese financial system, it is not fundamental in nature.

The financial structure developed by the policy makers in Japan may not be sophisticated in terms of free market fluctuations, but it has been effective. Funds have flowed to those sectors of the economy needing development and the investments made in plant and equipment has catapulted Japanese industry to the forefront of the world economy. Yet while funds poured into industry, the personal sector has received only a minimal amount of consumer credit.

As the pace of economic growth has been slowing in the past several years, the Japanese economy has begun to shift its gears from a private-sector orientation of rapid growth to a public-sector orientation of stable growth. National consensus in Japan has been supportive of a lower growth path, given the constraints of the energy crisis. As Japan moves towards the 1980s, a process of transition has begun to emerge in the operations and markets of the financial system. City banks have been expanding their business with smaller enterprises and individuals. Greater emphasis is being placed on consumer credit and the welfare of the general public. The financial market is showing the initial signs of liberalisation, and the rigid compartmentalisation of financial activity is gradually being dissolved. Particular attention should be paid to the process of the liberalisation of interest rates through CD issues and public bids of medium-term government bonds.

Furthermore, the overborrowed position of large enterprises has somewhat improved with the decline of the growth rate. A decrease in debt finance leads to a reduction in the demand for bank credit, which in turn alters the overloan posture of city banks. Concurrently, in the equity market, the declining rate of economic growth will serve to increase the trend, though yet small, of issuing stock at near market price. It will be of great help in the reduction of the debt to equity ratios of corporations in the future. It will take more time, however, to increase the reliance of Japanese financial institutions on market mechanisms and to reduce the influence of government regulations.

Finally, the process of internationalisation is worth noting in the recent trends of Japan's financial institutions and market. In the past decade, the Japanese economy itself has been greatly internationalised, reflecting the sharp increase of exports, imports and overseas investments. Thus, Japanese financial institutions have recently made rapid progress in their international businesses and operations.

Before turning to the new phase of internationalisation, their main business centred around trade finance for the foreign trade of Japanese enterprises. Their clients, too, were limited only to Japanese enterprises. This reflected a period of foreign currency shortages for Japan's financial institutions which had to rely upon mainly the intake of Eurodollars and borrowings from US banks to raise funds. Since 1970, however, international businesses have been expanded and diversified to include overseas lendings, especially international syndicated loans.

Today, international banking has become one of the main strategic targets of Japan's major banks. All city banks have branch offices in major foreign cities, like New York and London, where international foreign markets are well established. The total number of overseas branch offices (excluding locally-incorporated subsidiaries) increased sharply from 52 in 1965 to 122 in 1979. As of 1979, their assets in foreign countries accounted for nearly 15 per cent of total assets.[21]

There are two types of customers to Japanese financial institutions for their international businesses. On the one hand, in the case of transactions with domestic customers, they are engaged in the buying and selling of forward exchange and foreign currencies, the collection of export and import bills, opening of letters of credit, etc. On the other hand, when they transact business with overseas customers, Japanese financial institutions are engaged in overseas lendings, receiving foreign currency deposits and free-yen deposits, foreign-exchange finance, etc. Also, on behalf of both domestic and overseas customers, they act as trustees of yen-denominated bonds issued by foreigners and deal with the payment of their principal and interest.[22]

On the other hand, the operation of foreign banks in Japan has sharply increased in recent years. Indeed, the number of them rose from 15 in 1965 to 63 in 1979, and among 63 of present foreign banks, 22 came from the USA, 26 from Europe, 2 from Central and South America and 13 from Asia. When foreign banks want to start business in Japan, they are required to obtain a licence under the Japanese Bank Law as one of the ordinary banks. They are allowed to issue negotiable certificates of deposit for fund raising, although they cannot issue debentures. The main business they are engaged in in Japan is, first, foreign-exchange transactions, as authorised foreign-exchange banks, and second, lendings. Their lendings merely share about 3 per cent of total bank lendings in Japan, but they extend not only to foreign-affiliated firms but also to the leading Japanese enterprises. Since Tokyo is expected to grow as an important international financial market, the operation of foreign banks is likely to increase further.

Foreign-affiliated firms finance very little of their external fund (i.e. capital, debentures, short- and long-term borrowings) from foreign banks operating in Japan. The share of long-term borrowings from foreign banks accounts for only 0.3 per cent of total external funds in 1977 and, similarly, that of short-term borrowings, 3.9 per cent. Stated differently, foreign-affiliated companies collect their required funds from Japan's domestic financial market.[23]

NOTES

The author is indebted to the staff of the Special Economic Study Department at the Bank of Japan for collecting data, and to Mr Stanley Howard for editing the English in this paper.

1. L. R. Krause and S. Sekiguchi, 'Japan and the World Economy', in H. T. Patrick and H. Rosovsky (eds), *Asia's New Giant: How the Japanese Economy Works* (Washington, D. C. The Brookings Institution, 1976) provides additional coverage.

2. For more comprehensive discussion of Japan's postwar economic reconstruction, see H. T. Patrick, 'The Phoenix Risen from the Ashes: Postwar Japan', in J. B. Crowley (ed.), *Modern East Asia: Essays in Interpretation* (New York: Harcourt Brace & World, 1970); A. Boltho, *Japan: An Economic Survey 1953–1973* (London: Oxford University Press, 1975); K. Bieda, *The Structure and Operations of the Japanese Economy* (Sydney: John Wiley, 1970); E. F. Denison and W. K. Chung, *How Japan's Economy Grew So Fast: The Sources of Post-war Expansion* (Washington, D. C.: The Brookings Institution, 1976); and R. E. Caves and M. Uekusa, *Industrial Organization in Japan* (Washington, D. C.: The Brookings Institution, 1976).
3. For further coverage of this point, see P. H. Tzeizise and Y. Suzuki, 'Politics, Government, and Economic Growth in Japan', in H. T. Patrick and H. Rosovsky (eds), *Asia's New Giant*.
4. For a summary of this development, see M. T. Skully, 'Japanese Structure: Some Factors in its Development', *International Journal of Accounting*, (Spring 1981) pp. 67–98.
5. See G. Ackley and H. Ishi, 'Fiscal, Monetary and Related Policies', in H. T. Patrick and H. Rosovsky (eds), *Asia's New Giant*; H. T. Patrick, 'Cyclical Instability and Fiscal-Monetary Policy in Postwar Japan', in W. W. Lockwood (ed.), *The State and Economic Enterprise in Japan* (Princeton, N. J.: Princeton University Press, 1968); *Monetary Policy in Japan* (Paris: OECD, 1972); and T. Suzuki, *Money and Banking in Contemporary Japan* (London: Yale University Press, 1980).
6. More detailed discussion might be required to make such factors as mentioned in the text clearer. Three points are noted here. The first is concerned with the so-called bonus effects unique to Japan's wage payment system. Japanese workers and salaried employees generally receive bonus payments at least twice a year in addition to regular monthly wage and salary. Since the marginal propensity to saving expects to be higher in temporary incomes than in the usual type of regular wages, bonus payments would cause a rise in the saving rate. Second, generally speaking, a well-developed social security system tends to decrease the necessity of personal saving. On this point, the poor state of social security in Japan, which we have experienced in the past, is important. Third, emphasis is placed on the strong motivation to purchase our own land and housing, given the difficulty of owning them in the narrower space of Japan. We must save more to achieve our target. In addition to these points, it is argued that the Japanese income tax system might be able to stimulate personal saving with a sort of tax concession. Interest incomes from bank deposits and postal savings would be tax exempt, provided that the principal did not exceed 3 million yen. However, it is doubtful whether a tax concession could effect the promotion of saving. For a detailed study of these points, see T. Mizoguchi, *Personal Savings and Consumption in Postwar Japan* (Tokyo: Kinokuniya, 1969).
7. In recent years government borrowing has caused a serious problem in the financing of the public sector, i.e. the huge amount of fiscal deficit. More than one-third of government revenues in the general account of central government has been due to the issuing of public bonds since 1977. For

further discussion of Japan's past experience, see H. T. Patrick, 'Financing of the Public Sector in Postwar Japan', in K. Ohkawa and L. Klein (eds), *Economic Growth: The Japanese Experiences since the Meiji Era* (Homewood, Ill.: R. D. Irwin, 1968).

8. See G. Ackley and H. Ishi, 'Fiscal, Monetary, and Related Policies', in H. T. Patrick and H. Rosovsky (eds), *Asia's New Giant*.

9. *Banking System in Japan* (Tokyo: Federation of Bankers' Associations of Japan, 1979) provides more detailed coverage of the various banks' operations.

10. In postwar Japan, the large banks have played an important role as suppliers of the ever-increasing demand for capital by large enterprises, and they became major shareholders in these enterprises. Thus, in the 1960s distinct alliances of economic interests emerged between the largest firms and the largest banks. Major groups of main enterprises have gradually been organised under the names of specific banks, like the Mitsubishi, the Mitsui, and the Sumitomo groups and so on. The emergence of these groupings could be said to closely resemble the ex-Zaibatsu groups. See Richard E. Caves and M. Uekusa, 'Industrial Organization', in H. T. Patrick and H. Rosovsky (eds), *Asia's New Giant*; H. C. Wallich and M. I. Wallich, 'Banking and Finance', ibid.; and K. Yamamura, *Economic Policy in Postwar Japan* (Berkeley: University of California Press, 1967) ch. 7.

11. A recent study of Japan's 13 city and 3 long-term credit banks found them the largest shareholder of 257 of the companies listed on the Tokyo Stock Exchange: many of them exceeding the new investment guidelines of 5 per cent on bank share holdings (*Nihon Keizai Shinbun*, 16 April 1979).

12. Commercial banks as well as other private banking institutions can legally deal in public securities, like national bonds, local government bonds and government-guaranteed bonds. In practice, however, the present administrative guidance (*Gyosei-shido*) prohibits the banking institution from underwriting and dealing in these public securities. In contrast, they are not officially permitted by Article 65 of the Securities and Exchange Law to deal in securities other than public securities. On this point, banking business is separated from securities business in both practice and law.

13. Mutual banks (*Sogo Ginko*) insist that they should be officially treated as commercial banks, using the same name *Ginko*, not *Sogo Ginko*. The latter tends to give a less reliable image to bank customers.

14. More details on Japan's money market, particularly as related to the securities companies, can be found in M. T. Skully, *Merchant Banking in the Far East*, 2nd edn (London: Financial Times Business Publishing, 1980) ch. 4.

15. For more information see *An Introduction to the Japanese Bond Market* (Tokyo: The Nomura Securities Co., 1978).

16. See H. C. Wallich and M. I. Wallich, 'Banking and Finance', in H. T. Patrick and H. Rosovsky (eds), *Asia's New Giant*.

17. In 1965 the business performance of Yamaichi Securities Company drastically deteriorated and fell into a serious situation. In order to cope with this crisis, the Bank of Japan took an extraordinary step to make a special loan to Yamaichi, invoking Article 25 of the Bank of Japan.

18. See, M. Tatsuta, *Securities Regulation in Japan* (Tokyo: University of Tokyo Press, 1970).
19. The securities exchanges of Japan are located in Tokyo, Osaka, Nagoya, Kyota, Hiroshima, Fukuoka, Niigate and Sapporo. Tokyo, however, accounts for over 80 per cent of the total volume. See *Securities Markets in Japan* (Tokyo: Japanese Securities Research Institute, 1977) and *Japan's Securities Market 1979* (Tokyo: Securities Public Information Centre of Japan, 1979).
20. See *Industrial Groupings in Japan* (Tokyo: Dodwell Marketing Group, 1974) which lists Japan's major industrial groups and the degree of each member's affiliation, and which shows many companies have loose affiliations with more than one group. D. A. Adhadeff, 'Bank–Business Conglomerates–the Japanese Experience', *Banca Nazionale del Lavoro Quarterly Review*, No. 114, September 1975, pp. 232–67, provides more details on this development with respect to the banks.
21. See *Banking System in Japan* for specific details of the banks' overseas expansion and their branch locations, subsidiaries and affiliates.
22. H. Moya, 'Euro-yen Bond Issues: a Growing Market?', *Finance and Development*, December 1978, pp. 42–4, indicates that yen issues are now also conducted in Europe–usually with a Japanese securities company or bank affiliate.
23. *Trends of Foreign Enterprises in Japan* (*Gaishikei Kigyo No Doko* in Japanese) (Tokyo: Ministry of International Trade and Industry, 1979) contains more specific information.

4 Financial Institutions and Markets in South Korea

SANG-WOO NAM and YUNG-CHUL PARK

INTRODUCTION

(a) The Setting

The Republic of Korea occupies the southern portion of the Korean peninsula, with Japan to the east and mainland China to the west. The main commercial centres are Seoul, Inchon (Seoul's port city) and Pusan (the southern port city). The Koreans themselves are a homogeneous, ethnically mongoloid people with their own traditional language and alphabet, Hangul.

Korea is a strategically important country which has traditionally served as a land bridge between mainland Asia and Japan, and as a cultural bridge as well. Throughout its history Korea has maintained its unique individuality. Beginning at the end of the sixteenth century, it adopted a policy of strong isolationism as a result of several foreign invasions. Early in the present century, after several decades of uncertainty and upheaval, Korea was annexed to the Japanese Empire and did not regain its independence until the end of the Second World War on 15 August 1945.

When the Korean War broke out on 25 June 1950, the Western world had little knowledge of the country, and the circumstances of its introduction onto the world stage created an image of a war-torn, devastated country. So it was not until the mid-1960s that the government reforms, swelling exports and, perhaps most importantly, the affirmative attitude of the Koreans themselves improved Korea's international image.

Beginning from a position uncomfortably close to the bottom of the

MAP 4.1   South Korea

international income scale and without the benefit of significant natural
resources, Korea launched a series of economic development programmes which in less than 15 years has transformed the country from a
marginally subsistent agricultural economy into one of Asia's major
industrial nations. By 1979 real GNP, growing at 9.2 per cent per annum

since 1962, had risen from \$2.3 billion to \$60.1 billion in current prices; while per capita GNP, in current prices, had increased from \$87 to \$1597, one of the highest rates of sustained growth in modern economic history.

Though Korea's rapid growth has clearly been the result of a number of interacting economic, political and social factors which cannot be easily quantified, certain key elements can be singled out. The nation's commitment to industrialisation, while it was to a large extent dictated by circumstances, also reflected the fact that Korea did possess a very important resource: an educated, highly motivated and industrious populace, without whose strong drive, discipline, and general desire for higher living standards Korea's economic development would not have been possible.

Among the tactical factors involved in Korea's remarkable growth, the key role played by export expansion and an outward-looking development strategy stands out. One can say, in fact, that manufactured exports, which rose from \$15 million in 1962 to over \$13.6 billion in 1979–a real growth rate of 39.6 per cent per annum–have been, in a real sense, the engine of growth.

Agriculture was the traditional mainstay of the Korean economy for generations, and this sector still contributes some 20.5 per cent to GNP. It has grown at a steady pace of more than 4 per cent per annum since 1962, and there has been a substantial improvement in agricultural terms of trade during this period. Nevertheless, the mining and manufacturing sector has grown, in constant terms, at more than three times the pace of agriculture, and its share of GNP has surpassed that of agriculture since 1973.

The share of the mining and manufacturing sector rose from 16.2 per cent of GNP in 1962 to 28.0 per cent in 1979, while that of the agriculture, forestry and fishery sector declined from 36.6 to 20.5 per cent, and the social overhead capital and other services sector rose from 47.1 to 51.5 per cent.

The development of the industrial structure has led in turn to a redistribution of employment. Employment in the agriculture, forestry and fishery sector decreased from 63.5 per cent of the total labour force in 1963 to 35.8 per cent in 1979, while the share of the mining and manufacturing sector increased from 8.7 to 23.7 per cent and that of the social overhead capital and other services sector from 28.2 to 40.5 per cent.

The sustained high growth of the Korean economy has been led by the remarkable development of the manufacturing sector, which contributed an average of 38.9 per cent to the annual growth of GNP during this period. Particularly noteworthy is the growth of the heavy and chemical industries, which increased their share within the sector from 28.6 to 50.7 per cent between 1962 and 1979. The average annual growth rate of the manufacturing sector as a whole was 17.1 per cent and that of the heavy and chemical industries was 24.3 per cent, as compared with an average annual growth rate of 9.2 per cent for the economy as a whole.

It must be noted, however, that the high growth rate and the deepening industrial structure were attained at the cost of aggravating inflationary pressure in the economy. Wholesale prices and GNP deflator rose at the annual rates of 11 per cent and 18 per cent, respectively, during 1976–8. With rapid increases in commodity and service exports, the money supply expanded, but the excess liquidity was not effectively absorbed into the organised financial markets because of suppressed interest rates. The money supply increased at the annual rate of 32 per cent during 1976–8, which led to speculation in real estate, commodities, and any other scarce assets. Nominal wages also rose as fast as 32 per cent annually during 1976–8. These high rates of inflation and wage increase together with the fixed exchange rate since late 1974 had drastically deteriorated the competitiveness of Korean products in the world market. Meanwhile, the overemphasis on the heavy and chemical industries caused serious misallocation of limited financial resources. Small and medium industries supplying some critical daily necessities were unable to obtain investment funds.

The stabilisation programme adopted in April 1979 was designed to deal with the causes as well as the consequences of inflation. The programme aimed at restructuring the economy to provide a firmer foundation for sustained economic growth by restoring the function of the market mechanism to allocate resources more efficiently and equitably.

Though the major policy targets of the stabilisation programme were attained for the most part, inflation turned out to be much worse in 1979 than anticipated. Wholesale and consumer prices rose 24 and 21 per cent respectively. The new oil crisis, together with the price increases of commodities released from direct government control, was responsible for the major portion of the inflation rate.

The soaring oil price adversely affected not only the inflation rate, but also the balance of payments. With real exports registering negative growth (increased by 20 per cent at current prices), the current account deficit widened from $1.1 billion in 1978 to $4.2 billion in 1979. The growth in the real GNP at 1975 prices equalled 6.4 per cent in 1979, a significant drop from 11.6 per cent achieved in 1978.

(b) An Overview of the Financial Sector

(i) *Domestic savings mobilisation*

With sustained growth of income and a high rate of return on investment, real domestic savings have increased dramatically. During the period of the First Five-Year Economic Development Plan (1962–6), more than half of the gross domestic capital formation was financed with foreign savings (mainly transfers): domestic savings amounted to just 8 per cent of GNP. During 1977–9, however, the domestic saving ratio was 26.1 per cent, while as shown in Table 4.1, foreign savings accounted for a small portion – only 3.9 per cent.

TABLE 4.1 Savings ratio (percentage of GNP)

	1962–6	67–71	72–6	77–9
Total saving ratio	16.3	25.7	26.6	31.3
(1) Domestic saving	8.0	15.6	20.3	26.1
Government	0.6	5.6	4.1	6.5
Private	7.4	10.0	16.2	19.6
Households	0.0	2.3	5.2	9.4
Business	7.4	7.7	11.0	10.2
(2) Foreign saving	8.6	10.1	6.9	3.9
Net transfer	6.8	3.2	1.3	0.8
Net borrowing	1.8	7.0	5.5	3.1
(3) Statistical discrepancy	−0.2	0.0	−0.5	1.5

Government saving expanded rapidly during the Second Five-Year Plan period averaging 5.6 per cent of the GNP, but abated during the years of slower economic growth (1971–5) before increasing to 6.5 per cent of the GNP during 1977–9. The household saving ratio steadily increased from zero during 1962–6 to 9.4 per cent of GNP during 1977–9. Savings of the business sector, which constituted almost all of the domestic saving during the First Development Plan period and about half of it during the period of the Second Plan, further accelerated with the launch of the Third Plan, accounting for nearly 55 per cent of total domestic savings. Net transfers constituted most of the foreign savings during 1962–6, but were replaced by long-term borrowing that accounted for as much as 7 per cent of GNP during the Second Five-

Year Plan period. Foreign borrowing decreased to 3.1 per cent of GNP during 1977–9.

(ii) *Financial deepening*

The financial system in a developing country is expected to play an active role in economic development, rather than simply to react to stimuli in the real sectors of the economy. In recent years, there has been some concern over the slow growth of the Korean financial sector. The worry is that the financial system is retarding the growth of the real economy.

Financial development in Korea started with a growth in money supply. The high interest rate policy adopted in September 1965 was the key factor in the drastic improvement of the financial interrelation ratios. Indeed, as shown in Table 4.2, the ratio of broadly defined money (M2) to GNP jumped to 32.7 per cent at the end of 1969 from 8.9 per cent five years before. During this period, the volume of time and savings deposits almost doubled every year and constituted the majority of the increase in total domestic financial assets. In addition, the ratio of total domestic financial assets to GNP rose from 25.2 per cent to 55.5 per cent over this period. Interest rates were lowered gradually beginning in April 1968, and reached the pre-1965 level in 1972. Thus, the broad money/GNP ratio (M2/Y) declined until 1976 from the peak in 1973, when the economy recovered strongly from the previous slowdown without any serious inflationary pressure. The high inflation rate attributed to the energy crisis coupled with the depressed interest rates has been responsible for the relative contraction of money. Meanwhile, the volume of non-bank deposits and securities grew rapidly during

TABLE 4.2   Financial interrelation ratios (percentage)

	Ratio to nominal GNP	
End of year	*Broad money (M2)*	*Domestic financial assets*[a]
1964	8.9	25.2
1965	12.1	28.4
1969	32.7	55.5
1973	37.8	69.5
1975	32.2	60.9
1977	34.5	68.3
1979	34.0	73.4

[a] Domestic financial assets include currency, bank and non-bank deposits, and securities.

1972/73 when policy measures were effective in stimulating the stock market and in developing non-bank financial institutions including short-term finance companies. These policies were aimed at attracting private savings from the unorganised money market. Consequently, the ratio of total domestic financial assets to GNP rose drastically during this period to peak at 70 per cent of the GNP at the end of 1973, before there was a significant decline during the energy crisis. This ratio recovered to the 1973 level by the end of 1977.

(iii) *Monetary policy and financial system*

Monetary and credit management in Korea has relied more heavily on credit ceilings and other direct control measures than on indirect control methods. However, direct control has caused many adverse effects: imbalance in credit allocation among industrial sectors and specific firms, rigidity in credit management due to bank credit ceilings for individual firms, and limited incentive for competition among banks.

The rediscount policy in Korea has been of very limited use as most of the Bank of Korea (BOK) loans were automatic rediscounts of preferential loans made by banking institutions. The rediscount rate has not been used effectively to control the demand for rediscounts or to affect the interest rates of commercial banks. The BOK often permitted loans to commercial banks to remedy their reserve deficiencies in the face of excess loan demand. The reserve requirement has been a powerful policy tool in the virtual absence of other orthodox monetary controls including the rediscount policy and the open market operations. The Monetary Stabilisation Account, opened to supplement the inflexibility of the reserve requirement policy, has played an important role in absorbing temporary excess bank reserves. Conditions conducive to more effective open market operations have been fostered in recent years: the maximum discount rate was raised to 20 per cent per annum; the non-bank financial institutions were encouraged to participate in the open market operations; and government-guaranteed bonds were introduced as tradable instruments.

Artificially controlled interest rates form an essential part of financial repression and are responsible, to a large extent, for the ineffectiveness and inefficiencies of the financial sector in supporting the real sectors of the economy. Low real interest rates keep the size of savings from growing large enough to be distributed among sectors in decent sizes. The limited size of the organised financial markets restricts the scope of direct monetary management. Low interest rates accelerate inflation as, with unattractive financial assets, it is difficult to maintain the increase in money supply at a reasonable rate and to discourage people from engaging in speculative dealings in physical assets such as real estate. Furthermore, gross inefficiencies are inevitable as the small loanable fund is distributed among sectors without any specific criteria. The arbitrary nature of the rationing of capital and the structure of interest rates applied to specific sectors are likely to distort greatly resource allocation. The supply and demand imbalance for some commodities arising from this distortion was one of the major sources of economic instability in recent years. While many daily necessities were in short supply, there has been over-capacity in some heavy manufacturing industries. Therefore, the deceleration of investment in some heavy manufacturing industries was inevitable. In addition, the low level of real interest rates makes it difficult to adjust the rates to changing economic conditions, thereby restricting the effectiveness of monetary policy.

Direct government influence in every phase of monetary operations has weakened the role of the central bank. As a consequence, there has been a continuous tendency of rapid money supply growth to accommodate the ambitious expansion of the real sector, which has, in turn, created inflationary pressure on the economy.

FINANCIAL INSTITUTIONS

South Korea's financial sector is comprised of 5 nationwide city banks, 10 local banks, 33 foreign bank branches, 6 special banks, 3 development finance institutions, 6 life insurance companies, 13 non-life insurance companies, 18 investment and finance companies, 6 merchant banking corporations, a number of mutual savings and finance companies and credit co-operatives, the Korea Credit Guarantee Fund, 3 leasing companies, 27 securities companies, the Korea Securities Finance Corporation, and 2 securities investment trust companies–an indication of the relative importance of the major groups is shown in Table 4.3.

For discussion purposes, these institutions have been divided into two major groups: monetary institutions and other financial institutions. The monetary institutions include the central bank, the Bank of Korea and the deposit money banks: these include the domestic and foreign commercial banks as well as those specialist banks that compete with the commercial banks for much of their funding. The other financial institutions include the development and savings institutions and the insurance and investment companies.

TABLE   4.3   Total assets of financial institutions (as of the end of 1980; in million won)[a]

	Amount	Percentage of total
Commercial banks		
City banks	11938118	32.6
Local banks	1883071	5.1
Special banks		
The Korea Exchange Bank	3762754	10.3
The Small and Medium Industry Bank	1409354	3.8
The Citizens National Bank	1506326	4.1
The Korea Housing Bank	1180608	3.2
The National Agricultural Cooperatives Federation and member cooperatives	2038924	5.6
The Central Federation of Fisheries Co-operatives and member co-operatives	261643	0.7
Development institutions		
The Korea Development Bank	4623362	12.6
The Export-Import Bank of Korea	556481	1.5
The Korea Long-term Credit Bank	449063	1.2
Savings institutions		
Trust business	2088216	5.7
Mutual savings and finance companies	533453	1.5
Credit unions	1620358	4.4
Life insurance companies	991181	2.7
Investment companies		
Investment and finance companies	1242361	3.4
Merchant banking corporations	578659	1.6
Total	36663932	100.0

[a] Exclusive of the Bank of Korea.
Source: Bank of Korea.

(a) Banking Institutions

Korea's present banking system was established in June 1878 when Japan's Dai-Ichi Bank (now part of the Dia-Ichi Kangyo Bank) opened a branch office in the southern seaport of Pusan. It was soon followed by other Japanese- and later Korean-sponsored banks. This early Japanese influence and control of Korea's financial sector is still reflected in many aspects of Korean finance and financial practices.

The banking system today consists of three major components: the central bank, the commercial banks, and the special banks. For discussion purposes, the latter two are combined within the deposit money banks section.

(i) *The Bank of Korea*

The Bank of Korea (BOK) was established in June 1950 under the Bank of Korea Act, to serve as Korea's central bank and to formulate and implement the nation's monetary and credit policies.[1] Among other things, the Monetary Board, the top policy-making organ of the BOK, determines:

(i) Required reserve ratios for each banking institutions.
(ii) Maximum deposit and loan rates for banking institutions.
(iii) Rates of discounts and interest on loans of the BOK to banking institutions.
(iv) Volume of securities the BOK is to sell or buy in the open market.

In practice, however, the functions of the Board are, to a large extent, transferred to the Ministry of Finance, leaving the Board to play a consulting role. In addition to the orthodox monetary policy tools, the monetary authorities control interest rates of banking institutions and have other powerful and direct control measures in periods of inflation.

To control credit, Variable Reserve Requirements have been used more flexibly than any other measure. As was the case for five months from October 1966, when there was fear of serious inflation, marginal reserve ratios of more than 50 per cent may be imposed on banking institutions. There are two unique features about the reserve deposits in Korea. First, the BOK often pays interest on reserve deposits of banking institutions to compensate for the forgone earnings whenever bank profit figures are not satisfactory. Second, since Korean banks have been engaged in excessive lending with little slack in deposit reserves, a rise in required reserve ratios tends to produce additional borrowings from the BOK.

'Open market operations' in Korea are too limited in size and frequency to be called such by the standards of advanced economies. Mainly because of the underdeveloped capital market, transactions of securities – excluding Monetary Stabilisation Bonds – have been conducted only in extremely short run with individual banks on a *tête-à-tête* basis several times a year. Monetary Stabilisation Bonds, introduced in 1961 as a special negotiable obligation of the BOK, have played a major role in regulating the liquidity positions of banking institutions. As are the cases with government bonds and government-guaranteed bonds, the major share of the Stabilisation Bonds are distributed through bilateral dealings with banking institutions on the basis of fixed interest rates and with repurchase agreements.

The Monetary Stabilisation Account was established in the BOK as a complementary instrument to control temporary excess liquidity positions of banks. The funds compulsorily deposited in the Account are not regarded as a part of legal reserve requirements, but are subject to the interest rate of 16 per cent per annum.

Owing to insufficient internal funds and the underdevelopment of the capital market, Korean business firms rely heavily on banks for their financial requirements. With insufficient deposit inflows, the banking institutions have in turn greatly depended upon borrowings from the BOK. The interest rates of banking institutions have been predetermined in line with the BOK lending rates, being altered simultaneously in view of the need to change borrowing cost of business firms and to mobilise domestic savings. The Monetary Board sets the upper limits of interest rates on various types of bank loans and deposits while the actual rates, if necessary, are agreed upon by the Bankers' Association within the Board's limits. The bank rates thus determined have been significantly lower than the rates prevailing in the unorganised money market. Thus, chronic excess demand for bank loans (credit rationing) and associated abnormalities involved in loan dealings have been a problem. In September 1965, a drastic upward adjustment of bank rates was made in order to entice unorganised money market savings into banking institutions and to normalise bank operations. After three years, however, the rates started to be adjusted downward–mainly to alleviate financing cost of business firms. By August 1972, the rates reached the pre-1965 level. The rediscount policy of the BOK is characterised by its preference for bills related to designated industries in both available amount and in rediscount rates. Export-related bills are most favourably treated and account for about half of the total BOK lendings. Rediscounts of commercial bills, general loans, and loans for agriculture and fishery constitute the other half.

During periods of marked inflation, the BOK may resort to other direct credit control measures. It can fix ceilings on the aggregate outstanding volume of loans and investments of a banking institution for specified periods of time. Such ceilings may be specified for each industry. All loan applications in excess of the specified ceiling are submitted to the BOK for prior approval. The BOK may also determine the maximum maturities and the types and amounts of collateral to be required for loans by banking institutions. Direct controls of this kind over bank lending activities, which are detrimental to the autonomous growth of banks, have frequently been in effect over the last two decades.

(ii) *The deposit money banks*

Although the commercial and special banks are administered under different legislation, a significant portion of their operations are much the same. For discussion purposes, therefore, the major banking business of these banks has been combined within one section: the more specific details of each are contained respectively in the commercial and special bank sections.

Major banking business

Receipt of deposits: Demand deposits are received by Korean banks in three major classes: cheque, passbook and temporary deposits. Cheques, bills and notes are usable only for chequing deposit accounts and are held mostly by business enterprises. Passbook deposits are frequently utilised by individuals or enterprises without chequing accounts for depositing temporary surplus funds. Temporary deposits are mainly used by business firms for cash inflows which are destined to be paid out soon or accounting treatment of which is uncertain. Passbook and temporary deposits bear low interest rates of 1.8 and 1.0 per cent per annum, respectively.

Time deposits, instalment savings deposits, and deposits at notice are the major types of time and savings deposits. Time deposits are the most popular form of savings and have the highest deposit interest rates. With an automatic borrowing privilege for those who have deposited over one-third of the contract period, instalment savings deposits are widely used as a savings medium by both households and business firms. Deposits at notice are generally utilised by business firms with interest-seeking motives for the temporary operation of idle funds.

Issuance of debentures: Special banks are authorised to issue debentures up to 10 to 20 times their capital accounts. Bank debentures at present in circulation are Industrial Finance Debentures of the Korea Development Bank, and Housing Debentures of the Korea Housing Bank fully guaranteed by the government. Housing Debentures, in particular, serve as a major financial source for the Korea Housing Bank, next to deposits from the general public.

Lendings: Of the total bank lendings, 92 per cent were funded through banking sources such as deposits, issuance of bank debentures, borrowings from the BOK, etc., as of the end of 1979. Of the lendings, 8 per cent use funds from government sources, including foreign borrowings.

Short-term bank loans include discounts on bills, overdrafts, general loans on bills, loans on instalment savings, remunerations, and loans for short-term export financing. Discounts on bills are not popular because of BOK policy to limit the type of trade bills eligible for rediscounts. Overdrafts are also limited owing to the higher interest charge and the low level of transactions settled through chequing accounts. General loans on bills constitute the major portion of bank loans. Three months is the usual original term of bills which are supposed to supplement borrowing firms' working funds. These loans, however, are often utilised to meet long-term financial needs through roll-overs and renewals. Providing loans to small borrowers such as households and small merchants, remunerations are handled solely by the Citizens National Bank. Finally, loans for short-term export financing with maturities of three to six months are extended to exporters and those who produce export goods. These loans carry the most preferable interest rates and rediscount privilege and, with a rapid increase in exports, have accounted for a major part in the overall expansion of bank loans.

There are various types of long-term bank credits, including term loans, loans for machinery industry promotion, equipment of export industry, agriculture, small and medium enterprises and housing, National Investment Fund loans, and loans in foreign currency. Loans for machinery industry promotion are extended at preferential rates to both machine manufacturers in heavy industries and purchasers of domestically-produced machines. Started in 1971, term loans aim at meeting the increasing demand for medium- and long-term equipment loans by enterprises. Loans for equipment of export industry started in 1973 at a rate slightly lower than the general loan rate. National

Investment Fund loans also started in 1973 to finance export-oriented heavy and chemical industries out of the government budgets and the issuance of National Investment Bonds to be subscribed by financial industries. The Fund is administered by the BOK and is loaned to all banks to be reloaned at a preferential rate.

Loans in foreign currency are extended to export and other designated industries to facilitate importation of required equipment and facilities. Korea's own exchange holdings and borrowings from foreign banks are major sources of credit and interest rates on these loans float in line with those of international financial markets within an upper limit set by the BOK. Loans for agriculture, fishery, small and medium enterprises, and housing are almost exclusively handled by the respective special banks to be described below, with funds from both banking and the government sources.

Except for discounts on bills, banks, in principle, require collateral for their loans. Real estate is favoured most and accounts for a dominant, though declining, portion of the total collateral. The structure of bank loan rates is extremely complex, with rates varying according to the sources as well as the uses of funds. The rate differentials usually have nothing to do with loan risks or administrative or other costs involved. Most preferential interest rates are given to loans for export financing, machinery industry, equipment of export industry, small and medium enterprises, and agriculture.

Investments in securities: Commercial banks are allowed to invest up to 25 per cent of their demand deposit liabilities in stocks and bonds with maturities of over three years. Government bonds and Monetary Stabilisation Bonds of the BOK are excluded from the limitation. Banks, however, have little inducement to hold securities, mainly because of the low levels of yields and liquidity associated with security investment. Nevertheless, banks are the largest subscribers to government bonds and government-guaranteed bonds.

Commercial banks
Commercial banks are at present composed of 5 nationwide city banks, 10 local banks, and 32 foreign banks.

Nationwide city banks: There is strong uniformity among the five city banks in their organisation and management because of similar historical backgrounds and deep intervention by the government. At present, the government owns more than one-third of the total shares of four of the five city banks. The government share of the Commercial Bank of Korea was completely divested in 1972 as a first step towards private commercial banks. The five city banks dominate the commercial banking business, accounting for more than 75 per cent in total deposits and loans. Major fund sources are deposits from the public and borrowings from the BOK, mostly rediscounts on short-term bills related to export industries.

In 1976 the Seoul Bank, one of the big five, combined with the Korea Trust Bank. Only banking accounts of this bank are treated as a part of commercial banking business, and it has a unique source of funds – borrowings from the trust accounts of commercial banks. An indication of the relative importance of each of these banks is shown in Table 4.4.

TABLE 4.4 Nationwide city banks

		Domestic branches		
Bank	*Date established*	*Branches*	*Sub-branches*	*Total*
Cho-Heung Bank Ltd	19 February 1897	94	13	107
Commercial Bank of Korea Ltd	30 January 1899	73	17	90
Korea First Bank	1 July 1929	73	15	88
Hanil Bank	16 December 1932	72	12	84
Bank of Seoul & Trust Company	1 December 1959	121	15	136
Totals		433	72	505

Local banks: The introduction of local banks was to achieve a balanced dispersion of banking businesses and to promote regional development. Accordingly, their major clients are local enterprises and local public entities. The maximum interest rates on time deposits and some short-term loans are a little higher than those allowed to nationwide city banks. This is to help the local banks gain more business in their early years and also takes into account the higher costs due to their smaller scale of operations. A listing of these banks is provided in Table 4.5.

Foreign banks in Korea: The Seoul branch of the Chase Manhattan Bank, opened in April 1967, was the first among foreign banks operating in Korea. Promotion of a close relationship between the domestic

TABLE 4.5   Local banks

Bank	Head office	Established	No. of branches
Daegu Bank	Daegu	7 October 1967	26
Busan Bank	Busan	25 October 1967	48
Chungchong Bank	Daejeon	22 April 1968	20
Gwangju Bank	Gwangju	20 November 1968	19
Jeju Bank	Jeju	19 September 1969	n.a.
Gyeonggi Bank	Inchon	8 December 1969	n.a.
Jeonbug Bank	Jeonju	10 December 1969	20
Gangweon Bank	Chooncheon	3 April 1970	17
Gyeongnam Bank	Masan	22 May 1970	21
Chungbuk Bank	Chungjo	24 April 1971	22

economy and the international financial markets and improvement in the management of domestic banks through international competition were the major objectives of inducing foreign banks to enter Korea. They are required to maintain a certain range of over-bought positions and the foreign-exchange funds in excess of the upper limit must be sold to the BOK or the Korea Exchange Bank in exchange for domestic currency. Borrowings from head offices and deposits in won currency are their main fund sources, while their assets are mostly in loans in foreign and won currencies. Rediscount windows of the BOK are closed to foreign banks in Korea. Loans in foreign currency are extended mainly to export industries to facilitate importation of capital equipment.[2]

Despite the above restrictions on their operations, the foreign banks have nevertheless found the potential for Korea business very appealing and, as shown in Table 4.6, most of the world's major banks are now represented locally either through a branch or representative office.

Special banks

Special banks were established in order to provide intermediate- and long-term credits to meet the demands for funds from key industries or other strategic sectors which commercial banks alone would not adequately supply. Their operations are directed and supervised directly by the government, and regulations on reserve requirements and deposit and loan rates are applied to these special banks as to the commercial banks. Special banks play a significant role in the Korean banking system. Their combined total outstanding loans amount to 56 per cent of the commercial bank loans at the end of 1979. Like commercial

TABLE 4.6   Foreign banks in Korea

Name	Nationality	Date of licensing	Location
Branches:			
Chase Manhattan Bank	USA	21.7.67	Seoul
Bank of Tokyo	Japan	4.9.67	Seoul
Citibank	USA	8.9.67	Seoul
Mitsubishi Bank	Japan	20.10.67	Seoul
Bank of America	USA	1.12.67	Seoul
Chartered Bank	UK	29.1.68	Seoul
Fuji Bank	Japan	24.1.72	Seoul
Dai-Ichi Kangyo Bank	Japan	7.2.72	Seoul
Banque de L'Indochine et de Suez	France	1.8.74	Seoul
Banque Nationale de Paris	France	4.10.76	Seoul
First National Bank of Chicago	USA	1.11.76	Seoul
AMEX International Banking Corp.	USA	27.5.77	Seoul
Lloyds Bank International	UK	7.6.77	Seoul
Barclays Bank International	UK	5.9.77	Seoul
Indian Overseas Bank	India	19.9.77	Seoul
Bank of Credit & Commerce International (Overseas)	Grand Cayman	9.11.77	Seoul
Banque de Paris et des Pays-Bas	France	23.11.77	Seoul
Bank of America	USA	22.12.77	Busan
Citibank	USA	30.12.77	Busan
Grindlays Bank	UK	19.1.78	Seoul
International Bank of Singapore	Singapore	23.2.78	Seoul
Bank of Nova Scotia	Canada	27.3.78	Seoul
Continental Illinois of Chicago	USA	1.5.78	Seoul
Morgan Guaranty Trust	USA	20.6.78	Seoul
Credit Lyonnais	France	14.7.78	Seoul
European Asian Bank	West Germany	1.8.78	Seoul
Chemical Bank	USA	6.9.78	Seoul
Bank of Montreal	Canada	20.11.78	Seoul
Manufacturers Hanover Trust Company	USA	5.12.78	Seoul
Bankers Trust Company	USA	22.12.78	Seoul
Algemene Bank Nederland	Netherlands	16.3.79	Seoul
Union des Banques Arabes et Françaises	France	9.7.79	Seoul
Representative offices:			
Chase Manhattan Bank[a]	USA	15.4.71	Busan
Marine Midland Bank[a]	USA	23.12.71	Seoul
Yamaguchi Bank	Japan	7.9.73	Busan

TABLE 4.6 (*Contd.*)

Name	Nationality	Date of licensing	Location
Hongkong & Shanghai Banking Corporation	Hong Kong	29.10.75	Seoul
Sanwa Bank	Japan	24.2.76	Seoul
Security Pacific National Bank[a]	USA	29.1.77	Seoul
Saitama Bank	Japan	1.12.77	Seoul
United California Bank[a]	USA	16.1.78	Seoul
Bank of Tokyo[a]	Japan	22.2.78	Busan
Union Bank[a]	USA	10.4.78	Seoul
Wells Fargo Bank[a]	USA	19.6.78	Seoul
Mitsui Bank	Japan	24.10.78	Seoul
Sumitomo-Bank	Japan	6.9.78	Seoul
Royal Bank of Canada	Canada	3.11.78	Seoul
Taiyo Kobe Bank	Japan	20.3.79	Seoul
Kyowa Bank	Japan	7.5.79	Seoul
Hokkaido Takushok Bank	Japan	1.6.79	Seoul
First National Bank of Boston	USA	1.6.79	Seoul
Crocker National Bank[a]	USA	8.9.79	Seoul

[a] To be upgraded to branch status before the end of 1981.

banks, deposits are their major fund source. However, they receive government funds as a part of their financial resources in addition to their own funds raised through receiving deposits and issuing debentures. These banks include the Korea Exchange Bank, the Small and Medium Industry Bank, the Citizens National Bank, the Korea Housing Bank, the National Agricultural Cooperatives Federation and the Central Federation of Fisheries Cooperatives.

The Korea Exchange Bank (KEB): With increasing foreign trade, the KEB was established on 30 January 1967 with all of its capital subscribed by the BOK to take on all foreign-exchange business formerly conducted by the BOK. Being predominantly engaged in financing business firms involved in international trade both at home and abroad, the KEB controls a major portion of foreign assets and liabilities in Korea. The Bank is also engaged in general banking activities. Foreign currency deposits of the BOK, borrowings from foreign banks, and deposits from the public are its main financial resources. Loans in foreign currency made by the KEB are far larger than the combined total of the five city banks, and are almost as large as its loans in domestic currency.

The Small and Medium Industry Bank (MIB): The MIB was established on 1 August 1961 to provide loans to small and medium enterprises which are neglected by commercial banks mainly because of their high risks and lack of adequate collateral. The MIB also exclusively handles small industry funds of the government, and makes repayment guarantees for small and medium firms when they borrow from other banks. Its main resources include deposits from the public, borrowings from the government, and foreign funds.

The Citizens National Bank (CNB): The CNB was established on 1 February 1963 and evolved from a consolidation of '*mujin*' companies, which were traditional mutual savings and loan organisations serving the common people in Korea. It receives mutual instalment deposits and makes mutual remuneration loans to those having a mutual instalment deposit account. The Bank also makes general loans with funds raised through instalment savings and other deposits or borrowings from the government and the BOK.

The Korea Housing Bank (KHB): The KHB was founded on 10 July 1967 to take over the housing funds of the Korea Development Bank when government housing funds steadily decreased due mainly to the reduction in the USAID counterpart funds. The KHB finances housing for low-income families by receiving housing instalment and other deposits and issuing housing debentures and lotteries. The funds are supplied to those constructing or purchasing houses, grading housing sites, and producing construction materials.

The National Agricultural Co-operatives Federation and member co-operatives: The National Agricultural Co-operatives Federation (NACF) and its member co-operatives were established on 15 August 1961 through the merger of the former agricultural co-operatives and the Korea Agricultural Bank. In 1977 the NACF also absorbed the, formerly Post Office run, postal savings system into its operations. Through their credit departments, the Federation and its country co-operatives offer banking services to farmers, local government bodies and non-profit organisations, and specialise in the provision of finance for farming and agriculture-related projects.

The NACF obtains its funds from public deposits and, more importantly, borrowings from the government and the Bank of Korea. It may also issue government-guaranteed Agricultural Credit Debentures in amounts up to 20 times its paid-up capital to help fund its operations.

The Central Federation of Fisheries Co-operatives and member co-operatives: The Central Federation of Fisheries Co-operatives (CFFC) and its member co-operatives were established on 1 April 1962 to promote the living conditions of fishermen and productivity of marine product manufactures. The credit departments of the Central Federation and its fishery co-operatives offer banking services to fishermen, local government bodies and non-profit organisations, and specialise in the provision of finance to fishermen and related ventures as well as acting as agents for government bodies and other financial institutions within this area. The CFFC's operations are funded by public deposits and loans from the Bank of Korea government.

(b) Non-banking Financial Institutions

The non-bank or other financial institutions in Korea are still in their early stages of development. Until very recently, money in trust and life insurance was about all of the savings at non-bank financial institutions. Recently, with the marked growth of investment and finance companies and mutual credit companies, the relative importance of the non-bank financial institution portion of the financial sector has increased and now includes the Korea Development Bank, the Korea Long-term Credit Bank, the Export-Import Bank of Korea, the Korean Land Development Corporation, the investment and finance companies, merchant banks, mutual credit companies, the trust business, insurance companies, credit co-operatives, leasing compaines, and some specialised securities industry related institutions such as the securities companies, the Korea Securities Finance Corporation, and the securities investment trusts.

(i) *The Korea Development Bank* (KDB)

As the successor to the Industrial Bank of Korea established in 1918, the KDB was founded on 1 April 1954 with its capital wholly paid in by the government. Having concentrated on the rehabilitation of industrial facilities severely destroyed during the Korean War, its efforts have been directed to development projects. The KDB not only provides long-term credits but also subscribes and underwrites corporate debentures or public debts to finance major industrial projects. It also deals with foreign exchange banking business and makes repayment guarantees for business firms on corporate debentures and loans extended by other domestic financial institutions with foreign borrowings. A major financial source for the KDB is borrowing from government budgets, including USAID counterpart funds. The KDB also acts as an agent for introducting foreign capital into Korea, and borrows from overseas banks or other institutions. The Bank's own funds include capital accounts, proceeds from Industrial Finance Debentures, and special time deposits from the public.

(ii) *Korea Long-term Credit Bank (KLB)*

The KLB was established on 2 June 1980 as a private long-term credit bank by reorganising and expanding Korea Development Finance Corporation. The KDFC was organised in 1967 with the help from the World Bank to assist in the development and creation of private enterprises by providing medium- and long-term industrial financing and equity participation as well as technical and managerial consulting services. Before its reorganisation, the KDFC had mostly been involved in the relending of foreign currency resources they had mobilised from abroad. With a new charter, the KLB is allowed to mobilise loanable funds in the domestic money and capital markets by securities underwriting and accepting time deposits from those to whom they have extended loans.

(iii) *The Export–Import Bank of Korea*

Established in July 1976 as a special government financial institution, it promotes the export–import trade of Korea by providing loans, guarantees, insurance and other financial facilities. Its medium- and long-term loans are extended to domestic suppliers or foreign buyers in connection with the export of designated Korean capital goods and technical services, to domestic importers for their import of raw materials and to domestic investors for their enterprises abroad. Guarantees are provided to domestic financial institutions against loss incurred in financing either the domestic suppliers or the foreign buyers, while export credit insurance is to insure domestic firms against non-payment or other loss for their exports.

At the end of 1979, paid-in capital and borrowings from National Investment Fund and others accounted for 83 per cent of the total liabilities and capital, while 64 per cent of total assets were in loans and discounts.

(iv) *Korea Land Development Corporation*

The Korea Land Development Corporation was established on 27 March 1979 under the Korea Land Development Corporation Act, to expand the country's land development efforts and to assume the former business operations of the Korea Land Bank. the Corporation is involved with the purchase, management, and sale of land; making loans for land purchases and development, and assisting the government with the management of its property holdings. It obtains its funding in part through the issuance and sale of land debentures.

(v) *Investment and finance companies*

Short-term finance business was started in 1973 with a view to absorbing the unorganised money market (UMM) funds and to effectively meeting short-term capital needs of corporations. At present, the companies are engaged in supplying their funds, raised mainly by issuing their own short-term papers, to prime enterprises through discounts on commercial papers. Though their interest and discount rates are supposed to be market-determined, the maximum ceiling is predetermined by the government. The growth of finance companies has been spectacular; they are supposedly attracting many funds away from the UMM, though the growth seems to be slowing owing to government intervention on rates. A list of these institutions is provided in Table 4.7.

(vi) *Merchant banking corporations*

Merchant banking corporations were introduced in 1976 because of the need to diversify the channel of borrowing from abroad after experiencing a serious foreign-exchange shortage caused by the oil crisis during 1973/4. At the end of 1979 there were six corporations, all of which were joint ventures with foreign investors with an equity share less than 50 per cent. A listing of these institutions is provided in Table 4.8.

Korea's merchant banks were given authority to offer a wide range of financial services and patterned after their British counterparts: a position unique among Korea's normally highly segregated financial institutions. These operations include money market activities, won lending, foreign currency work, the underwriting and securities

TABLE 4.7   Investment and finance companies in Korea

Korea Investment & Finance Corporation[a]	1972
Seoul Investment & Finance Corporation	1973
Pusan Investment & Finance Corporation	1973
Hang Yang Investment & Finance Corporation	1973
Yung Nam Investment & Finance Corporation	1973
Dai Han Investment & Finance Corporation	1973
Orient Investment & Finance Corporation	1973
Central Investment & Finance Corporation	1973
Gwang Ju Investment & Finance Corporation	1974
Tong-Hae Investment & Finance Corporation	1974
Jae Il Investment & Finance Corporation	1977
Jeon Bug Investment & Finance Corporation	1979
Dae Gu Investment & Finance Corporation	1979
Gyeong Nam Investment & Finance Corporation	1979
Dae Jeon Investment & Finance Corporation	1979
Gyeong Gi Investment & Finance Corporation	1980
Hang Do Investment & Finance Corporation	1980
Chung Bug Investment & Finance Corporation	1980

[a] Unlike other short-term finance companies, the Korea Investment & Finance Corporation is a major factor in the underwriting business. This is in part due to its development finance role and foreign shareholders. These include the US investment bank, Goldman Sachs & Co. (5 per cent); the Japanese securities company, Nomura Securities (5 per cent); Banker Trust (5 per cent); PICA (5 per cent); and the World Bank's International Finance Corporation (20 per cent).

TABLE   4.8   Merchant banks in Korea

	Commenced business
Korea Merchant Banking Corporation	14 September 1976
Korea Kuwait Banking Corporation	2 May 1977
Saehan Merchant Banking Corporation	7 November 1977
Korean French Banking Corporation	21 November 1977
Asian Banking Corporation	3 March 1978
Korea International Merchant Bank	14 September 1979

Source: M. T. Skully, *Merchant Banking in the Far East*, 2nd edn (London: Financial Times Business Publishing, 1980) p. 393.

business, financial advice, investment trust management, and leasing services. The money market and its associated short-term finance work is the most developed of these activities and provides the vast majority of the industry's operating income. Since 1978, however, foreign currency loans and the issuance of debentures have increased significantly to account for 23 per cent of the total liabilities and net worth of the industry at the end of 1979.[3]

(vii) *Mutual credit companies*

These companies evolved through the rearrangement of the UMM lenders and started in business in 1969. Their primary function is to absorb small-scale UMM funds through instalment savings and to extend credit loans with instalments. However, these companies were outside government control and caused problems; they frequently got into financial trouble with insufficient capital and engaged in unlawful dealing with the unorganised money market. To protect the public interest sound companies were brought into the official financial system under the Mutual Savings and Finance Company Act of 1972 as mutual savings and finance companies. Their principal business today is to manage the traditional lottery-styled mutual credit associations or '*kyes*' formerly the unorganised money market, as well as to accept mutual instalment savings and advance small unsecured loans or discount bills for members. These operations are subject to strict government controls regarding the loan ceilings to a single individual, net worth, reserve requirements, and interest rates.

(viii) *Trust business*

With the establishment of the Korea Trust Bank in 1968, the five city banks were prohibited from making new trust contracts. The sources of trust funds include money, real estate, securities, and other assets in trust. Money in trust (specified and non-specified) accounts for more than 80 per cent of the total liabilities of the Korea Trust Bank. Slightly more than half of the funds are lent to business firms, and more than 20 per cent of the funds are invested in securities, mostly debentures. The interest rates on money in trust are slightly higher than those on time deposits in banks. In 1976 the Korea Trust Bank was merged with the Seoul Bank renamed the Bank of Seoul and Trust Company.

(ix) *Insurance companies*

The Korean insurance industry has expanded rapidly since 1962 and today 'ranks second in Asia and 28th in the world in terms of scale'.[4] As shown in Table 4.9, it consists at present of 6 life and 13 non-life insurance companies.[5] Their operations are tightly controlled, under the

Insurance Business Law, by a statutory body, the Korean Insurance Corporation and the Ministry of Finance.

Although the life insurance industry is dominated by the six life companies, several government-sponsored self-insurance arrangements – such as the workmen's compensation insurance scheme, the government employees' pension plan, and the military servicemen's insurance programme – are also active in this field. The combined underwriting reserves of the life companies constitute more than 80 per cent of their liabilities and net worth and their major assets consist of securities, real estate and loans held in about equal proportions. The premium rates charged on policies are uniform for all companies and heavily government-controlled; pure endowment insurance is the most popular form of cover.

The non-life companies are most active in fire and marine insurance but offer more specialised policies as well; the premuims involved in each case are set by a government-sponsored committee. The 12 operating companies are also required to reinsure a portion of each policy with the now privately owned, Korean Reinsurance Corporation.

(x) *Credit co-operatives*

Credit co-operatives are non-profit organisations established by small independent business firms, or by the members of a company, church, local community, or other organisation. Savings of the members are loaned out to other members of a co-operative. Having started in 1960, the modern credit co-operative movement in Korea gained further support by the enactment of the Law on National Credit Co-operatives in 1972. The co-operatives are now expected to enhance public confidence and to absorb some of the UMM funds. They are subject to government regulations regarding the credit ceiling of a single person, the maximum interest rates, and reserve holdings. Of the 44,218 credit co-operatives in operation at the end of 1977, 1396 were general credit co-operatives, 1580 agricultural or fishery co-operatives, and 41,242 village credit unions. The first group's association, the Korean Association of Credit Co-operatives, is the local members of the World Council of Credit Unions.

(xi) *Korea Credit Guarantee Fund*

The Korea Credit Guarantee Fund was established under the Korea Credit Guarantee Fund Act to assume the credit guarantee programme

TABLE 4.9 Insurance companies in Korea

	Date established in Korea
Non-life insurance companies (domestic)	
The Oriental Fire & Marine Insurance Co.	1922
The First Fire & Marine Insurance Co.	1939
The Shin Dong-A Fire & Marine Insurance Co.	1946
Dae Han Fire & Marine Insurance Co.	1946
International Fire & Marine Insurance Co.	1947
The Korea Fire & Marine Insurance Co.	1948
The Ankuk Fire & Marine Insurance Co.	1952
Hae Dong Fire & Marine Insurance Co.	1953
The Eastern Marine & Fire Insurance Co.	1955
Pan Korea Marine & Fire Insurance Co.	1959
Korea Automobile Insurance Co.	1962
Korean Reinsurance Co.	1963
Korea Fidelity & Surety Insurance Co.	1969
Life insurance companies (domestic)	
Dae Han Life Insurance Co.	1946
Hung Kuk Life Insurance Co.	1950
The First Life Insurance Co.	1954
Dong Bang Life Insurance Co.	1957
Dae Han Education Life Insurance Co.	1958
Dong Hae Life Insurance Co.	1973

previously conducted by the Medium Industry Bank, and commenced separate operations on 10 June 1976. The Fund is designed to provide credit guarantees against default for those borrowers with insufficient loan collateral. It also conducts credit investigations of these borrowers and will provide some forms of management consulting advice to its customers.

A major source of money for the Fund has been the payment by the commercial banks of a levy of 0.5 per cent on all general (non-government-sponsored) loans – regardless of whether they were guaranteed or not. It was intended that these payments would cease at the end of 1980 but the levy period has now been extended indefinitely.

(xii) *Leasing companies*

As part of its efforts to diversify Korea's sources of medium- and long-term foreign capital, the government encouraged the establishment of specialised foreign affiliated leasing companies and in 1973 Korea's first leasing company, the Korea Industrial Leasing Company commenced operations; it was followed in 1975 by Whashin Tiger Leasing Inc. and the Korea Development Leasing Corporation.[6]

Since their establishment, the leasing companies have proved very successful in the inducement of foreign capital but certain restrictions on the import of additional overseas funds and legal technicalities have hampered their recent growth. Also in 1978, additional competition was introduced for such business with the licensing of merchant banks to enter certain aspects of the industry.

(xiii) *Securities companies*

The securities companies are joint stock companies licensed by the Ministry of Finance to buy and sell securities for their own accounts or on consignment; to act as brokers or agents in the sale or purchase of securities – to underwrite securities – to arrange subscription for the sale of securities; and to finance their customers' purchase of securities. As shown in Table 4.10, there are 27 securities firms operating as members of the stock exchange, but the seven major securities firms dominate the industry. They, together with the merchant banks, are also responsible for virtually all underwriting activities.

(xiv) *Korea Securities Finance Corporation*

The Korea Securities Finance Corporation was established in 1955 to assist the securities companies in financing their operations. Today it is the principal organisation for securities finance in Korea. With borrowings from banks and to a lesser extent issuing its own commercial paper, the company channels the funds necessary for the clearing of brokers' margin transactions, assists the underwriters and subscribers of new issues, and lends to securities companies and individuals against the collateral of their securities.

(xv) *Securities investment trusts*

The securities investment trust business was established in 1970 by the Korea Investment Corporation, and there are now two specialist organisations operating in this area: the Korea Investment Trust Company (established in 1974) and the Daehan Investment Trust Company (established in 1977).

TABLE 4.10 Securities companies in Korea

Bukook Securities Co.
Dae-A Securities Co.
Daebo Securities Co.
Daehan Securities Co.
Daeshin Securities Co.
Daeyu Securities Co.
Dongbang Securities Co.
Dongnam Securities Co.
Dongsuh Securities Co.
Dongwha Securities Co.
Dongyang Securities Co.
Hanheung Securities Co.
Hanil Securities Co.
Hanshin Securities Co.
Hanyang Securities Co.
Hyosung Securities Co.
Ilkuk Securities Co.
Jail Securities Co.
Kukil Securities Co.
Kukje Securities Co.
Kunseul Securities Co.
Sambo Securities Co.
Seoul Securities Co.
Shinheung Securities Co.
Sinyoung Securities Co.
Taipyung Securities Co.
Yuwha Securities Co.

These companies raise their funds through the sale of their trusts' beneficial interests to the public, not unlike a unit trust. The funds raised and the securities purchases, though, are maintained by the Bank of Seoul and Trust Company which acts as the trustee for each issue.

In 1976 the merchant banks also entered the investment trust business but as of 1979 their combined efforts did not even account for a quarter of the business.

FINANCIAL MARKETS

The financial markets in Korea can be divided into three major subgroups: the money market, the securities market, and foreign-exchange business.

(a) Money Markets

The Korean money market is comprised of three major sub-markets: the call market, the private or unorgainsed money market, and the short-term finance market. The call market serves as Korea's inter-bank market and allows the country's banks to manage their daily liquidity positions. The private or unorganised money market is far from unorganised but its street or kerb nature is such that the government has been unable to control its operations: its interest rates are thus probably the only true reflection of the demand for funds within the economy. The short-term finance market is the government-approved equivalent of the unorganised market and is centred around the operations of the investment and finance companies and merchant banks.[7]

(i) *The call money market*

The interbank market in Korea is run by the call transaction centre of the Bankers Association of Korea. The five nationwide banks are traditionally the heaviest borrowers in the market and the special banks, the major suppliers of call funds. The market's maximum interest rate is set at 25 per cent per annum but transactions may be conducted at lower rates as desired.[8]

(ii) *The unorganised money market*

The unorganised money market (UMM) has been an important source of financing for Korean firms and individuals. Indeed one study states it to be considerably bigger than the underground financial markets found in the Philippines and some other Asian countries and to be used by relatively large businesses rather than the petty traders.[9] This is mainly because of government suppression of, and the resulting limited-role played by, the institutional financial markets. There always has been excess demand for bank loans. Firms frustrated by lack of collateral or delays and red-tape involved in loan application procedures, or for other reasons, turn to the UMM market.

Credits to consumers and farmers are especially neglected by organised financial institutions. '*Kye*' is a very popular financial arrangement among individuals. It is a zero-sum scheme of mutual instalment savings and loans, with the saving of some members financing the dissaving of others. Most of the active unorganised credits in the agricultural sector are made in kind, mainly crops and land, to protect lenders against inflation. Farmers borrow from relatives, other farmers, traders, and money lenders for consumption, expenses of farm operations, and farm fixed investments.

There have been several attempts to estimate the size of the UMM based on corporate tax return data and household budget and other surveys. A rather reliable estimate of the UMM could be obtained by the Presidential Emergency Decree of August 1972 which required all of the UMM loans outstanding to business firms to be reported to the National Tax Office. By the decree, loans made to a firm by its major stockholders or executives were to be converted into capital subscriptions to the firm. Other loans of more than three million won were rescheduled to be repaid in eight years with a three-year grace period at the interest rate of 1.35 per cent per month. Small loans of less than three million won were repayable in a maximum period of three years. The reported volume of credit was 354 billion won. This figure does not include the UMM credits within the household sector, and it is believed that many small borrowings were simply not reported. One peculiar feature disclosed by the decree was that almost 30 per cent of the total business UMM loans were so-called disguised UMM loans – those made by major equity holders or executives of the borrowing firms. This phenomenon seems to arise from the interest and tax structures faced by business firms and individuals. In the following, we will focus on the UMM loans to business firms only.

Firms seem to borrow from the UMM for working capital needs mainly to purchase raw materials. Average term of the loans is two to three months. However, it was revealed that the unit sizes of the loans are sometimes very large – suggesting that the UMM loans might be used for fixed investments as well. Interest rates are supposed to be rather sensitive to the risk differentials among borrowers, changing demand and supply conditions in the money market, and the rate of inflation. They typically range from 2.5 per cent to 5.0 per cent per month.

Professional money lenders and relatives or friends of the company men are the major categories of lenders. In contrast with organised financial institutions, these lenders usually do not insist on collateral. According to a survey, fewer than 10 per cent of the loans were secured by real properties or inventories. These professional money lenders seem to be efficient in evaluating credit-standing of borrowers, loan collection, and pricing. However, the UMM is very inefficient in other respects: it is an extremely fragmented market, and information is far from being freely available to potential borrowers and lenders, and transaction costs seem to be significant.

(iii) *The short-term money market*

The short-term money market was established in Korea in 1972 as part of the government's efforts to 'formalise' the unorganised money market. It was intended that the short-term market would attract funds from individuals, corporations and institutions that had previously been invested in the private market. Its operations centre on the dealership and trading operations of the investment and finance companies and to a lesser extent, since 1976, the merchant banks. For practical purposes, this market might well be called the promissory note market as the transactions involved the purchase and sale of promissory notes issued by the investment and finance corporation and merchant banks and their customers. As with most aspects of Korean finance, the rates at which these securities are discounted – be they issued by the institutions themselves or rediscounted (with or without recourse) customer paper – are closely controlled by the government.

(b) Securities Market

The Korea Stock Exchange (KSE) opened in 1956.[10] During the first five years, only government bonds mostly issued during the Korean War were traded on the Exchange. Throughout the 1960s, shares of the KSE, the Korea Securities Finance Corporation, the government-owned Korea Electric Company, and commercial banks dominated the Exchange. No corporate debentures were issued in the open market before 1972. In short, the securities market played only a minor role in mobilising private savings until the early 1970s. On the demand side, there were such attractive alternatives as the UMM loans and real estate investment. On the supply side, despite tax and other concessions, family corporations were reluctant to go public mainly due to the fear of losing perfect control over their corporations, of losing the ability to pay appropriate levels of dividends, and of the leakage of secret information to rival companies. From the beginning of the 1970s, the securities market began to enhance its role thanks to the following measures taken by the government.

There have been a series of measures to create demand for securities. Starting in 1968, in order to discourage real estate investment, capital gains on designated land are taxed at the heavy rate of 50 per cent. Regulations on real estate were reinforced in 1974 when property and acquisition tax rates for such real estates as idle land and luxury houses were raised to a great extent. Furthermore, by the Presidential

Emergency Decree in August 1972, the UMM loans to a business enterprise made by its large shareholders and executives were converted into capital subscriptions, and other UMM loans were rescheduled to be repayable over a maximum period of eight years.

The Law on Fostering the Capital Market of 1968 provided other incentives. Private shareholders of the government-controlled enterprises are guaranteed to receive preferential dividends up to a prescribed rate. Furthermore, dividends received by small shareholders from publicly held or the Exchange-traded corporations are exempted from tax. Starting in 1972, tax exemptions were introduced for the interest income from small corporate bond holdings.

Finally in 1974, the government announced a plan to provide credits of up to 50 per cent of the required capital for private investors subscribing to newly placed securities in the issue market or opening an instalment security savings account. By providing tax concessions and financial supports it also established a joint underwriting system in which the Korea Investment Corporation[11] larger-scale securities companies, banks, investment and finance companies and insurance companies all broadly participated. In addition, new issues in most cases were sold at the par values (that is, at the cost of issuing firms) and were significantly underpriced. It has resulted in an over-subscription phenomenon by those with a short-term speculative motive.

There also have been measures to increase the supply of shares. By the Law on Fostering Capital Market of 1968, tax concessions were given to corporations open to the public. In addition to preferential corporate income tax rates, an additional 20 per cent is allowed in general depreciation allowances on fixed assets. In addition, the Public Corporation Inducement Law of December 1972 empowered the Minister of Finance to designate eligible corporations and force them to go public. Those who were designated and actually went public enjoy some tax benefits, while those who were designated but did not go public are subject to heavier personal and corporate income taxes and restrictions on access to bank credits.

Thanks to these measures, the growth of the Korean stock market during the last decade has been very rapid. The number of companies listing their stocks at the Exchange increased from 42 at the end of 1969 to 355 ten years later. New stock listings have been particularly numerous since 1972 when the Public Corporation Inducement Law was enacted. Similarly the number of shareholders, which was only 54 thousand in 1969, rose to 963 thousand at the end of 1978 before falling slightly to 872 thousand one year later. The total market value of listed stocks has also shown enormous growth with fast increases in both the quantity and the price of listed stocks with the exception of 1979 when the composite stock price index fell. The turnover of market value in the stock market has tended to stabilise since 1965 as the room for grossly speculative dealings has become narrower, although the rate rose from 0.38 in 1974 to 0.78 in 1977 before it decreased back to 0.55 in 1979.

The government and public bond market had declined to a negligible size by 1968 but, thereafter, it has grown steadily with an increasing number of issues. Because of relatively low coupon rates on these bonds, most of them were bought up by government-controlled financial institutions rather than by individual investors. Therefore the growth of the market has been relatively slow. For many years, few corporations issued bonds on the open market. Instead, business firms depended heavily on indirect financing through banks at subsidised interest rates. However, owing to the downward adjustment of bank deposit rates in 1971 and 1972 and the introduction of a corporate bond guarantee system, large firms with good credit ratings could finally afford to issue bonds at competitive interest rates. Since 1978, public offerings of corporate bonds have surpassed the paid-in capital increase of the listed companies. By 1979 the number of listed corporate bonds had increased to 792 issues offered by 356 corporations worth 45 and 38 per cent of the book and market value of listed equity capital respectively.

The Securities and Exchange Commission and its executive body, the Securities Supervisory Board, were established in early 1977 to remedy structural weaknesses remaining in the capital market and, thereby, to maintain fairness in transactions and protect the investors. To encourage the corporate disclosure essential for a competitive market and the optimal price determination of new issues, registration is required for corporations wishing to list their securities on the Exchange, unlisted corporations wishing to sell securities or to merge with a listed firm, and other designated firms.

In addition, the government's supervision and guidance of the operations of securities companies has increased: auditing of listed corporations by certified public accountants has been required, and an improved system of margin transactions and subscription to new equity issues has been established.

(c) Foreign Exchange

Prior to March 1962, all foreign-exchange transactions in Korea were handled by the central bank, the Bank of Korea. The commercial banks were subsequently authorised to conduct such transactions and in 1967 the Korean Exchange Bank was established as a specialised bank within this area.

1980 saw another major change to the Korea foreign-exchange business as the government freed the won from its former link with the US dollar and announced its goal of a freely floating exchange rate system. At present the won is pegged to the International Monetary Fund's Special Drawing Rights quotations but this will eventually be replaced by a trade-weighted basket of the currencies of its major trading partners. In line with these new changes, an expanded forward cover system for importers and exporters' won–US dollar transactions was introduced in mid – 1980. This coverage should be expanded in 1981 to include certain other transactions and similar coverage in Japanese yen, German marks and British sterling.

Today under the Foreign Exchange Control Act, the commercial banks ' authorisation falls within two catagories: Class A and Class B licensing. The former may establish correspondent bank accounts overseas and handle their own transactions whereas the latter must use Class A banks for these purposes. Interestingly, since 1977 merchant banks have been given Class A licensing. Such authorisation is particularly necessary if one wishes to be active in the on-leading for foreign currency.

Foreign currency loans have been very important in achieving Korea's recent history of economic growth as its long-term development plans, established in early 1960, required enormous amounts of foreign exchange to be implemented. Also at this time, the United States had made it clear that aid in the form of grants would gradually be decreased and be replaced by development loans. Therefore the government started to prepare institutional arrangements to encourage the inflow of foreign loans. As a tax benefit, interest income accruing to foreign lenders is to be tax-exempt for the first five years after the introduction of a loan, and subject to only 50 per cent of the appropriate tax burden for the following three years. On the other hand, to protect foreign lenders from default and foreign-exchange risks, bank guarantees have been made for the repayment of foreign loans. In addition, various types of investment guarantees provided by the US and Japanese governments to their nationals for their loans to (or investments in) Korea undoubtedly helped to make the default risk of foreign lenders practically negligible. At the end of 1979 the total outstanding external debt reached US$ 14.7 billion. The debt service ratio was stable at the 11 to 12 per cent level during 1974–8 before it rose to 14.7 per cent in 1979.[12]

Every enterprise wishing to use a foreign loan first has to obtain the approval of the Economic Planning Board. Once the loan is approved, the BOK or the KEB issues a guarantee to the foreign lender, and the KDB or a commercial bank issues a guarantee to the BOK. In this process, however, the banks involved play no critical role. Loan arrangements are made directly between the borrower and lender, and then approved by the government. The banks issue the repayment guarantees passively on the instructions of the government without careful evaluatiion of the projects.

Interest rates on these foreign loans typically have been 1.0–2.5 percentage points higher than those on comparable loans in the Eurodollar market. The interest rate differentials, without any significant risks, have been large enough to attract many foreign lenders. Korean enterprises have also been eager to borrow abroad since foreign loans are much cheaper than domestic borrowings and they have limited access to the foreign exchange badly needed for some projects. However, it is suspected that foreign loans are in general much more expensive than the contracted interest rates. Most foreign loans are in the form of suppliers' credit, and the delivered equipment and machines very often do not comply with domestic requirements. Furthermore, in the early years at least, borrowers were usually supposed to compensate government officials for their favour of loan approval. Finally, additional cost arising from the possible exchange devaluations within the repayment period may be high considering the experience of periodic upward adjustments in the exchange rate expressed in won per US dollar.

ANALYSIS

Reform of the financial system has been one of the most frequently raised issues in the recent policy discussions in Korea. To many observers the growth of the financial sector lags behind that of the real economy. For one thing, the ratio of bank deposits or other financial assets to sales of non-financial business enterprises has sharply declined. The rate of increase in general bank loans has been lower than the rate of current GNP growth. Despite the small number of nationwide commercial banks, the site of individual banks is very small: total deposits of the five nationwide commercial banks is roughly equivalent to the deposits of a local bank in Japan.

It is believed that the dominance of government banking institutions is responsible, to a large extent, for the sluggish growth of the banking sector. Only local banks and the branches of foreign banks in Korea are truly private and then account for only 15 per cent of the total bank loans and discounts. Since the voting right of an individual private shareholder is restricted to the maximum 10 per cent by the Provisional Law on Financial Institutions, the government or quasi-government authorities, holding about 30 per cent of the shares in each of the five nationwide commercial banks, has little difficulty in running these banks as it wishes.

Because of direct government involvement in the management of the government-owned financial institutions, there is a general lack of autonomy in personnel management, budget formulation and execution, and asset management in these institutions. For example, elected bank presidents and directors, changes in the maximum employable number of bank employees, the budgets of banks, and bank acquisition of real estate for business operations all require the approval of the director of the Office of Bank Supervision and Examination. The uniformity and rigidity in the control of bank organisation, budgets, and personnel management without regard for their varying functions and conditions limit inter-bank competition, impede any innovative efforts in banking management, and tend to invite excessive and unlawful government interference. Unsound lending due to external pressure, lax manpower management, irrational outlays and other types of business inefficiency which reflect the absence of the profit motive have been widespread phenomena.

Another related area of concern is the continuation of preferential loans. New categories of preferential loans have been created without due consideration of the availability of additional funds and without clear criteria for granting such loans. Owing to this expansion of preferential loan categories, they now account for more than 40 per cent of total loans and have greatly reduced the availability of the general loans. Interest rates on preferential loans vary greatly as a differential rate is applied every time a new type of loan is provided. Thus, different interest rates are charged on a similar types of loans granted for similar purposes.

Since general consensus has been built up concerning the need and basic direction of the financial reform, it is expected that the Korean financial sector will undergo substantial changes in the coming decade. The role of the government in monetary matters will largely be limited to the formulation of overall macroeconomic policy, whereas the formulation and the implementation of detailed monetary policy, as well as the supervision of banking institutions, will to a large extent be left to the central bank. Government intervention in personnel management, budgeting processes, and the business operations of financial institutions will be minimised.

The thrust of monetary control will gradually shift from existing direct credit controls towards indirect measures such as open market operations and flexible adjustments of the rediscount and other interest rates. An adequate supply of securities available for open market operations and a realistic interest yield on those securities are crucial for the activation of these operations. For the rediscount rate adjustment to be an effective tool of monetary management, the BOK should be freed from the obligation of providing export and other preferential financing. Banks and the non-bank financial institutions will be given gradually greater autonomy in determining interest rates according to changes in deposits, demand for loans and inter-market flow of funds. Though the present financial situation requires the continuation of the preferential loan system, the total amount, as well as the priority in the allocation, of such loans will have to be determined in advance and the interest rate structure will be rationalised. For more effective monetary management and to avoid excessive credit squeeze on the non-preferential sectors, the provisions for preferential credit have to be more selective, limited to industries such as machinery and some other heavy and chemical industries in which Korea is known to have relatively greater comparative advantage among industries.

The above measures will promote sound and competitive business practices in the financial markets, and will be a precondition for the denationalisation of the commercial banks. The denationalisation of existing commercial banks is a necessary step toward the modernisation of the entire financial system and the growth of internationally competitive financial institutions. As a first step, the Provisional Law on Financial Institutions will have to be repealed and temporary measures should be taken concerning the government ownership of banks and the government's voting right at the general meetings of the banks' shareholders.[13] Establishment of new commercial banks wholly owned by the private sector will also be encouraged.[14] Non-bank financial intermediaries will be stimulated to expand their operations and to develop new financial assets to meet the diversified demands of savers. Capital markets will continuously be fostered, and the direct financing of long-term business investment through these markets will be encouraged. In order to maintain a close relation between the Korean economy and those of foreign countries, financial institutions should grow and upgrade themselves to international standards, in terms of scale and quality of financial services. In this regard, the opening of overseas branch offices would be beneficial.[15] Moreover, businesses will be encouraged to turn to the international capital markets for their ever-expanding demand for long-term investment funds.

TRENDS AND PREDICTIONS

The prospect for the future trend of financial growth and deepening will depend heavily on the level of nominal interest rates as well as the inflation rate. If financial institutions are freed from excessive government regulation, inflationary pressure is constrained and, at the same time, interest rates are allowed to be freely determined in the market or adjusted to a level near the equilibrium rate, an increasing rate in the process of financial deepening is likely. Otherwise, financial deepening will proceed at a very slow pace or may even move backward.

In the near future, it is expected that the money supply will maintain its share while time and savings deposits will grow faster than total financial assets provided that adequate incentives are given through higher real interest rates. Insurance, trust and short-term finance company deposits are expected to grow most rapidly among all categories of financial assets, reflecting their high income elasticities and the infant stages of development of these instruments. Public and corporate bond markets are also expected to grow at a rapid rate as the authorities issue more public debentures to more efficiently manage the money supply through open market operations. In addition, more firms are able to raise debt in the market. Steady expansion of the stock market largely through rising capital gains will also contribute to the growing share of securities in total financial assets. Finally, foreign debt holdings will increase at a very slow rate, sharply reducing their ratio to total financial assets outstanding.

With respect to corporate capital structure, there has been deep concern over the extremely high corporate financial leverage. At book values, the debt–equity ratio of Korean corporations in manufacturing was as high as 3.77 in 1979. The financial leverage is even higher than that of Japanese corporations whose reliance on external borrowings can hardly compare with the cases of other developed countries. During 1979/80 when tight credit together with severe repression hit the economy hard, some of the highly leveraged firms went bankrupt. As an attempt to improve the corporate capital structure, the government, in September 1980, made it compulsory for major corporations to report their holdings of real estate and to dispose some of their real estate held for non-operational purpose.

The effect of this measure is yet to be seen. However, the excessive holdings of borrowings and real estate for Korean corporations seem to have been dictated by the environment: chronic inflation, relatively high cost of internal funds, repressed interest rates on organised financial market loans, imposition of personal income tax on retained earnings of privately-held corporations, tax deduction for interest payments and insufficient corporate depreciation allowances based on book values. Therefore, together with an effort to develop a sound stock market, attentions should be directed to the tax and interest rate structures and other factors affecting corporate financing behaviour.

NOTES

1. Jae Yoon Kim (ed.), *Financial System of Korea* (Seoul: Bank of Korea, 1978) provides additional details on the Bank of Korea's establishment and operations.
2. Sang-Kyo Lee, 'Korea Carves out a Niche for Foreign Banks', *Asian Banking*, September 1980, pp. 70–5, and 'Foreign Banks in Korea', *Korea Exchange Bank Monthly Review*, August 1978, pp. 1–12, provide more details on this subject.
3. M. T. Skully, *Merchant Banking in the Far East*, 2nd edn. (London: Financial Times Business Publishing, 1980) ch. 9, provides a detailed discussion of these institutions' operations in Korea.
4. 'Korea Insurance is No. 2 in Asia', *Asian Money Manager*, October 1979, p. 32.
5. The American International Underwriters and American Foreign Insurance Association are also authorised to conduct business within Korea. Three other foreign insurance companies are jointly operating with Korean insurance companies: Royal Insurance of the UK with Oriental Fire Insurance, Tokyo Marine Insurance of Japan with Korea Fire Insurance, and Continental Insurance of US with First Fire Insurance. The American Home Assurance Co., Hartford Fire Insurance Co., American Defender Life Insurance, American Fidelity Life Insurance Co., First National Life Insurance Company of America, Midland National Life Insurance Company, Prudential Insurance Company of America, Trans World Assurance, and United Life Insurance Co. are also represented in Korea but restrict their business to foreign residents – mainly those associated with the United States military.
6. 'Korea's Leasing Industry', *Korea Exchange Bank Monthly Review*, September 1978, pp. 1–8, provides additional details on their operations.
7. A more detailed discussion of the short-term money market, particularly as related to merchant banks, may be found in M. T. Skully, *Merchant Banking in the Far East*, pp. 397–400.

8. *The Korean Economy: Review and Prospects* (Seoul: Korea Exchange Bank, 1980) p. 107.
9. *Capital Markets in Asia's Developing Countries* (Hong Kong: Business International, 1976) p. 143, and M. T. Skully, 'Seoul's Street Money Lenders', *Far Eastern Economic Review*, 20 May 1977, pp. 53–5, also provide details on the market's earlier operations and the introduction of the short-term finance companies.
10. Kim Tae-Cheon (ed.), *Securities Market in Korea* (Seoul: Korea Securities Dealers Association, 1977) provides more details on the Stock Exchange's operations and the securities industry in general.
11. The Korea Investment Corporation was established in 1968 as a Joint venture of the government and the banks to assist in the development of the securities market. It provided best effort arrangements and outright or stand-by underwriting, guaranteed corporate bonds, provided credits to subscribers of public offerings, and made general loans against the collateral of designated securities. It was also responsible for the establishment of the first investment trust operations (later assumed by the Korea Investment Trust Company) and the stabilisation of stock price movements on the exchange. Prior to its closure in 1976 it was a leading participant in the distribution of new shares and corporate bonds.
12. Further discussion of Korea's foreign borrowing position may be found in 'Korea's Borrowing in International Financial Markets', *Korea Exchange Bank Monthly Review*, June 1979, pp. 1–20.
13. In December 1980 the government announced a plan to transfer its majority shareholdings in four of the five nationwide banks to private hands over the next three years and to lessen the government controls over the operations of these institutions. The first of these banks will be placed under private ownership in 1981 and the other banks will be handed over to the private sector step-by-step as financial conditions permit.
14. In December 1980 the government announced plans to allow the establishment of one joint venture bank with foreign participation to operate within the Korean market. The ownership is expected to be 51 per cent Korean and 49 per cent foreign. A large American bank is expected to be the foreign partner and the Korean shareholders may be from the banking sector and individuals.
15. Many of the Korean banks already have branch representation overseas. At the end of 1980 these included: the Korean Exchange Bank, 15; the Cho Heung Bank, 3; the Commercial Bank of Korea, 4; Korea First Bank, 6; the Hanil Bank, 5; and the Bank of Seoul and Trust Company, 3. In addition, many have majority and minority shareholdings in foreign banks, merchant banks, and other financial institutions overseas, as well as many representatative offices.

5 Financial Institutions and Markets in Taiwan

CHING-ING HOU LIANG and MICHAEL T. SKULLY

INTRODUCTION

(a) The Setting

Located approximately 100 miles off the Chinese mainland, Taiwan's 17.2 million people enjoy the fourth highest per capita income in Asia. As this tobacco leaf-shaped island's 35,854 square kilometres contains only limited mineral resources, its economic development record is all the more impressive.

In 1946 it had a population of 6 million people and was basically a two-crop agricultural economy, dependent on rice and sugar cane: what manufacturing that existed related to processing these products. With the transfer of the capital of the Republic of China to Taipei in December 1949, however, Taiwan began its transformation, concentrating on agricultural production and infrastructure in the 1950s, industrialisation specialising in consumer durable and other labour-intensive production in the 1960s, and shifting from labour-intensive light industry to more sophisticated and heavy industry in the 1970s.[1] The success of these changes is reflected in the country's economic growth rate which, starting with the government's first four-year plan in 1953, averaged 6.1 per cent per annum for the first decade and 10.1 per cent for the second.

Having only limited amounts of natural gas and coal, Taiwan's enviable growth trend was broken with the oil crisis and economic instability of the 1970s and in 1974 the GNP grew by only 0.6 per cent. Fortunately the government's resulting Economic Stabilisation

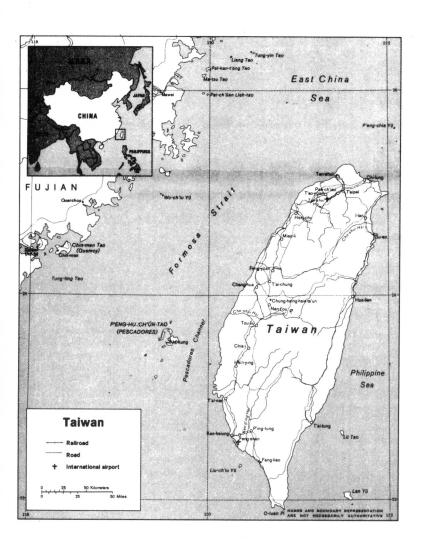

MAP 5.1   Taiwan

Source: United States Department of State, Bureau of Public Affairs, July 1980.

Programme, which entailed tight credit through a large across-the-board upward adjustment of bank rates as well as once-and-for-all substantial price increases on government-controlled goods and services, was able to bring inflation back to more moderate levels and economic growth returned as well. Thus in 1978 and 1979, when many other countries were suffering from stagnation and recession, Taiwan's real gross national product grew by 13.8 per cent and 8.03 per cent respectively. Today it is the twentieth largest trading and the sixteenth largest exporting country in the world.

(b) An Overview of the Financial Sector

The development of a country's financial system often reflects the nation's historical background. In China, for example, 'flying money' (remittances) was widely practised during the reign of Shen-Chung of the Tang Dynasty in the ninth century. Paper money, called 'Chiao-Tze' and 'Hwei-Tze', was issued by the Emperors of the Sung Dynasty in 1001 and 1127, even though it was short-lived. Finally 'Piao-Haw' (bill exchangers) and 'Chien-Chung' (native bankers) appeared in northern China and the Shanghai area in the eighteenth and nineteenth centuries.[2]

It would be erroneous, however, to say that China's banking system evolved from 'Chien-Chung'. It instead developed under the influence of the British colonial banks. The financial system in Taiwan today is a mixture of the reactivated banking institutions of mainland China, Taiwan's own financial system developed under the Japanese colonial government before the Second World War, and newly-established financial institutions.

As a middle-income developing country, Taiwan's financial sector has been undergoing a process of rapid transition. Table 5.1 provides some key indicators of Taiwan's success in financial deepening.[3] The most important measure, as shown in the table, was to offer savers a positive real rate of return; thus financial deepening advanced progressively when wholesale price stability was achieved in the 1960s.[4] The M_2 to GDP ratio increased from 30.5 per cent in 1961–5 to 37.8 per cent in 1966–70. M_2 deflated by the wholesale price index, which represents the real lending capacity of the organised banking sector,[5] grew 12 times during the period. This strengthened liquidity position provided an important base from which the commercial banks' credit expansion could proceed. Increased credit availability and relative price stability in

TABLE 5.1   Key indicators of financial deepening, 1961–79

	1961–5	1966–70	1971–5	1976–9
1. Ratio of M_1 to GDP (%)	14.3	15.0	17.6	21.9
2. Ratio of M_2 to GDP (%)	30.5	37.8	49.8	66.6
3. Percentage change in wholesale price index	1.03	1.89	12.57	5.72
4. Interest rate on one-year deposits (%)	12.91	9.83	10.91	10.56
5. Real return on holding one-year deposits (%)	11.88	7.94	−1.66	4.84
6. M_2 at 1976 constant prices (billions of NT dollars)	53.5	119.4	268.8	565.2
7. Ratio of net private national saving to national income (%)	9.5	12.2	16.9	16.3
8. Government bonds outstanding as percentage of GDP	1.9	4.2	2.4	1.2
9. Corporate bonds outstanding as percentage of GDP	0.2	0.3	0.3	1.2
10. Market value of stocks outstanding as percentage of GDP	20.0[a]	8.6	12.1	14.9

Notes: [a] The stock market was established in 1962.

M_1 = Net currency issued + demand deposits adjusted.

M_2 = M_1 + quasi-money.

M_2 at 1976 constant prices is deflated by the wholesale price index.

The percentage figures relate to the ratio of financial instruments outstanding to GDP.

GDP is used as the denominator owing to the unavailability of national wealth statistics.

Owing to the overall revision of *Financial Statistics Monthly, Taiwan District, The Republic of China*, the data of money supply and deposits are not available prior to July 1961.

Sources: DGBAS: (1) Commodity Price Statistics Monthly, *Taiwan District, The Republic of China;* (2) *National Income of the Republic of China.* Economic Research Department, The Central Bank of China: *Financial Statistics Monthly, Taiwan District, The Republic of China.*

turn helped reduce interest rates. The dampening of inflationary expectations contributed not only to the extraordinary financial growth, but also to the rise of the net private saving ratio from 9.5 per cent of national income in 1961–5 to 12.2 per cent in 1966–70.

Since the value of corporate bonds and shares outstanding as percentage of GDP show no clear growth trend over this period, the banking system's contribution to economic growth has been considerable. Indeed a principal characteristic of Taiwan corporate finance is a heavy dependence on bank credit.[6]

FINANCIAL INSTITUTIONS

As shown in Table 5.2, Taiwan's financial institutions can be broken into 12 different subgroupings with the domestic banks being the most important.[7] These subgroups, though, can be classified into two groups, monetary and other financial institutions, with the Central Bank of China serving as the nucleus of the financial system and acting as the lender of last resort.[8]

TABLE 5.2   Major financial institutions in Taiwan (by total assets in October 1980)

Institutional type[a]	NT$ billion	Percentage of total
Central Bank of China	426.9	20.5
Domestic banks	1080.6	51.9
Foreign banks	89.3	4.3
Medium business banks	61.4	3.0
Postal savings system	131.3	6.3
Investment and trust companies[b]	66.1	3.2
Bill finance companies	4.3	0.2
Life insurance companies	20.9	1.0
Fire and marine insurance companies	7.4	0.4
Credit co-operative associations	111.7	5.4
Credit departments of farmers' associations	79.8	3.8
Total[c]	2079.7	100.0

[a] Excludes mention of the securities finance companies, the first of which commenced operation during 1980.

[b] Figures for investment and trust companies are for September 1980 and include the assets of the China Development Corporation.

[c] There are some elements of doubt in counting the total figures. Savings deposits, for examples, are collected by the postal savings system and redeposited with the Central Bank which in turn channels them into the long- and medium-term loan fund used to support long- and medium-term commercial bank lending.

Source: Economic Research Department, the Central Bank of China, *Financial Statistics Monthly, Taiwan District, The Republic of China* (November 1980).

(a) Banking Institutions

The banking or monetary system in Taiwan consists of six major subgroups: the central bank; domestic banks; local branches of foreign banks; medium business banks; credit co-operatives; and the credit departments of farmers' and fishermen's associations.[9]

(i) *The Central Bank*

The Central Bank of China was founded in Canton in 1924 and commenced normal central bank functions for the Republic of China in 1928. With the removal of the central government from the mainland to Taipei in 1949, though, many of its functions were delegated to the Bank of Taiwan, then the provincial government's most important as well as the largest bank on the island. The Central Bank of China resumed its functions on 1 July 1961.

The Central Bank of China performs all normal central banking functions.[10] It issues currency, formulates interest rate policy, determines reserve ratios against deposits, and provides lender of last resort facilities to banking institutions. The Central Bank supervises financial institutions and conducts periodical examinations of their operation, paying special attention to the soundness of their business practices, and their compliance with monetary regulations. The Central Bank is also the fiscal agent of the national government for currency issue, handling treasury receipts and disbursements, managing the country's holding of foreign-exchange, performing economic research, compiling financial statistics, and advising the government on economic and monetary matters.

In conducting its operations the Bank is required under Article 1 of the Central Bank Law to: promote monetary stability; promote a sound financial and banking system; maintain internal and external stability for the value of the currency; and, consistent with the above, foster economic development.

In terms of monetary management the Central Bank's operations are conducted primarily through four distinct policy areas: interest rate controls; reserve requirements; open-market operations; and selective credit controls.

The Bank's influence on bank interest rates is effected in two ways. First, the Bank adjusts the interest rates on its own rediscount and other credit accommodation facilities offered to the banking system in light of the monetary situation and, equally important, makes these changes public. Secondly, the Bank may, at its discretion, prescribe a uniform upper limit for interest rates on bank deposits and approve the range of the interest rates on bank loans as proposed by the Bankers' Association.[11]

The Bank's power to require the banks to keep reserves against bank deposits also has an important impact as they can be adjusted within certain limits in the light of monetary conditions between 15 and 40 per cent for chequing deposits, 10 and 35 per cent for demand deposits, 5 and 20 per cent for savings deposits, and 7 and 25 per cent for time deposits. In addition, since July 1974, the Bank has been able to prescribe extra reserve requirements (not subject to the normal limits) on any incremental increase in cheque and demand deposits after a specific date: the first of these, a 5 per cent ratio of liquid assets to deposits, was introduced on 1 August 1977.[12] It can also stipulate in what forms these extra reserves may be maintained. This enables the Bank to correct over-liquidity more rapidly and also encourages the secondary trading of acceptable reserve securities within the money market.

Although the Bank has had the power to conduct open-market operations as a means of monetary policy, 1979 was the first time it was used. These operations may include the purchase and sale of government and government-guaranteed securities, financial debentures issued by banks, and bank bills guaranteed or accepted by banks. When required for monetary adjustment, the Bank may also issue and trade in its own certificates of time deposit, savings bonds, and short-term bonds.

Finally, under its selective credit controls the Bank may impose maximum loan ratios on the appraised value of commodities or real estate used as collateral for secured bank loans. Similarly it can prescribe and regulate the down-payment and period of credit offered on bank loans for the purchase or construction of buildings and the purchase of durable consumer goods, and prescribe regulations on the accommodations extended by banks to securities dealers or securities finance companies.

(ii) *The domestic banks*

As was shown in Table 5.2, the domestic banks form the backbone of Taiwan's financial sector, comprising some 51.9 per cent of the total assets of major financial institutions. Aside from commercial banking operations, most of the 15 domestic banks operate savings and foreign-exchange departments, and three have trust departments. However, the fact that 11 of these are majority government-owned has meant that some degree of specialisation has developed.[13] The Bank of Communications for example, once primarily a commercial bank, is now chartered as a development bank to foster the development of the manufacturing, mining, transportation industries and public utilities. It extends medium- and long-term credit and guarantees to capital-intensive precision industries, invests in pioneering firms, and renders advice to customers to improve their management and expedite technical innovation. The Farmers Bank of China specialises in financing agricultural development and promoting rural construction. The Land Bank of Taiwan specialises in land and agricultural credit, promoting agricultural development, handling housing programmes and assisting the government in carrying out its land and agricultural policies. The Co-operative Bank of Taiwan serves as 'a central banking institution' for co-operatives, provides credit to agriculture and fisheries and, on authorisation of the Central Bank, examines the operations of credit cooperatives and credit departments of farmers' and fishery associations. The City Bank of Taipei acts as the fiscal agent of the Taipei Municipal Government and handles the flotation of the city's bonds. The Bank of Taiwan, the *de facto* central bank between December 1949 and June 1961, acts as the fiscal agent for the provincial government. Finally the Central Trust of China, besides commercial banking and foreign-exchange, is engaged in the trust and insurance business, serves as an agent for government procurements, and performs regular trading business for both public and private enterprises. The newest of the government-owned banks, the Export–Import Bank of China, was founded in January 1979 and is involved in: extending medium- and long-term credit and guarantees to the exports of plant and equipment and overseas construction projects; export insurance; and country risk surveys and credit investigation. As financing of plant and equipment on a deferred-payment basis involves higher credit risks, the specialised Export–Import Bank supplements the International Commercial Bank of China and other commercial banks' involvement in this area. It also, where possible, participates with foreign banks in overseas lending to preclude political reasons being used for non-payment.

The remaining three government banks, the First Commercial Bank of Taiwan, Chang Hwa Commercial Bank, and the Hua Nan Commercial Bank, are partially owned by the provincial government and provide extensive commercial banking facilities throughout the island; as shown in Table 5.3, they have the largest branch structures of the domestic banks.

The four non-government-owned commercial banks – the Shanghai Commercial and Savings Bank, the International Commercial Bank of China, the Overseas Chinese Commercial Banking Corporation and the United World Chinese Commercial Bank – are relatively small compared with the state banks; the Shanghai Commercial and the United World Chinese, for example, have only one branch each. The International Commercial Bank, which was reorganised from the Bank of China into

TABLE 5.3 Domestic banks (figures as of 31 October 1980)

Bank	NT$ million deposits	No. of branches
Bank of Taiwan	122641	52
City Bank of Taipei	40531	17
Bank of Communications	18186	9
The Farmers Bank of China	23714	17
The Central Trust of China	3906	3
Land Bank of Taiwan	70341	50
The Co-operative Bank of Taiwan	85591	64
The First Commercial Bank	71219	99
Hua Nan Commercial Bank	64198	81
Chang Hua Commercial Bank	70748	98
Export–Import Bank of China	*	1
International Commercial Bank of China	15788	14
Overseas Chinese Commercial Banking Corporation	5619	8
Shanghai Commercial and Savings Bank	1595	1
United World Chinese Commercial Bank	7477	1

* Cannot accept deposits.

Source: Central Bank of China (1980).

a private banking corporation on 18 December 1971 is the largest of the four and through its six overseas branches and agencies in New York, Chicago, Tokyo, Osaka, Bangkok, and Panama, is also active in international trade and foreign-exchange.

As shown in Table 5.4, 60.1 per cent of the domestic banks' assets are held in the form of loans and advances and of these NT$646,048 million, 75 per cent were made to private enterprises. Of the total loans, 1.1 per cent were in the form of discounts, 0.7 per cent in advances on imports, 60.5 per cent in short-term advances and the remaining 37.7 per cent in medium- and longer-term loans. While approximately 60 per cent of the banks' advances are officially secured loans, much of the unsecured, particularly short-term, loans in fact utilise post-dated cheques as *de facto* security. Indeed, such short term advances are used in Taiwan in place of an overdraft: the latter facility is seldom granted.

In terms of funding, deposits of various forms, particularly savings deposits, comprise almost half of the banks' capital and liabilities; shareholders' funds amount to only 4 per cent. Though as yet not an important source of funding, the domestic banks have also raised some funds overseas in the form of Eurodollar borrowings, floating rate notes and certificates of deposit.

TABLE 5.4 Domestic banks' assets and liabilities (August 1980)

	Percentage of assets	*NT$ million*
Types of assets		
Cash in vault	1.1	12396
Claims on financial institutions	7.5	80728
Government securities	1.2	13215
Other securities	5.5	58660
Loans and discounts	60.1	646048
Foreign assets	24.1	259453
Fixed assets	0.5	4970
Total assets (net)	100.0	1075470
Type of liability		
Cheque accounts	7.1	76280
Passbook deposits	4.5	48325
Time deposits	10.6	114052
Savings deposits	19.3	207357
Foreign currency deposits	0.3	3140
Government deposits	6.9	74280
Amounts due financial institutions	34.3	369095
Presettlement for imports	1.8	19414
Foreign liabilities	8.3	89577
Other items	6.9	73950
Total liabilities (net)	100.0	1075470

Source: *Financial Statistics Monthly, Taiwan District, The Republic of China* (September 1980) pp. 17–20.

(iii) *The foreign banks*

Foreign banks are allowed to establish branch or representative offices in Taiwan but are restricted to one per bank and this must be located in Taipei or Kaohsiung. At present 21 foreign banks have established branch operations: their names, home countries, and local establishment dates are shown in Table 5.5. They are authorised to handle foreign-exchange transactions and extend loans to customers. They may also accept local currency demand deposits, but not time deposits, up to 12.5 times their local paid-in capital to a maximum amount of NT$1 billion. These funds are supplemented by inter-bank borrowings and, depending on local monetary conditions, offshore borrowings.

Though technically there is no difference between the powers of the

TABLE 5.5   Foreign banks in Taiwan, 1980

	Nationality	Date established in Taiwan
Banks with branches		
The Dai-Ichi Kangyo Bank Ltd	Japan	10 September 1958
Bank of America	USA	31 March 1965
Bangkok Bank Ltd	Thailand	25 April 1965
Citibank NA	USA	28 February 1967
American Express International Banking Corp.	USA	21 June 1967
Metropolitan Bank and Trust Company	Philippines	30 September 1967
Chase Manhattan Bank NA	USA	5 December 1972
Continental Illinois Bank and Trust Co.	USA	31 January 1973
Irving Trust Company	USA	8 February 1973
United California Bank	USA	16 July 1974
Chemical Bank	USA	16 November 1974
The Toronto Dominion Bank	Canada	4 March 1975
International Bank of Singapore	Singapore	16 October 1978
Rainier National Bank	USA	2 April 1980
First National Bank of Boston	USA	19 April 1980
Seattle-First National Bank	USA	21 April 1980
Grindlays Bank Ltd	UK	20 August 1980
European Asian Bank	Germany	22 September 1980
Société Générale	France	25 September 1980
Banque de Paris et des Pays-Bas	France	6 October 1980
Hollandische Bank Unie NV	Holland	17 December 1980
Banks with representative offices		
Bankers Trust Company	USA	15 December 1973
Singer & Friedlander Ltd	UK	25 March 1974
Bank of California NA	USA	2 April 1976
Security Pacific National Bank[a]	USA	7 October 1976
Manufacturers Hanover Trust Company	USA	27 December 1979
Bank of Canton of California	USA	to open

[a] Plans to upgrade to branch status.

various foreign banks, the more recent arrivals seem to be at some disadvantage. As one regional magazine reported the Ministry of Finance's attitude, 'if they do not engage in an unspecified amount of term lending, they will not be granted licenses for current accounts'.[14] Also, although the government encourages banks from countries not already represented in Taiwan, other foreign banks may find entry, either by a branch or representative office, more difficult in the future. Basically, branch applicants are expected to conduct some US$100 million of business a year for at least three years with Taiwan of which at least US$60 million is comprised of medium- to long-term lending to major Taiwan enterprises; some US$500 million of business in the year prior to applying, and a total of US$1000 million worth of business over the three previous years. Even to open a representative office, there is a requirement for a minimum of US$100 million (including US$20 million in medium- to long-term loans) of Taiwan business to be maintained. These requirements may be waived to some extent, however, should the bank's country of residence not be already represented in Taiwan and if it allows reciprocity for Taiwanese banks.[15]

(iv) *Medium business banks*

While the medium business banks are relatively new financial institutions within Taiwan, they developed from the country's long-standing mutual loans and savings companies. These in turn were an outgrowth of the old mutual finance pools organised by private individuals and common to most Asian countries. Under Article 96 of the Banking Law, medium business banks' main functions consist of extending medium- and long-term credit to improve machinery and equipment, financial structure, management and business operations of medium business enterprises; traditionally the mutual loans and savings companies were a major source of funds for small business.

There are at present eight medium business banks in operation: their names and number of branches are shown in Table 5.6. As reflected in the names, their operations and branches are restricted within a certain district of the island. The exception to this, the partly government-owned Medium Business Bank of Taiwan, however, has branches throughout the island: the Bank of Taiwan is its majority shareholder. At the end of October 1980, the medium business banks had assets of NT$61,444 million, 75 per cent of which were in loans and 9 per cent in securities.

(v) *Co-operatives*

As with much of Taiwan's financial system, the first credit co-operative was established during the Japanese occupation in 1908. There are now three different varieties: credit co-operative associations; the credit departments of farmers' associations; and the credit departments of fishery associations.

TABLE 5.6   Medium business banks

Established	Name	Reorganised	Branches
28 April 1946	Medium Business Bank of Taiwan	1 July 1976	71
4 May 1948	Taipei Business Bank	7 November 1977	23
7 January 1949	Medium Business Bank of Hsinchu District	2 December 1977	14
1 August 1953	The Medium Business Bank of Taichung District	1 January 1978	20
1 November 1952	The Medium Business Band of Tainan District	1 January 1978	14
1 November 1950	The Medium Business Bank of Kaohsiung District	30 June 1978	13
1 November 1952	The Medium Business Bank of Hualien District	1 January 1979	4
12 January 1952	The Medium Business Bank of Taitung District	1 January 1979	3

There are at present some 75 credit co-operative associations with 199 branches mainly in the urban areas of Taiwan. They may accept deposits and grant loans only to their members and offer some banking services such as cheque accounts, passbook deposits and time savings accounts. At the end of October 1980, credit co-operatives had assets of NT$111,719 million, 66 per cent of which were loans to members and 32 per cent deposits with other financial institutions.

The credit departments of the local farmers' associations in 298 of Taiwan's townships assist in extending agricultural credit in Taiwan. They accept deposits from and extend loans to farming members, handle remittances, and serve as the agents for the Land Bank of Taiwan, the Co-operative Bank of Taiwan, the Farmers Bank of China and other government agencies. As the demand for farm credit is highly seasonal and a farmer's credit standing may appear poor, commercial banks are less willing to service this sector. As the various government agencies are specialists in agricultural lending and loan on the basis of the farmer's future production, these agency arrangements play a vital role in agricultural development as do the various agricultural extension services normally associated with these associations. At the end of October 1980, credit departments of farmers' associations had assets of NT$79,301 million, 50 per cent of which were loans to members and 39 per cent deposits with other financial institutions.

The credit departments of fishery associations serve a similar function to those of the farmers' associations and the associations themselves are also very much involved in the supply, processing, and marketing of the goods concerned. There are at present four fishery association credit departments in operation.

(b) Non-banking Financial Institutions

The banking system is capable of creating money autonomously whereas non-banking financial institutions create credit only as a result of borrowing 'idle' money and making it 'active'. The main effect of an increase in the credit of non-banking financial institutions is to increase the velocity of circulation of a given money stock.[16] The criterion on which the distinction is based has important analytical significance, even though the distinction between the banks and the non-banking financial institutions is difficult to draw precisely in practice. For discussion purposes, Taiwan's postal savings system, investment and trust companies, insurance companies, bill finance companies, and securities finance companies have been included within the non-banking section and are officially classified as 'other financial institutions'.

(i) *The postal savings system*

The postal savings system, run by the Directorate General of Postal Remittances and Savings Banks, was established in China in 1930 and commenced operations on Taiwan in June 1962. Through 898 post offices and 1481 postal agencies, the system accepts savings deposits and handles remittances both locally and to overseas countries, but does not extend loans. The savings deposits raised are then redeposited with the Central Bank to be channelled into the long- and medium-term loan funds which extends credit to investment projects through commercial banks at a preferential interest rate. At the end of October 1980, the postal savings system had assets of some NT$131,293 million.

(ii) *Investment and trust companies*

Taiwan's investment and trust companies date back to 1971 when they were established to encourage longer-term savings and investment.[17] Their areas of operation are quite broad and in many respects fulfil a role similar to a merchant or investment bank in other countries. These operations include: trust deposits management; direct and syndicated medium- and long-term loans and guarantees in local and foreign currencies; leasing; underwriting and private placements of securities; dealing in securities on the stock exchange and in the money market; retirement fund management; investment advice; debt and equity securities registration, custodianship and trustee services; real estate sales, investment, appraisal, construction and management; credit cards; and financial and corporate advice. Their main source of funds come from 'discretionary' trusts which offer guaranteed rates of return slightly higher than commercial bank savings deposits of similar maturity. This modest margin has been a major factor in the companies' rapid expansion over recent years and suggests a high degree of interest-sensitivity on the part of Taiwan's savers.

As shown in Table 5.7, there are at present eight investment and trust companies in operation in Taiwan, five of which have foreign financial institutions as minority shareholders.[18] At the end of October 1980, these companies had assets of NT$66,103 million, 58 per cent of which was in loans to private enterprise, 27 per cent in securities investments and 9 per cent in real estate. Prior to 1979, their business was confined to Taipei. Many have since expanded their operations and the number of branches is expected to increase rapidly over the next few years.

Though considered as one of the eight investment and trust companies, special mention must be made of the oldest of these firms, the China Development Corporation. It was established in 1959 to assist private industrial and commercial enterprises with medium- and long-term loans in both local and foreign currencies. It is also involved with equity participation, guarantee operations, and other investment and trust-company styled business. Unlike the trust companies, though, it neither accepts deposits nor trust funds. Similarly it makes loans for less than a year maturity and invests directly in company shares rather than through the market. In addition to its own capital base, the Corporation obtains funds from the government and international financial institutions. This support is also reflected in its shareholdings with government institutions owning 10.6 per cent, foreign institutions 14.57 per cent and others 75.37 per cent.

(iii) *Insurance companies*

The present insurance industry in Taiwan dates from the postwar period when the Taiwan Fire and Marine Insurance Company and Taiwan Life Insurance Company were established, in 1948 and 1947, by the provincial government to assume the unexpired policy business of the 14

TABLE 5.7 Investment and trust companies

Name	Date established	No. of branches	Foreign institutional shareholders (% owned)	
Cathay Investment and Trust Company	28 July 1971	5	—	
Taiwan First Investment and Trust Company	22 June 1971	1	Citibank	(40.00)
Overseas Investment and Trust Company	6 August 1971	3	COB FINANCE Co. Ltd	(19.00)
China United Trust and Investment Company	12 October 1971	2	Wobaco Trust Ltd Irving Trust Co. Individuals	(12.40) (20.00) (4.60)
China Investment and Trust Company*a*	1 March 1966	5	H. S. Development & Finance Co. The Nikko Securities Co. Ltd Private Investment Corp. for Asia (PICA) SA Continental International Finance Corp.	(15.81) (2.85) (4.76) (5.13)
Taiwan Development and Trust Company*b*	December 1964	—	—	
Asia Trust and Investment Corporation	7 July 1972	3	—	
China Development Corporation	14 May 1959	—	Morgan Guaranty International Finance Corp. Wells Fargo Bank International Corp. C. V. Starr & Co. Incorporated Private Investment Corp. for Asia (PICA) SA	(10.18) (2.99) (1.10) (0.30)

a Known as China Securities Investment Corporation until 1 July 1971.
b Government-owned. Assumed present operations and functions of the old Taiwan Land Development Corporation on 3 July 1972.

Japanese life and 12 property insurance companies previously in operation. Following the move of the central government to Taipei in 1949 the government-owned China Fire and Marine Insurance Company and two private companies, Taiping Insurance and China Mariners Assurance, also moved to Taiwan. These firms were further supplemented by the Central Trust of China's insurance activities[19] and the postal savings system's individual and group life and endowments programmes. After the restriction on new insurance companies was removed in 1961 a number of local private companies were formed and there are now 9 life and 14 fire and marine insurance companies in Taiwan with 47 and 56 branches respectively; these are listed in Table 5.8.

TABLE 5.8   Insurance companies in Taiwan

	Established in Taiwan
Fire and marine insurance companies	
Taiwan Fire & Marine Insurance Co. Ltd	5 January 1948
China Mariners' Assurance Corp. Ltd	May 1949
The Taiping Insurance Co. Ltd	5 January 1951
Cathay Insurance Co. Ltd	19 April 1961
Malayan Overseas Insurance Corp.	27 April 1961
The Taiwan Insurance Co. Ltd.	May 1961
Mingtai Fire & Marine Insurance Co. Ltd	22 September 1961
Central Insurance Co. Ltd	1 March 1962
The First Insurance Co. Ltd	September 1962
Kuo Hua Insurance Co. Ltd	December 1962
Union Insurance Co. Ltd	20 February 1963
New Light Fire & Marine Insurance Co. Ltd	May 1963
South China Insurance Co. Ltd	1 May 1963
China Insurance Co. Ltd	1 November 1972
Life insurance companies	
Taiwan Life Insurance Co. Ltd	1 December 1947
Life Insurance Dept/Central Trust of China	May 1949
Life Insurance Dept/Postal savings system	1 March 1962
The First Life Insurance Co. Ltd	26 May 1962
Cathay Life Insurance Co. Ltd	15 August 1962
Overseas Life Insurance Corp.	27 April 1963
Nan Shan Life Insurance Co.	1 July 1963
Kuo Hua Life Insurance Co. Ltd	20 July 1963
Shin Kong Life Insurance Co. Ltd	30 July 1963

Source: *Financial Institution in Taiwan, The Republic of China* (Taiwan: Central Bank of China, July 1980) pp. 25–6.

In 1979, the total life business premiums from the industry's 1,580,000 policies stood at NT$459,000 million (US$12.7 billion). However, in Taiwan life business includes personal and group accident coverage as well as endowment, ordinary life, and health insurance; endowment policies are the most popular and account for 90 per cent of all business. The reserve funds of insurance companies are used primarily for bank deposits, loans, equity and securities investments, subject to regulation by law. At the end of October 1980, life insurance company assets totalled NT$21, 250 million, 29 per cent of which was real estate, 40 per cent loans, and 10 per cent corporate securities.

A local government reinsurance fund was established in 1956 under the management of the Central Trust of China and, on 31 October 1968, reconstituted as the Central Reinsurance Corporation. Today, besides its reinsurance activities, the Central Reinsurance Corporation also assists the Ministry of Finance in the examination and regulation of the insurance industry; the examination of the insurers' asset management is conducted by the Central Bank.

(iv) *Bill finance companies*

In order to encourage the growth of the money market, the government in 1976 authorised the establishment of bill finance companies to deal in treasury bills, negotiable certificates of deposits, bankers' acceptances, and commercial paper. In addition to dealing, the bill finance companies also advise firms on the use of commercial paper and act as underwriters, guarantors, endorsers, and registrars of these securities. They may also act as brokers in the inter-bank/inter-financial institution market in respect to call loans.

The first of the three companies, the Chung Hsing Bill Finance Corporation, was established on 20 May 1976, primarily with the support of government-owned banks and enterprises. Another two firms, the International Bills Finance Corporation and Chang Hwa Bills Finance Corporation, were founded subsequently in 1977 and 1978, the former receiving its support from the private sector and the latter from government institutions.

(v) *Securities finance companies*

In another effort to encourage the development of the securities market, securities finance companies were introduced to Taiwan's financial sector on 21 April 1980 with the establishment of the Fuh-Hua Securities Finance Company. Previously the purchase of securities with loan funds through a form of margin account was available through the Bank of Communications, the Bank of Taiwan, and the Land Bank of Taiwan, but now this is the exclusive business of the securities finance companies. In addition, the Company is authorised to provide accommodation for the sale of securities and to serve as a custodian.[20]

FINANCIAL MARKETS

Table 5.9 differentiates the major categories of financial instruments outstanding by issuer which are evidences of claims against or of ownership in them.[21] As shown in the table, claims on the banking system account for more than three-quarters of total claims outstanding in 1979; while claims on non-banking financial institutions represent only 6.9 per cent. Amounts of government bonds, corporate bonds and commercial paper outstanding were even smaller with 5.5 per cent. The market value of corporate stock account for the remaining 12.9 per cent of financial instruments.

Financing choices in Taiwan have been weighted heavily in favour of debt rather than equity, and of non-negotiable debt through bank borrowing rather than negotiable debt. These general observations show that both the money market and the capital market in Taiwan are not fully developed. Similarly a true foreign-exchange market was only recently established.

(a) The Money Market

For individual economic units, the money market provides an important source of short-term borrowings on advantageous terms, promotes a more intensive use of cash balances, and perhaps facilitates real capital formation. For commercial banks, the money market is especially important in managing their liquidity positions: it makes the banking system more sensitive to the central bank policy action by allowing banks to operate with lower margins of excess reserves. For the monetary authorities, money market conditions also reflect the success of government monetary policy and allow central bank to influence money and credit conditions.[22] As the economic structure becomes more complex internally, and more dependent on foreign trade and international financial development externally, the monetary autho-

TABLE 5.9 Financial instruments outstanding in Taiwan (December 1979)

	Amount outstanding (NT$ billion)	Percentage of total financial instruments outstanding
I. Claims on the banking system		
A. Money		
Currency in hands of public	88.3	6.4
Net deposit money	166.4	12.0
B. Quasi-money[a]		
Time deposits	122.1	8.8
Savings deposits	402.4	29.1
Foreign currency deposits	3.2	0.2
C. Capital accounts and others		
Capital accounts	91.5	6.6
Government deposits	134.9	9.8
Treasury bills	2.0	0.1
Bankers' acceptances	2.8	0.2
Negotiable CDs	20.7	1.5
II. Claims on other financial institutions		
A. Life insurance company reserves	26.7	1.9
B. Fire and marine insurance company reserves	5.0	0.4
C. Trust funds	53.0	3.8
D. Borrowing of bills finance companies	0.8	0.1
E. Capital accounts and others	9.5	0.7
III. Claims on non-financial institutions		
A. Government bonds	13.3	1.0
B. Corporate bonds	19.3	1.4
C. Commercial papers	42.7	3.1
D. Corporate stock (market value)	178.8	12.9
Total	1383.4	100.0

[a] Quasi-money does not include certificates of time deposit and savings bonds which are included in time and savings deposits of the banking system.
Source: Economic Research Department, The Central Bank of China, 1980.

rities will require an increasing range of policy instruments for the financial management of the economy.

The widespread use of the post-dated cheque in Taiwan as a credit instrument has been a major factor impeding the rapid growth of organised money market in Taiwan.[23] The post-dated cheque in fact is a form of commercial paper. The major reason creditors accept post-dated cheques is that failure to pay is a criminal offence. By contrast, dishonouring a trade bill or promissory note involves only civil penalties. It is unlikely that the popularity of the post-dated cheque will wane while interest rates remain lower in the organised than in the unorganised money market and such apparent disadvantages exist in using other instruments.[24] The unorganised money market rates in July 1980, for example, stood at 2.5 per cent per month on loans against post-dated cheques, 2.55 per cent on unsecured loans and 1.9 per cent for deposits with firms.

The formal money market in Taiwan dates back to December 1970 when ten financial institutions were appointed 'government bond dealers' as part of the government's effort to create a market for other than inter-bank transactions. Their activities were confined primarily to longer-term government securities but from 18 October 1973, when the first NT$200 million of treasury bills were issued, these 91- and, later, 182-day securities soon came to dominate the market. Thus at the end of 1975 they constituted 76 per cent of all credit instruments on the market.[25]

Though popular, treasury bill rates, as they were fixed by the government, did not truly reflect market rates and other securities, such as bankers' acceptances and certificates of deposit, and had not been issued in sufficient quantities to achieve active secondary trading. Therefore new instruments were required. Commercial paper was chosen and, under the encouragement of the then Prime Minister, Chiang Ching-Kuo, specialised bill finance companies were created to promote their use and underwrite their issue: the first commenced operations in 1976.[26] The government has since taken further measures to encourage the market's development. In February 1977, for example, money market instruments were given special tax treatment, attractive to corporate and high-income individuals. This was followed in November by Ministry of Finance regulations enabling Taiwan Stock Exchange Category A listed companies to issue commercial paper more easily. In July 1978, an increase in the Banking Law's liquid assets to liabilities ratio from 5 to 7 per cent forced more money market transactions and in December the Central Bank began buying money market instruments instead of using its accommodation arrangements to increase the money supply. Other changes in money supply management also forced the banks to make greater use of bankers' acceptances. However, as shown in Table 5.10, commercial paper still remains most important.

TABLE 5.10 Money market instruments outstanding (figures in NT$ million)

	1975	1976	1977	1978	1979	1980 (October)
Treasury bills	1700	3100	4800	7400	2000	2107
Commercial paper	—	1625	8754	14910	42725	58691
Bankers' acceptances	137	580	1182	2130	2766	4595
Negotiable certificates of deposit	399	2167	6595	22422	20746	16398

Source: Economic Research Department, The Central Bank of India, *Financial Statistics Monthly, Taiwan District, The Republic of China* (November 1980).

The result of these various measures is that the money market has grown dramatically over 1976–8 and, as one observer commented, 'has reached a point of sophistication whereby the business and industries can have a dependable supply of short-term funds and the investors can have an effective mechanism for investment which not only ensures liquidity and high yield but also entails minimal risks'.[27]

(b) The Capital Market

There are significant deficiencies in certain aspects of the long-term capital market in Taiwan. Many short-term loans extended by banks are regularly rolled-over, and by implicit or explicit agreement often become *de facto* long-term loans. Since firms prefer bank financing and as private debt issues typically require bank guarantees, the corporate bond market is very small in size. Public demand for government bonds has also remained weak owing to their low interest rates and corporate and government bonds have largely been purchased by financial institutions. Nevertheless the use of corporate bonds has increased over recent years with the NT$24,231 million outstanding at the end of October 1980 compared with NT$13,182 million in 1978; an indication of their increased popularity and the importance of 100 per cent bank guarantees on such issues is shown in Table 5.11. To encourage their greater use by the corporate sector, the bond market in Taiwan must adopt more flexible new-issue prices, promote the use of convertible bonds, and develop more secondary trading of these debt securities on the stock exchange; their recent classification as a liquid asset for bank ratio purposes should encourage their continued growth in the future.

The formal securities market, the Taiwan Stock Exchange, was formed on 23 November 1961 by 43 government and private banks and enterprises, and commenced trading on 9 February 1962. At the end of

TABLE 5.11   Corporate debentures outstanding (figures in NT$ million)

	1976	1977	1978	1979	1980	(August)
Debentures secured by banks	5152	7392	11682	17838	21732	
Taiwan Suget Co. debentures	—	—	1500	1500	1500	
Debentures not secured by banks	200	—	—	—	—	
Totals	5353	7392	13182	19338	23232	

Source: *Financial Statistics Monthly, Taiwan District, The Republic of China* (September 1980) p. 91.

its first year 18 companies were listed. As an incentive for listing, public companies were offered a 10 per cent reduction on corporate tax for two years and their shareholders allowed to receive the first NT$6000 of dividend income tax free. However, as listings involved considerable initial expense as well as continued disclosure and reporting costs, the number of listed companies increased slowly. Indeed only in 1973 when the share index more than doubled in value did more than 10 companies join the board. As shown in Table 5.12, the growth in numbers continued, helped along in 1977 by further listing incentives: the 10 per cent tax reduction (now 15 per cent) extended to three years, and the tax-free dividend ceiling raised to NT$24,000. The recent establishment of specialised securities finance companies to finance margin accounts should also assist the market's development.

Companies listed on the Taiwan Stock Exchange fall into two groups: Category A and Category B securities. The former is the more difficult to achieve but has greater status and certain advantages in respect to raising additional capital. The requirements for each are shown in Table 5.13.

TABLE 5.12   Taiwan Stock Exchange: selected statistics

	1976	1977	1978	1979	1980	(October)
Number of listed companies	77	82	87	96	102	
Transaction value	145941	172178	361646	205487	138118	
Total market value	94534	120988	153338	179809	214449	

Source: Economic Research Report of the Chinese Central Bank, *Financial Statistics Monthly, Taiwan District, The Republic of China* (October 1980).

TABLE 5.13   Listing requirements on the Taiwan Stock Exchange, 1980

For Category A stocks:

1. *Capital*: The amount of paid-in capital exceeds NT$ 100 million.
2. *Earning ability*: The ratio of net profit after tax to the amount of paid-in capital for the past two years exceeds 10 per cent.
3. *Capital structure*: The ratio of net worth to total assets for the preceding year exceeds one third.
4. *Repayment ability*: The ratio of current assets to current liabilities for the preceding year exceeds 100 per cent.
5. *Distribution of shares*: The total number of registered shareholders exceeds 1000 and at least 15 per cent of the total subscribed capital stocks must be held by a minimum of 500 registered shareholders each holding shares with a total amount of par value lying between NT$ 10,000 and NT$ 300,000.

For Category B stocks

1. *Capital*: The amount of paid-in capital exceeds NT$ 50 million.
2. *Earning ability*: The ratio of net profit after tax to the amount of paid-in capital for the preceding year or for the current year if its operation was commenced in the current year for a period of over half a year but less than one year exceeds 6 per cent.
3. *Distribution of shares*: The total number of registered shareholders exceeds 600 and at least 15 per cent of the total subscribed capital stocks must be held by a minimum of 300 registered shareholders each holding shares with a total amount of par value lying between NT$ 10,000 and NT$ 300,000.

Source: Taiwan Stock Exchange (1980).

On the trading side of the market, the exchange members are also divided into two categories: brokers and traders. Traders deal on their own account while brokers deal on behalf of their clients. Some financial institutions occupy positions in each: investment trust companies, for example, comprise 7 of the 12 securities traders while banks account for 13 of the 27 securities houses. Of the trading volume on the exchange, some 70 per cent is from individuals and the remaining 30 per cent from institutions.[28]

An important function of the stock market is to help diffuse ownership and equalise the distribution of wealth and income. However, the Taiwan exchange remains relatively underdeveloped and has not been a great source of funds for the business sector. Its small size also exposes it to considerable price instability which dissuades some companies from listing. A tradition of a low proportion of equity funding and a reliance on bank borrowing, much like in Japan, and a desire for close management control and little public disclosure has further worked against the Exchange's success. Restrictions on Overseas Chinese and other foreigners' purchases also deny the market an important source of trading volume and investment funds. In addition, the government has yet to undertake an effective programme designed to increase investors' equity purchases or corporations' listing and issuing shares: both the accounting and disclosure requirements for listed firms as well as tax incentives are felt to be inadequate. Furthermore the Securities and Exchange Commission is inadequately staffed and the brokerage and underwriting profession is also weak.[29] Adequate accounting data and professionalism are important prerequisites if the stock market is to do a good job in valuing equities and thereby in allocating capital.

(c) Foreign-exchange Market

External equilibrium can be achieved by adjustment through domestic inflation or by appreciation and devaluation of the NT dollar against the US dollar. As a matter of fact, the two adjustment paths reflect alternative choices with a short-run trade-off between income growth and price stability.

The government officially severed the direct and rigid link between the NT dollar and the US dollar and adopted a floating exchange rate system on 1 February 1979. The NT dollar had been linked to the US dollar primarily because the United States was Taiwan's most important trading partner and most foreign trade transactions are denominated in US dollars. As a result, pegging was not only institutionally the simplest thing, but also helped reduce uncertainties in economic and trade calculations. This system, however, had at least two shortcomings.[30] First, the pegged exchange rate movements did not reflect developments in Taiwan's balance of payments, but rather those of the US. Secondly, exchange rate fluctuations interfered with the pursuit of internal policy objectives, since the fluctuations were exogenous and independent of government policy. Thus the domestic economy was subject to undesired and largely unpredictable inflationary and deflationary impulses transmitted through the foreign sector. The exchange rates of the two major trading partners, the United States and Japan, experienced drastic fluctuations in 1978/79. As a result pegging became incompatible with internal policy objectives and the NT dollar was floated to avoid the harmful effects of the large fluctuations in the US$/yen exchange rate. Thus, while exchange rates were once adjusted disruptively by government decision, exchange rate changes now are continuous and moderate, avoiding drastic variations over the short run.

The implementation of a floating exchange rate system, by also establishing a new foreign-exchange market on 1 February 1979, has enabled the exchange rates to move in response to changes in demand and supply conditions. It also has enabled the Central Bank to gain more effective control over the money supply and allowed more autonomy and latitude for monetary and fiscal policies. In order to help importers and exporters adapt to the new system and reduce the exchange risk, the Central Bank began to provide forward cover on US dollars from August 1978, and subsequently revised the regulations to meet their requirements.

The difference between the previous arrangements and the new foreign-exchange market is that, under the old system, earners of foreign-exchange were required to sell it to, and demanders of foreign-exchange purchase it from, the Central Bank at the basic rate, with the appointed banks handling the transactions on behalf of the Central Bank. Under the new regulations, foreign-exchange earners may hold their proceeds in a special foreign-exchange passbook or time deposits accounts offering very attractive rates of interest. The depositors can withdraw these for their own use in accordance with the related provisions, or sell the foreign-exchange through appointed banks in the foreign-exchange market to buyers holding import permits or other approved certificates for foreign-exchange settlement. Thus foreign-exchange is no longer wholly bought by or sold to the Central Bank. Supply and demand now form the base of the foreign-exchange market, but the variation in exchange rates is moderate since domestic economic considerations and the international competitiveness of export industries are duly considered in fixing the maximum limit for daily movements in exchange rates.

As shown in Figure 5.1, the foreign-exchange market consists of two major sub-markets: the bank customer market and the inter-bank market. The latter can be further divided into transactions between the appointed banks themselves and those between these banks and the Central Bank. The Foreign Exchange Centre established by the Bank of Taiwan, the International Commercial Bank of China, the First Commercial Bank, the Hua Nan Commercial Bank, and the Chang Hwa Commercial Bank, acts as the overall coordinator of the market and facilitates transactions between the appointed banks and the Central Bank: in 1980 there were 33 appointed banks in Taiwan.[31]

The Central Bank's function is to maintain an orderly market, to

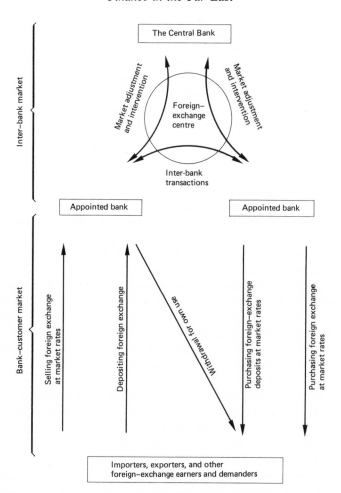

FIGURE 5.1   The framework of transactions in the foreign-exchange market in
Taiwan

avoid large and sudden fluctuations in exchange rates, and to maintain
exchange rates compatible with the domestic and international policy
objectives. Its foreign-exchange department also sets the overnight and
cumulative position limits for the appointed banks. These maintain the
permissible inventories of foreign-exchange to serve their clients' daily
transactions as well as finance buyers' credits or raw material imports.

The move to a floating exchange rate is a sort of watershed in the
financial development of the Republic of China. Even so the exchange

market still remains tightly controlled by the Central Bank to insure against abrupt changes: the principal purpose of this cautious step towards liberalisation is to substitute markets for government regulations. It is hoped that the strategy of liberalisation will unleash further economic growth, and help the monetary authority maintain a more independent policy in safeguarding the currency.

ANALYSIS

New methods of organisation and new institutions must be developed in the process of economic development so as to increase economic efficiency and perform new economic functions. In other words, the deepening of finance involves specialisation in financial functions and institutions, and in the process the organised domestic institutions and markets gain in relation to the unorganised kerb market.[32] As a middle-income developing country, the development of the financial institutions in Taiwan, the Republic of China, is well under way and will continue undergoing a process of rapid transition, representing adjustment to changing conditions.

The principal matters emerging from this study of the financial institutions in Taiwan may be summarised as follows:

1. Corporate bonds and market value of stocks outstanding as percentage of GDP have not revealed a clearly increasing trend during the period under review. Financing choices in Taiwan remain weighted heavily in favour of debt rather than equity, and of bank borrowing rather than negotiable debt. A low proportion of bond and equity financing and a correspondingly heavy dependence on bank credit remains a principal characteristic of corporate finance in Taiwan.

2. The commercial banks have been the backbone of the Taiwan's financial sector, and provide a well distributed network throughout the island. The commercial banks provide various types of credit, while most of the so-called specialised banks also engage in commercial banking. The specialisation in finance, however, is far from complete.

3. The private sector's heavy dependence on bank credit and the underdevelopment of flexible markets for money substitutes have contributed to the effectiveness of monetary policy. It also must be noted that any effort to interpret the financial market's behaviour on

the basis of a price system may be misleading because Taiwan's interest rates are officially controlled. The banks in turn circumvent controls to some extent by such devices as compensating balances and by treating all aspects of the bank and its customer relations as part of a package.[33] Therefore a shift towards interest rate liberalisation and more market-oriented techniques has become increasingly appropriate. In the absence of substantial financial liberalisation these methods may prove less effective in meeting the future needs of the economy.

4. Domestic and international environments of the economy have been subject to an accelerated pace of change over recent years. Inadequate and out-of-date institutional arrangements should be changed as rapidly as possible to adapt to the new environments. The government has recently established a foreign-exchange market to let the exchange rate find its own level so as to promote easier balance-of-payments adjustment, and greater independence from external disturbances which will render the operation of monetary policy more effective. Increased export incentives can take the form of extending medium- and long-term credit to foreign buyers of plant and equipment on more flexible terms and reforming export insurance and guarantee systems. Banks also need to become more 'supply-leading' rather than 'demand-following' to encourage investment and technical innovation.[34] Failure to recognise the dynamic nature of comparative advantage doctrines would freeze capital, labour and other scarce resources in industries where opportunities are declining, and lead to the neglect of advantageous new export opportunities. Finally, it has to be stressed that the strategy of liberalisation should reach beyond the financial sector and be linked with such complementary measures as trade liberalisation.[35]

In late 1980, after this chapter had been prepared, the government took further steps to liberalise the financial system by freeing the banks of much of their specific controls. As mentioned, the Central Bank had the power to, and does, specify the various interest rates that the banks can charge or pay for loans and deposits. Under the new system, however, the Central Bank will just set the maximum lending and deposit rates. The Bankers' Association of Taipei's Interest Rate Screening Committee will then determine the specific details. For example, in late 1980 it set a 13.5 to 16.2 per cent range of lending rates with narrower bands within that range for specific types of loans. In addition to determining these ranges and setting the deposit rates, the

Association may also recommend changes in the Central Bank's interest rate ceilings.

While the above should allow the banks more flexibility in responding to market changes, a more important move is the total freeing of the interest rates paid on negotiable certificates of deposits and bankers' debentures – regardless of the Central Bank's maximum rates for bank deposits. This should promote greater use of these securities for funding purposes and substantially improve the former's attractiveness in the money market. Similarly on the lending side, banks will be able to set their own discount rates in respect to promissory notes and trade bills; again encouraging their use and trading potential.

These changes may not appear significant, but within a financial sector where most operations have traditionally been tightly regulated, they are very important indeed. Besides their effects on the money market and the new potential for inter-bank competition, they represent yet another indication that the government will allow the financial system to become increasingly market-oriented.

TRENDS AND PREDICTIONS

Since the Shanghai Communiqué in 1972 one question that hung over Taiwan's economic and political future was: what would happen if the United States chose to recognise the People's Republic of China instead of the Republic of China? The general feeling was that such a move might end the country's enviable record of economic growth. As one observer in 1977 explained, 'if the US were to derecognize us, our economy would be drained. Foreigners would not come to invest, and even our own people would not invest.'[36]

The United States's derecognition of the Republic took place on 1 January 1979, but as yet none of the many feared economic consequences has taken place. Instead, as the director of the Industrial Development and Investment Centre, Lawrence Lu, explained, 'the derecognition of the Republic of China by the US government had little impact on the economy of Taiwan. Domestic and foreign investors have shown continued confidence.'[37] Indeed the level of foreign and overseas investment, which had peaked in 1973 at US$248 million, has returned stronger than ever, exceeding the old high with US$329 million in 1979 and US$446 million in 1980. Similarly, while as a result of derecognition the Republic of China now has official relations with only 21 countries, it retains important commercial links with more than 140; and trade continues at higher levels than before.

Also of importance is the government's own reaction to this matter at the economic policy level. The recently completed 'big ten' infrastructure and heavy industrial projects,[38] for example, have since been replaced by 12 new projects. The 'big twelve' include the expansion of existing works as well as new activities and are estimated to cost NT$245 billion. Besides broadening Taiwan's economic base, such projects soften the economic impact of any overseas recessions or other export downturns and attract more overseas investment and loan capital to Taiwan. Furthermore, increased foreign borrowing not only assists Taiwan's development but, as one writer put it, has also 'created a situation where powerful bankers have a continuing interest in its survival and prosperity'.[39] Foreign bankers obviously view the country's future favourably as now many non-US banks are competing actively for Taiwan loan business and the country's public sector borrowings have dropped below a 0.75 per cent margin over the London Interbank Offered Rate. As such margins argue strongly for favourable economic conditions in the future, Taiwan's economy and its financial sector can be expected to continue on their present development trend. Indeed, as the respected American national newspaper the *Christian Science Monitor* recently suggested, Taiwan might even go on to become one of 'tomorrow's big powers'.[40]

NOTES

1. Samuel Pitto, *Economic Development of Taiwan, 1860–1970* (New Haven, Conn.: Yale University Press, 1978) provides details of these earlier developments.
2. Frank M. Tamagna, *Banking and Finance in China* (New York: Institute of Pacific Relations, 1942) provides more details of China's early financial development.
3. E. S. Shaw, *Financial Deepening in Economic Development* (New York: Oxford University Press, 1973) p. vii. Financial deepening relates to the accumulation of non-financial wealth.
4. Fu-chi Liu, *Studies in Monetary Developments of Taiwan* (The Institute of Economics, 1970) pp. 1–38, discusses Taiwan's monetary policy and its effects during this early period.
5. R. I. McKinnon, *Money and Capital in Economic Development* (Washington, D. C.: The Brookings Institution, 1973) p. 114.
6. South Korea's traditional corporate structure has similarly developed, possibly also reflecting its status as a Japanese colony between 1894 and 1945.
7. Although not discussed, there are also a number of government-related funding programmes, such as the Government Development Fund and the Credit Guarantee Fund for small- and medium-sized businesses.

8. Prior to July 1978, financial institutions in Taiwan were classified as either monetary or non-monetary institutions. The former group comprised the Central Bank of China, the domestic banks and credit co-operative associations. The latter consisted of the medium business banks/mutual loan and savings companies, the credit departments of farmers' and fishermen's associations, the postal savings system, local branches of foreign banks, investment and trust companies, the China Development Corporation, and general and life insurance companies.

9. Under the Banking Act there are formally four categories of banks: commercial banks, savings banks, specialised banks, and trust and investment companies. However, as the trust and investment companies are considered as 'other financial institutions' by the Central Bank, and not monetary institutions, they are discussed in the non-banking sector.

10. In carrying out these functions, the bank works closely with the Ministry of Finance and particularly its Department of Monetary Affairs. Interestingly, the governor of the Central Bank is traditionally a former finance minister (J. A. Caldwell, 'The Financial System of Taiwan, Republic of China: Structure, Function and Issues for the Future', a paper dated 21 April 1975, p. 14).

11. The Bankers' Association's general agreement on interest rates and other charges removes much of the price competition incentives between the domestic commercial banks.

12. Liquid assets in this respect include excess reserves maintained at the Central Bank of China, net due from other banks, treasury bills, negotiable certificates of deposits, bankers' acceptances, commercial paper guaranteed by banks and dealers, government bonds, corporate debentures (since August 1980), and other securities approved by the Central Bank.

13. Under Article 87 of the Banking Law, promulgated on July 4 1975, the government may approve the establishment of specialised banks or designate existing banking institutions to facilitate specific types of credit.

14. *Insight*, September 1980, p. 18.

15. Ibid.

16. W. T. Newlyn, *The Financing of Economic Development* (Oxford: Clarendon Press, 1977) pp. 26–7.

17. Though a number of investment and trust companies operated in China before the government's move to Taiwan, the present companies and their operations were reconstituted under the Ministry of Finance's 'Rules Governing Trust and Investment Companies' and 'Criteria Governing Establishment of Trust and Investment Companies', promulgated on 30 November 1970. The Central Trust of China and the Bank of Taiwan are also active in the trust business.

18. Under Article 11 of their regulations, investment and trust companies are allowed foreign investors among their shareholders provided that no one foreigner holds more than 20 per cent, and that the total foreign holding does not exceed 40 per cent of the company's capital (*Regulations Governing the Trust and Investment Companies in Taiwan, the Republic of China* (Taiwan: Department of Monetary Affairs of the Ministry of Finance, 1974) p. 3).

19. The Central Trust of China's insurance operations include special coverage for military personnel, a government employees' insurance department and the Workers' Compensation Bureau.

20. *Financial Institutions in Taiwan, the Republic of China* (Taiwan: The Central Bank of China, 1980) p. 24.

21. R. W. Goldsmith, *Financial Structure and Development* (New Haven, Conn. Yale University Press, 1969) p. 3.

22. J. Parthemos, 'The Money Market', in J. R. Monhollon and G. Picou (eds), *Instruments of the Money Market* (Richmond, Cal.: Federal Reserve Bank of Richmond, 1974) pp. 5–12.

23. The money market consists of both an organised and an unorganised segment. The former consists primarily of the government, financial institutions, and major companies, while the latter usually involves individuals and smaller businesses.

24. The post-dated cheque's demise as a financial instrument could be hastened by removing all criminal penalties (W. G. Mellon, 'Some Comments on the Evolution of Financial Markets and Institutions in the Republic of China' an unpublished paper, 1976, p. 7).

25. *China Trust Monthly*, October 1979, p. 1.

26. Bancom Development Corporation, a Filipino investment house experienced in developing the money market, assisted in the planning of the commercial paper market and the training of the initial dealers.

27. Lo Lian-fu, 'The Burgeoning Money Market in Taiwan', *China Trust Monthly*, October 1979, p. 2.

28. Phil Kurata, 'Investors Flee the Market', *Far Eastern Economic Review*, 5 December 1980, p. 117.

29. J. A. Caldwell, 'The Financial System in Taiwan: Structure, Functions and Issues for the Future', *Asian Survey*, vol. XVI, no. 8, August 1976, pp. 742–3.

30. A. D. Crockett and S. M. Nsouli, 'Exchange Rate Policies for Developing Countries', *Document of International Monetary Fund*, DM/75/68, 1 August 1975, p. 11.

31. Ronald H. C. Ho, 'The Financial System in Taiwan, Republic of China: Its Functions and Operations', a speech to the Asian Institute of Management given in Manila in late 1980, p. 26.

32. E. S. Shaw, *Financial Deepening in Economic Development*, p. 8.

33. Characteristics of commercial banking in Taiwan are fairly similar to those in Japan; see H. C. Wallich and M. I. Wallich, 'Banking and Finance', in H. T. Patrick and H. Rosovsky (eds), *Asia's New Giant: How the Japanese Economy Works*, (Washington, D. C.: The Brookings Institution, 1976) p. 255.

34. H. T. Patrick, 'Financial Development and Economic Growth in Underdeveloped Countries', *Economic Development and Cultural Change*, vol. 14, no. 2, January 1966, pp. 174–7.

35. Kua-shu Liang and Ching-ing Hou Liang, 'Export Expansion and Economic Development in Taiwan', *The Oriental Economist*, vol. 46, no. 817, November 1978 pp. 32–9.

36. Dr Tsa Wei Ping, director of Taipei's Institute of International Relations, as cited in *Modern Asia*, October 1977, p. 34.

37. *China Trust Monthly*, November 1979, p. 1.

38. The ten projects included: the North–South Freeway, rail electrification, North Link Railway, Taichung Harbour, nuclear power plants, integrated steel mills, Kaohsiung shipyard and petrochemical project – see *Economic Development in the Republic of China* (Taipei: Economic Planning Council Executive Yuan, 1976) pp. 42–62. See also 'Ten Projects: a Brighter and More Prosperous Tomorrow', *ICBC Economic Review*, November–December 1976, pp. 3–15.
39. Philip Bowring, 'Taiwan: In Credit Where It Counts', *Far Eastern Economic Review*, 17 June 1977, p. 80.
40. Cited in K. M. Yu, 'New Investment Opportunities in Taiwan', *ICBC Economic Review*, January–February 1980, p. 1.

Bibliography

Adam, T. F. M. and Hoshii, Iwao, *A Financial History of the New Japan* (Tokyo: Kodansha International, 1972).

Adhadeff, D. A., 'Bank-Business Conglomerates – the Japanese Experience', *Banco Nazionale del Lavoro Quarterly Review*, Sep. 1975.

Allen, G. C. and Donnithorne, A. G., *Western Enterprise in Far Eastern Economic Development* (London: George Allen and Unwin, 1954).

Asia 1980 Yearbook (Hong Kong: Far Eastern Economic Review, 1980).

Banking Structures and Sources of Finance in the Far East, 3rd edn (London: Financial Times Business Publishing, 1980).

Banking System in Japan (Tokyo: Federation of Bankers' Associations of Japan, 1979).

Barnet, M. E., Price, N. L. and Gehrke, J. A., 'Japan – Some Background for Security Analysts', *Financial Analysts Journal*, Jan. – Feb. 1974.

'Beijing's Banks Capitalise on Xianggang', *Asian Banking*, July 1980.

Bennett, Gordon, *China's Finance and Trade: A Policy Reader* (London: Macmillan, 1978).

Bieda, K., *The Structure and Operation of the Japanese Economy* (London: John Wiley, 1974).

Boltho, A., *Japan: An Economic Survey, 1953–1973* (Oxford University Press, 1975).

Borsuk, Mark, 'How the *Gensaki* Market Works', *Euromoney*, May 1978.

Bowring, Philip, 'Tighter Regulations on Money Supply', *Financial Times*, 9 July 1979.

Bratter, Herbert M., *Japanese Banking* (Washington, D.C.: US Government Printing Office, 1931).

Bronte, Stephen, 'Peking Samurais Twinkles in Underwriters' Eyes', *Far Eastern Economic Review*, 22 Sep. 1978.

——, 'The Most Powerful Man in Japan', *Euromoney*, June 1979.

Brown, W. L. C., 'The Turkeys Which Voted for an Early Christmas', *Far Eastern Economic Review*, 4 Apr. 1980.

Caldwell, J. A., 'The Financial System in Taiwan: Structure, Functions and Issues for the Future', *Asian Survey*, Aug. 1976.

Capital Markets in Asia's Developing Countries (Hong Kong: Business International, 1976).

Caves, R. E. and Uekusa, M., *Industrial Organization in Japan* (Washington, D. C.: The Brookings Institution, 1976).

Chalkley, Alan, 'Hong Kong's Unfinished Business', *The Banker*, Dec. 1976.

Chang, F. S. Y., 'China Development Corporation in Ten Years', *Industry of Free China*, 25 Jan. 1970.

Chen, Tong Yung, *The Economy of Hong Kong* (Hong Kong: Far East Publications, 1977).

Cheng, C., 'The Banking System of the Republic of China', *Economic Review* (Taipei), Jan.–Feb. 1966.

'China: Little Red Passbooks', *The Economist*, 9 May 1981.

'China's Financial Institutions', *The China Business Review*, July–Aug. 1980.

'China's Foreign Insurance', *China Economy and Trade*, vol. 6 (1980).

Cho, Jiho, 'A Study of the Efficient Hypothesis in the Korean Stock Market', unpublished PhD thesis, Saint Louis University, Missouri, 1980.

Cohen, Jerome A., 'The Bank of China Clears Up its Legal Status', *Euromoney*, Dec. 1980.

Crockett, A. D. and Nsouli, S. M., 'Exchange Rate Policies for Developing Countries', International Monetary Fund paper, dated 1 Aug. 1975.

Cusac, Richard, 'Economic Prospects and Financial Markets in the Year of the Ram', a speech to the Hong Kong Society of Security Analysts, 16 Jan. 1979.

Denison, E. F. and Chung, W. K., *How Japan's Economy Grew So Fast: The Sources of Post-war Expansion* (Washington, D.C.: The Brookings Institution, 1976).

Donnithorne, Audrey, *China's Economic System* (London: C. Hurst, 1981).

Eckstein, Alexander, *China's Economic Relations* (Cambridge University Press, 1977).

Economic Development in the Republic of China (Taipei: Economic Planning Council Executive Yuan, July 1976).

Emery, Robert F., *The Financial Institutions of Southeast Asia: A Country by Country Study* (New York: Praeger, 1970).

Feurerwerker, Albert, *The Chinese Economy, 1912–1949* (Ann Arbor, Mich.: University of Michigan, 1968).

'Financial Innovation and Monetary Indicators in Japan', *Federal Reserve Bank of New York Quarterly Review*, spring 1981.

Financial Institutions in Taiwan, the Republic of China (Taipei: The Central Bank of China, 1980).

Flow of Funds in Taiwan, Republic of China, 1965–1971 (Taipei: The Central Bank of China, 1973).

'Focus on China', *Far Eastern Economic Review*, annual supplements.

'Focus on Hong Kong', *Far Eastern Economic Review*, annual supplements.

'Focus on Japan', *Far Eastern Economic Review*, annual supplements.

'Focus on South Korea', *Far Eastern Economic Review*, annual supplements.

'Focus on Taiwan', *Far Eastern Economic Review*, annual supplements.

'Foreign Banks Prosper in Korea', *Korea Exchange Bank Monthly Review*, Aug. 1978.

'Foreign Banks in Korea', *Korea Exchange Bank Monthly Review*, June 1980.

Forrai, George, 'How Good a Tax Haven is Hong Kong?', *Asian Finance*, 15 Mar. 1980.

Fuji, T., 'Japan's New Monetary Climate', *The Banker*, Aug. 1981.

Geertz, Clifford, 'The Rotating Credit Association: a "Middle Rung" in Development', *Economic Development and Cultural Change*, Apr. 1962.

Geiger, T. and Geiger, F. M., *The Development Progress of Hong Kong and Singapore* (London: Macmillan, 1975).

Goldsmith, R. W., *Financial Structure and Development* (New Haven, Conn.: Yale University Press, 1969).

Goodstadt, Leo, 'Hong Kong Banking: Controls Come to the Rock of Laissez-Faire', *Euromoney*, Apr. 1979.

——, 'Hope Springs Eternal in China's Bond Market', *Asian Banking*, May 1980.

——, 'Hong Kong Government's Plans to Put Deposit-Taking Companies in their Place', *Asian Banking*, July 1980.

——, 'China's Resilient Bankers Emerge from the Shadows', *Asian Banking*, June 1980.

——, 'Asia's Mutual Funds Bloom in Hong Kong', *Asian Banking*, Sep. 1980.

——, 'Inflation Conundrum for China's Banks', *Asian Banking*, Feb. 1981.

——, 'People's Bank Reveals All . . . Almost', *Asian Banking*, Aug. 1981.

Gurley, John G., *China's Economy and the Maoist Strategy* (New York: Monthly Review Press, 1976).

Gurwin, Larry, 'The Score is Hong Kong 3: Singapore 1', *Institutional Investor*, Apr. 1979.

Haddon-Cave, Phillip Sir, 'A Reprieve from Recession', *Far Eastern Economic Review*, 19 Sep. 1980.

Hayashi, Shozo, 'A Hard Look at the Bond Rush', *Asian Finance*, 15 July 1979.

Hayden, Erich, 'Tokyo's Tentative Offshore Future', *Asian Banking*, July 1981.

Holzer, Peter J., 'Hong Kong as a Syndication Centre', *Singapore Banking and Finance 1978* (Singapore: Institute of Banking and Finance, 1979).

Hong Kong 1980 (Hong Kong: Government Printer, 1980).

Howe, C., *China's Economy: A Basic Guide* (London: Paul Elek, 1978).

Hsiao, K. H., *Money and Monetary Policy in Communist China* (New York: Columbia University Press, 1971).

Industrial Groupings in Japan (Tokyo: Dodwell Marketing Group, 1974).

Insurance in China (New York: Chubb, 1980).

Introduction to the Japanese Bond Market, An, (Tokyo: Nomura Securities, 1978).

Jao, Y. C., *Banking and Currency in Hong Kong: A Study of Post-war Financial Development* (London: Macmillan 1974).

——, 'The Rise of Hong Kong as a Financial Centre', *Asian Survey*, July 1979.

——, 'Financial Structure and Monetary Policy in Hong Kong', unpublished working paper, 1980.

——, 'Hong Kong as a Regional Financial Centre: Evolution and Prospects', unpublished working paper, 1980.

Japan Company Handbook, The (Tokyo: Oriental Economist, 1979).

Japanese Financial System, The (Tokyo: Bank of Japan, 1978).

'Japan's Bond Repurchase *(Gensaki)* Market', *Mitsubishi Trust Report*, July 1979.

Japan's Securities Market, 1979 (Tokyo: Securities Public Information Centre of Japan, 1979).

Kann, Eduard, *The Currencies of China: An Investigation of Gold and Silver Transactions Affecting China, with a Section on Copper* (New York: AMS Press, 1975).

Kim, Chang-Joon, 'A Study of Money and Bank Credit as Target

Variables in the Korean Economy', unpublished PhD thesis, University of Cincinnati, 1980.

Kim, Jae Yoon, *Financial System of Korea* (Seoul: Bank of Korea, 1978).

Kim, Pyung-Joo, 'Does Monetary Policy Work and How: Toward a Model of Monetary Management in Korea', unpublished PhD thesis, Princeton University, N.J., 1976.

Kim, Si Dam, 'Interest Rate Reform in a Financially Undeveloped Economy: the Korean case', unpublished PhD thesis, State University of New York at Binghampton, 1979.

Kim, Tae-Cheon, *Securities Market in Korea* (Seoul: Korea Securities Dealers' Association, 1977).

Kim, Yong Kap, 'The Stock Exchanges in Asia: Problems and Solutions – the Korean Case', a paper to the First Asian Securities Industry Forum in Manila, 10–16 Nov. 1976.

Kindleberger, C. P., *The Formation of Financial Centers* (Princeton, N.J.: Princeton University Press, 1974).

King, F. H. H., *Money in British East Asia* (London: British Colonial Office, 1957).

Komaki, Rikizo, 'Foreign Banks: Patience Please', *The Banker*, Aug. 1981.

'Korea Insurance is No. 2 in Asia', *Asian Money Manager*, Oct. 1979.

'Korea Securities Market 1977', *Korea Exchange Bank Monthly Review*, May 1978.

'Korea's Borrowing in International Financial Markets', *Korea Exchange Bank Monthly Review*, June 1979.

'Korea's Leasing Industry', *Korea Exchange Bank Monthly Review*, Sep. 1978.

'Korea's Nationwide City Banks', *Korea Exchange Bank Monthly Review*, Oct. 1979.

Korean Economy: Review and Prospects, The (Seoul: Korea Exchange Bank, 1980).

Krause, L. R. and Sekiguchi, S., 'Japan and the World Economy', in H. T. Patrick and H. Rosovsky (eds), *Asia's New Giant* (Washington, D.C.: The Brookings Institution, 1976).

Kulkarni, V. G., 'China's Bankers Step Out of their Shell', *Bankers' Handbook for Asia, 1979–80* (Hong Kong: Asian Finance Publications, 1980).

Kurata, Phil, 'Investors Flee the Market', *Far Eastern Economic Review*, 5 Dec. 1980.

Lee, Mary, 'A New Relaxed Feeling of Having One's Heart at East', *Far Eastern Economic Review*, 21 Mar. 1980.

——, 'A Crack Down on Loan Sharks', *Far Eastern Economic Review*, 12 Dec. 1980.

Lee, Sang-Kyo, 'Korea Carves Out a Niche for Foreign Banks', *Asian Banking*, Sep. 1980.

Lethbridge, D., *The Business Environment in Hong Kong* (Oxford University Press, 1980).

Lewis, John, 'China: Tapping a New Market', *Far Eastern Economic Review*, 20 Mar. 1981.

Liu, Fu-chi, *Studies in Monetary Developments of Taiwan* (Taipei: The Institute of Economics, 1970).

Lo, L. F., 'The Burgeoning Money Market in Taiwan', *China Trust Monthly*, Oct. 1979.

Lockwood, W. W., *The State and Economic Enterprise in Japan* (Princeton, N.J.: Princeton University Press, 1968).

Loong, Pauline, 'A Second Look at the Role of Socialist Banking', *Far Eastern Economic Review*, 19 Dec. 1980.

——, 'Have Dollar, Will Sell', *Far Eastern Economic Review*, 9 Jan. 1981.

Ludlow, H. H. and Stepanek, J. B., 'Inside the Bank of China', *The China Business Review*, July–Aug. 1980.

McBride, Jo, 'The Growing Rewards of Ping-Pong Economics', *Asian Banking*, July 1980.

McElderry, Andrea L., *Shanghai Old Style Banks (Ch'ien Chuang) 1800–1935: A Traditional Institution in a Changing Society* (Ann Arbor, Mich.: University of Michigan, Chinese Study Center, 1976).

McKinnon, R. I., *Money and Capital in Economic Development* (Washington, D.C.: The Brookings Institution, 1973).

Mansfield, John, 'Breaking the Rules of the Bank Cartel', *Asian Money Manager*, Dec. 1980.

'Merchant Banking in Korea', *Korea Exchange Bank Monthly Review*, Aug. 1980.

Mellon, W. G., 'Some Comments on the Evolution of Financial Markets and Institutions in the Republic of China', unpublished paper, 1976.

Min, Byoung Kyun, 'Financial Restriction in Korea, 1965–1974', unpublished PhD thesis, University of Hawaii, 1976.

Minard, Lawrence, 'The Korean Stock Exchange: A Piece of the Action', *Forbes*, 3 Apr. 1978.

Miyashita, Tadado, *The Currency and Financial System of Mainland China* (Seattle: University of Washington Press, 1966).

Mizoguchi, T., *Personal Savings and Consumption in Postwar Japan* (Tokyo: Kinokuniya, 1969).

Monetary Policy in Japan (Paris: OECD, 1972).

Monroe, Wilbur, F., *Financial Markets and the World Economy* (New York: Praeger, 1973).

Mosley, Bill, 'Hong Kong and Shanghai Banking Corporation', *South China Post*, 9 Mar. 1978.

Moya, H., 'Euro-yen Bond Issues: a Growing Market?' *Finance and Development*, Dec. 1978.

Newlyn, W. T., *The Financing of Economic Development* (Oxford: Clarendon Press, 1977).

Nikko Securities, *Memorandum on Yen-Denominated Foreign Bonds*, Sep. 1979.

'Non-Monetary Financial Institutions in Korea', *Korea Exchange Bank Monthly Review*, Oct. 1978.

Park, Jae-Yoon, 'A Structural Estimation of Money Demand and Supply Functions for Korea', unpublished PhD thesis, Indiana University, 1975.

Parthemos, J., 'The Money Market', in J. R. Monhollon and G. Picou (eds), *Instruments of the Money Market* (Richmond, Va.: Federal Reserve Bank of Richmond, 1974).

Patrick, H. T., 'The Phoenix Risen from the Ashes: Postwar Japan', in J. B. Crowley (ed.), *Modern East Asia: Essays in Interpretation* (New York: Harcourt, Brace and World, 1970).

——, 'Financial Development and Economic Growth in Underdeveloped Countries', *Economic Development and Cultural Change*, Nov. 1978.

People's Republic of China: A Business Profile, The (Hong Kong: Hongkong and Shanghai Banking Corp., 1980).

Pitto, Samuel, *Economic Development of Taiwan, 1860–1970* (New Haven, Conn.: Yale University Press, 1978).

Rabushka, Alvin, *Hong Kong: A Study in Economic Freedom* (University of Chicago, 1979).

Regulations Governing the Trust and Investment Companies in Taiwan, the Republic of China (Taiwan: Department of Monetary Affairs of the Ministry of Finance, 1974).

Report on the Advisory Committee on Diversification, 1979 (Hong Kong: Government Printer, 1979).

Rowley, Anthony, 'Hong Kong's Tighter Take-over Code', *Far Eastern Economic Review*, 2 June 1978.

——, 'New Influence on Interest', *Far Eastern Economic Review*, 12 Dec. 1980.

Schroder, Klaus R., 'The Tokyo Money Markets: Liberalization Comes Crawling In', *Euromoney*, Jan. 1979.

Securities Market in Japan 1977 (Tokyo: Japan Securities Research Institute, 1977).

Shaw, E. S., *Financial Deepening in Economic Development* (New York: Oxford University Press, 1973).

Skully, M. T., 'Seoul's Street Money Lenders', *Far Eastern Economic Review*, 20 May 1977.

——, 'How the Chinese Communists Play the Capitalist Game', *Rydge's*, July 1978.

——, *Merchant Banking in the Far East*, 2nd edn (London: Financial Times Business Publishing, 1980).

——, 'Japanese Structure: Some Factors in its Development', *International Journal of Accounting*, spring 1981.

Stammer, D. W., 'Money and Finance in Hong Kong', unpublished PhD thesis, Australian National University, 1968.

Stanley, C. John, *Late Ch'ing Finance: Hu Kuang-yung as an Innovator* (Cambridge, Mass.: Harvard University, 1961).

Suzuki, T., *Money and Banking in Contemporary Japan: The Theoretical Setting and its Applications* (London: Yale University Press, 1980).

Tamagna, Frank M., *Banking and Finance in China* (New York: Institute of Pacific Relations, 1942).

Tatsuta, M., *Securities Regulation in Japan* (University of Tokyo Press, 1970).

'Ten Projects: a Brighter and More Prosperous Tomorrow', *ICBC Economic Review*, Nov.–Dec. 1976.

Trends of Foreign Enterprises in Japan (*Gaishikei Kigyo No Doko* in Japanese), (Tokyo: Ministry of International Trade and Industry, 1979).

Wagel, Srinivas, *Finance in China* (New York: Garland Publications, 1980).

Wesley-Smith, Peter, *Unequal Treaty 1897–1898* (Hong Kong: Oxford in Asia, 1980).

Wilson, Dick, 'Hong Kong Loses its Berlin Complex', *Australian Financial Review*, 17 Nov. 1978.

Wong, K. A., 'The Stock Market in Hong Kong', unpublished PhD thesis, University of Liverpool, 1975.

——, 'The Methods and Costs of New Issue in Hong Kong', *Stock Exchange of Singapore Journal*, Jan. 1979.

Yamamura, K., *Economic Policy in Postwar Japan* (Berkeley, Calif.: University of California Press, 1967).

Yu, K. M., 'New Investment Opportunities in Taiwan', *ICBC Economic Review*, Jan.–Feb. 1980.

Yu, Seungpil, 'The Development of Korea Large Corporations: Investment Behaviour, Capital Structure and Rate of Return', PhD thesis, Columbia University, 1979.

Index

213